THE HISTORY OF
BRITISH EUROPEAN
AIRWAYS

THE HISTORY OF BRITISH EUROPEAN AIRWAYS

Charles Woodley

Pen & Sword
AVIATION

First published in
Great Britain in 2006
By Pen & Sword Aviation
An imprint of Pen and Sword Books Ltd
47 Church Street
Barnsley
South Yorkshire
S70 2AS
England

ISBN 1 84415 186 7

Typeset in the UK by Mac Style, Nafferton, E. Yorkshire.
Printed and bound in the UK by CPI UK.

Pen & Sword Books Ltd incorporates the imprints of Pen & Sword Aviation, Pen & Sword
Maritime, Pen & Sword Military, Wharncliffe Local History, Pen & Sword Select, Pen & Sword
Military Classics and Leo Cooper.

For a complete list of Pen & Sword titles please contact
Pen & Sword Books Limited
47 Church Street, Barnsley, South Yorkshire, S70 2AS, England
E-mail: enquiries@pen-and-sword.co.uk
Website: www.pen-and-sword.co.uk

Contents

	Acknowledgements	6
	Introduction	7
I	BEA's Predecessors	9
II	The Beginnings of BEA	12
III	The Northolt Era	16
IV	The Heathrow Years – Mainline Operations by Aircraft Type	30
V	German Internal Services	85
VI	The Scottish Network	89
VII	Scottish Air Ambulance Operations	96
VIII	Channel Islands Operations	99
IX	Scilly Isles Operations	104
X	Helicopter Operations	108
XI	All-cargo Operations	116
XII	BEA Airtours	131
XIII	BEA's Structure	137
XIV	BEA's Financial and Operating Performance	141
XV	BEA's Fleet Policy	143
XVI	BEA Livery Changes	145
XVII	Training BEA's Crews	146
XVIII	BEA People	149
XIX	The British Airways Amalgamation	155
XX	BEA's UK Bases	157
Appendix I	BEA Chairmen	170
Appendix II	Selection of BEA Scheduled Services in 1952	171
Appendix III	Route Maps illustrating the Development of the Networks	172
Appendix IV	Technical Details of Major Aircraft Types	177
Appendix V	BEA Fleet List	182
	Bibliography	204
	Index	205

Acknowledgements

Many people have helped me with this book, by supplying photographs, data, documents, assistance, or simply encouragement, all of which were very gratefully received. I would like to thank:

Peter Coles at Pen and Sword Publishing, for commissioning this book and supplying encouragement and guidance.

Michael J. Crump, Head of Design Management at British Airways.

Paul Jarvis at the British Airways Archives and Museum, for arranging permission to reproduce British Airways copyright photographs and logos, Keith Hayward, Howell Green and others at the British Airways Archives and Museum, for research on my behalf and for their help and kindness during my visits.

Derek King, for compiling a BEA fleet list for me with his usual thoroughness.

Angela Poole, for supplying much material on Captain Eric Poole, and images of BEA aircraft and people.

The late Roger Jackson, for supplying many images from the A.J. Jackson Collection.

Phil Lo Bao, for permission to reproduce maps and diagrams from his book *An Illustrated History of British European Airways.*

Klaus Vomhof, for material on BEA charter flights and German internal services.

David Harrison at British Airways, for publishing my letter in *Touchdown* magazine.

Brian A.L. Jones, for loaning many photographs.

Steve Williams, for supplying images from his personal collection.

Kev Darling, for his CD of images.

Leslie Jones for supplying many images and period articles. David Bowler and Peter Dann, for BEA coach information and photos.

Anthony Kelly, for also supplying many photographs.

Captain Peter McKeown, Captain Douglas Evans, Michael Boden-Pritchett, Martin Ingles, Les Young, Patrick Tierney, Graham Stephenson, Robin Mackenzie, Doug Woodrow, Captain N.R. Clark, George Greenslade, Charles Miles, Eric Thomas, Guy Clark, Lyn Lovie, Mrs A. Sharp, Allen Clarke, Charles Owens, R.C. Humphries, Eric A Thomas, Helaine Michaels, Mr J.W. Jenkins, and, of course, my wife Hazel, for her patience and support. The many Air-Britain members who answered my questions on the AB-IX noticeboard. Anyone with an interest in aviation history should visit the Air-Britain website for details of the advantages of membership.

If there is anyone I have overlooked, please accept my apologies and thanks.

Introduction

British European Airways (BEA), was Britain's state-owned airline for short-haul and medium-haul routes for just over thirty-eight years. During this period it pioneered many important technical and operational innovations, including automatic landing techniques and scheduled services by helicopter, but always seemed to be overshadowed by its more glamorous long-haul counterpart British Overseas Airways Corporation (BOAC).

The BEA story began on 1 January 1946, when the wartime restrictions on civilian flying were revoked, and the British European Airways Division of BOAC was formally constituted. On 4 February 1946 it took over the services to continental Europe, operated until then by RAF Transport Command from Croydon, and transferred the operating base to Northolt Aerodrome. This was the beginning of an association with Northolt that was to last over eight years. Dakotas were used initially, but from September 1946 the new Vickers Vikings were phased in, and by January 1950 Northolt was the busiest airport in the United Kingdom. At the end of October 1954, however, BEA operated its last service out of Northolt and transferred its operating base to the new London Airport at Heathrow.

It was from this airport in the early 1950s that BEA revived the pre-war Imperial Airways 'Silver Wing' De Luxe service to Paris, using 'Elizabethan' class Airspeed Ambassadors. The lunchtime flights featured gourmet food and champagne, and were deliberately slowed down so that the passengers could enjoy a leisurely meal. The Ambassador's front-line service was relatively short-lived, however, as it was soon eclipsed by the revolutionary Vickers Viscount, a turboprop that offered new standards of speed and smoothness of flight. BEA was the first operator of the Viscount, and for five years after its introduction there was no other turbine-powered airliner in service on short/medium-range routes.

The BEA management was eager to gain publicity by competing in the air races that took place in the 1950s, using the prototype Viscount 700 for the Transport Handicap section of the 1953 London-Christchurch (New Zealand) Air Race. The distance was covered in under forty-one hours. In July 1959 a team of bowler-hatted BEA senior executives took part in the *Daily Mail* London-Paris Air Race, using a Comet 4B loaned from the manufacturer, plus a London bus, taxis and other forms of public transport, to race from Marble Arch to the Arc de Triomphe. In the 1960s, there was even talk of entering for the Transatlantic Air Race using several Tridents in relay, but this project never came to fruition.

In the early 1960s, the large-capacity turboprop Vickers Vanguard was used to great effect on domestic trunk routes from London to Belfast, Edinburgh and Glasgow. Substantial traffic growth on these routes was contributed to by the introduction of cheap Off-Peak and Night Tourist Fares. Comet 4Bs were used as a stop-gap measure to counter jet competition from the Caravelles of Air France and other airlines until the introduction of the Trident in 1964. This three-engined jet was the first to be designed from the outset for eventual fully automatic landings in poor visibility, and on 10 June 1965 a BEA Trident made the world's first autoflare touchdown (albeit in good visibility) whilst carrying fare-paying passengers on a commercial service. In April 1970 BEA was awarded the Queen's Award to Industry for Technological Achievement in recognition of its contribution to the development of autoland techniques.

After World War Two the reborn German national airline Lufthansa was prohibited from operating services into or out of Berlin. In its place, BEA, Pan-American Airways and Air France competed on routes from Berlin to the other major German cities. The introduction of Boeing 727 jets by Pan-American eroded the competitive position of BEA's Viscount-operated services, but a worthy successor to the Viscount was found in the new Super One-Eleven jet, which became the mainstay of the German internal network and was also used to open new direct services from Manchester.

Almost from its inception, BEA pioneered the commercial application of helicopters. The BEA Helicopter Experimental Unit was set up in 1947 to examine the potential of rotary-winged services. Its experiments with mail-carrying and later passenger-carrying scheduled flights led to the eventual use by BEA Helicopters of Sikorsky S-61Ns on scheduled services to the Scilly Isles and on North Sea oil charter contracts. Another long-established aspect of BEA was the operation of all-cargo services, commencing with Dakota flights from Northolt in 1947, and leading to the eventual introduction of specialised Argosy and Merchantman turboprop equipment.

Throughout its history, BEA operated subsidised social services connecting the Scottish highlands and islands with the major cities, and also maintained Rapide (and later Heron) aircraft and crews on standby for Scottish Air Ambulance flights. When the advent of package-tour charter flights eroded revenue on BEA's scheduled services to holiday destinations, the company responded in 1969 by launching its own charter subsidiary, BEA Airtours. Initially operating former BEA Comets on services to the Mediterranean, BEA Airtours was to progress to 'round-the-world' charters, using long-haul Boeing 707s.

In 1969 the 'Edwards Report' was published, recommending the setting up of a National Air Holdings Board to supervise the activities of BEA and BOAC and their subsidiaries. By 1971 this had been established as the British Airways Board, and it was only a matter of time before the two national airlines lost their individual identities.

At midnight on 31 March 1974 the full amalgamation was accomplished, and BEA and BOAC formally ceased to exist. For BEA the wheel had turned full circle.

CHAPTER ONE

BEA's Predecessors

British European Airways was a post-war creation, but British air services to continental Europe had been operating since the end of the World War One. In the early 1920s the Hambling Committee was appointed by the British government to look into the state of the British air transport industry. This committee decided that a merger of the existing airline companies into a unified national airline was the only way to compete with the European competition. The British companies were offered an incentive of £1 million spread over a period of ten years, with the stipulation that the new airline must only operate aircraft of British design. Thus, on 31 March 1924, Imperial Airways was formed from the merger of Instone Air Line Ltd, Daimler Airways, the British Marine Air Navigation Company and Handley Page Air Transport. The new airline was based at Croydon Airport, and commenced operations on 26 April 1924 with a Croydon-Paris service using single-engined de Havilland DH 34 aircraft. The company inherited 1760 miles of cross-Channel routes, and during that year Imperial Airways operated services to

Railway Air Services Dakota G-AGZB at Croydon. (Air-Britain)

Paris, Brussels, Cologne, Basle and Zurich, using Handley Page W.8b twin-engined machines. In 1926 the airline introduced the twenty-passenger, three-engined Armstrong Whitworth Argosy, and on 1 May 1927 this type was used to inaugurate the famous 'Silver Wing' lunchtime service to Paris.

In the summer of 1930 Imperial Airways experimented for four months with domestic services linking Croydon with Birmingham, Liverpool and Manchester. By 1931 the mainstay of the fleet was the Handley Page HP 42, which was built in two versions, for use on European and long-distance routes. The HP42W carried thirty-eight passengers on European routes. For a decade both HP 42 variants operated with a perfect safety record. However, they were slow, with a cruising speed of only 100 mph, and could not compete with the Douglas and Fokker types being introduced by their competitors. Other types were also in use, including the de Havilland DH 86, which was used to inaugurate a daily Croydon-Brussels-Cologne-Prague-Vienna-Budapest service in 1935.

In 1938 the Armstrong Whitworth Ensign monoplane was introduced on the Paris route, and the de Havilland Albatross also entered service. This all-wooden monoplane design was the first British 200 mph airliner, and cut the London-Paris flight time down to just one hour. By that time, however, Imperial Airways was finding that its competitive position on European routes was being increasingly hampered by its imposed policy of operating only British-built aircraft. A recommendation was put forward that the airline should continue to operate long-distance services, but hand over its European routes to British Airways, which was operating more competitive foreign types. Shortly after this, however, the decision was taken to merge Imperial Airways and British Airways into the British Overseas Airways Corporation, which was formed on 24 November 1939.

British Airways had been founded on 1 October 1935 as Allied British Airways out of a merger of Spartan Air Lines and United Airways, and competed with Imperial Airways on European routes. It was initially based at Heston, but transferred its operations to the new Gatwick Airport in 1936. At that time it was using a mixed fleet, which included DH 86s for passenger services and Junkers Ju 52/3ms for cargo flights and airmail services to Germany. In order to compete effectively with rivals such as KLM and Deutche Luft-hansa, the airline used foreign types such as the Fokker F.8, and ordered four examples of the Fokker F12 for new services to Malmö, Amsterdam, Hamburg, Copenhagen, Stockholm, Cologne and Hanover. It later re-equipped with a modern all-American fleet of Lockheed L10 Electras and Lockheed L14s, later to become better known as Hudsons in their wartime maritime patrol role.

In early 1930 Imperial Airways had become perturbed by the parliamentary powers that had been granted to the railway companies to operate cross-Channel air services. Approaches were made to the London Midland and Scottish Railway and the London and North Eastern Railway, which led to the eventual registration on 21 March 1934 of Railway Air Services Ltd. One director was nominated by each of the constituent companies: the London Midland and Scottish Railway; the Great Western Railway; the London and North Eastern Railway; the Southern Railway; and Imperial Airways. The new company was based at the Imperial Airways terminus beside Victoria Station in London. Services commenced on 20 August 1934 over the route Glasgow (Renfrew)-Belfast (Aldergrove)-Manchester (Barton)-Birmingham (Castle Bromwich)-Croydon, using DH 86 biplanes. In the years leading up to World War Two, a varied fleet was operated, comprising DH 84 Dragon IIs, DH 86s, DH 89 Dragon Rapides, Avro XIXs and

Douglas Dakotas. With the outbreak of war, all domestic air services were taken over for the duration by the Associated Airways Joint Committee (AAJC).

In October 1944 a plan was presented to the government by the Railway Company Association, under which Railway Air Services in a new form would operate post-war domestic and European air services, in partnership with other airlines and short-sea shipping interests to give complete interchangeability of tickets over their joint rail, sea and air networks. The proposed company would purchase new British aircraft as soon as they became available. It would operate all its routes without government subsidy, provided that agreement could be reached between governments that no subsidies would be granted to competing European airlines. An initial capital of £5 million was to be provided, and route development was to proceed in stages eventually to encompass twenty-seven domestic and twenty-five European routes. Purchase of the new Vickers Viking airliner was contemplated, and an artist's impression of the type in Railway Air Services colours was published. However, the scheme was eventually rejected in favour of the formation of British European Airways.

CHAPTER TWO

The Beginnings of BEA

On 2 March 1945 Britain's wartime coalition government published a White Paper entitled 'British Air Transport', in which it outlined its policy on civil air transport once the war was won. The White Paper proposed that British airline operations should be the prerogative of three public corporations. The British Overseas Airways Corporation (BOAC), which had been established in January 1939 and had operated priority government services throughout the war, would be responsible for all long-haul services except those to South America. These would be the responsibility of the British South

A BEA Commer Commando coach outside Airways Terminal in the late 1940s. (BEA photocopyright British Airways, via Brian A.L. Jones)

Ju 52/3m G-AHOH returning to its hangar at Croydon. (via Mrs Angela Poole)

American Airways Corporation (BSAAC). European and domestic services would be operated by the British European Airways Corporation, soon to become generally known as BEA. Following its victory in the 1945 General Election the new Labour government announced on 1 November 1945 that it would be implementing the proposals in the White Paper by introducing the 1946 Civil Aviation Bill.

On 1 January 1946 the wartime restrictions on civil flying in the UK were revoked, and on the same date the BEA Division of BOAC was formally constituted. Arrangements were put in hand for it to take over the services to continental Europe operated from Croydon by No. 110 Wing, 46 Group, RAF Transport Command. On 15 January 1946 BOAC board members Sir Harold Hartley and Gerard d'Erlanger began to formulate their plans for BEA. The takeover of the RAF services took effect on 4 February 1946. The London terminus was transferred from Croydon to RAF Northolt, and additional routes were added on that date. The list of destinations now comprised Amsterdam, Brussels, Helsinki, Lisbon, Madrid, Paris, Gothenburg and Stockholm. All these routes were served by Dakotas, which initially retained their RAF markings, and their crews their RAF uniforms. From 4 March 1946, however, BOAC colours and uniforms began to be seen on the Dakotas.

On 1 August 1946 the Civil Aviation Act 1946 received Royal Assent, and the British European Airways Corporation was established 'with a view to providing civil air services in various parts of the world, and in particular in Europe (including the British Islands)'. The original Board comprised: Sir Harold Hartley (Chairman), W. Whitney Straight (Deputy Chairman), Gerard d'Erlanger (Managing Director), Wing Commander A.H. Measures, and I.J. Hayward. From that date, BEA operated its own services to mainland Europe, and the very first BEA service is believed to have been the 0840 hrs

Ju 52/3m G-AHOC. (via Mrs Angela Poole)

Northolt-Marseilles-Rome-Athens schedule. BEA was initially organised into two divisions, the Continental Division, based at Northolt, and the United Kingdom Division, based at Speke Airport, Liverpool. Under the Act, the independent airlines were banned from operating scheduled services, except under 'associate agreements' with BEA, and BEA was supposed to have taken over from them all the UK internal routes operated under the control of the wartime Associated Airways Joint Committee. However, BEA was by no means in a position to take these services on at that time, and for a further six months or so the independent airlines continued to operate their routes on BEA's behalf.

In December 1946 the BEA board appointed a Scottish Advisory Council and a Northern Ireland Advisory Council to assist BEA (and BOAC and BSAAC) in meeting the needs of these areas for air transportation. The two advisory councils had as their chairmen Sir Patrick Dolan and W. A. Edmenson respectively. On 31 March 1947 Sir Harold Hartley and Whitney Straight resigned from the BEA board to take up new appointments as Chairman and Chief Executive of BOAC. Gerard d'Erlanger and J. H. Keeling were appointed Chairman and Deputy Chairman of BEA, and J. V. Wood was appointed Managing Director.

Despite the move to Northolt, some new routes were still being inaugurated from Croydon. On 18 November 1946, Railway Air Services, operating on behalf of BEA, opened Croydon-Liverpool-Belfast (Sydenham) services, using former *Luftwaffe* Junkers Ju 52/3m aircraft. From 16 December the Belfast terminus was transferred to the new Nutts Corner airport. From 20 March 1947, by which time BEA was operating the service in its own right, the stop at Liverpool was withdrawn. In BEA service the Ju 52/3m was known as the 'Jupiter' Class, and featured Royal Blue furnishings. On 19 May 1947, however, the type was replaced by Dakotas operating out of Northolt. It was finally withdrawn from BEA service altogether on 31 August 1947. BEA's last scheduled services out of Croydon with its own aircraft took place on 1 November 1947, when three

Ju 52/3m G-AHOF landing at Croydon in 1946/7. (via Mrs Angela Poole)

Dakota scheduled flights to Guernsey were operated, the final one by G-AGIF. However, this was still not quite the end of the airline's association with the airport, as during the summers of 1948 and 1949 Olley Air Services operated de Havilland Doves on seasonal services to Deauville on BEA's behalf.

BEA's initial fleet consisted of twenty-four Dakotas and eight Vickers Viking 1As inherited from the BEA Division of BOAC. The new airline suffered from a severe shortage of Dakota spares in the early days, resulting at one point in 25 per cent of the fleet being grounded. Dakotas had to be leased from BOAC for quite some time, and others were chartered from independent operators such as Skyways.

On 1 February 1947 BEA was ready to begin operating domestic schedules in its own right. It took over the services, aircraft and staff of the airlines of the Associated Airways Joint Committee, with the temporary exception of Allied Airways (Gandar Dower) Ltd, and Channel Island Airways. The companies taken over on that date were Railway Air Services, Scottish Airways, Isle of Man Air Services, Great Western and Southern Air Lines, Highland Airways, North Eastern Airways, West Coast Air Services, and Western Isles Airways, although the last four companies were not actually operating at the time. A fleet of assorted aircraft was inherited, comprising two Dakotas, eight Junkers Ju 52/3ms thirteen Avro 19s, thirty-nine de Havilland Dragon Rapides, one de Havilland Dragon, and one De Havilland Gypsy Moth. BEA's first domestic service in its own right was the 1325 hrs scheduled flight from Northolt to Prestwick and Renfrew Airport in Glasgow. This was operated by Dakota G-AGYZ under the command of Captain J. Ramsden.

On 1 April 1947 BEA took over Channel Island Airways, followed on 12th April by Allied Airways (Gandar Dower) Ltd.

CHAPTER THREE

The Northolt Era

During World War Two RAF Northolt in Middlesex had developed from a fighter station (until 1944) into a major base for transport aircraft. Early in 1945 work commenced on a new runway, 31/13, and the existing runway, 26/08, was resurfaced. Later, an apron was constructed on the south side of the airfield, and numerous prefabricated buildings were erected alongside the A40 London-Oxford road. Meanwhile, construction work had begun at Heathrow on what was to become London's major airport. While this work was in progress, and because of space constraints at Croydon, Northolt was selected as the temporary London terminal for European air services.

On 1 March 1946 Northolt Aerodrome entered a new era, as a civil airport on loan from the RAF to the Ministry of Civil Aviation, with the BEA Division of BOAC beginning a weekly service to Madrid and Gibraltar. This was followed within two weeks by a three-times weekly service to Stavanger and Oslo on 11 March, a four-times weekly service to Copenhagen on the following day, and a weekly schedule to Marseilles, Rome and Athens on 14 March. For all these services sixteen-seater Dakotas were used, with about half of

Viking 1B G-AJBR 'Sir Bertram Ramsay' in flight. (BEA photo-copyright British Airways)

Flight deck of a Vickers Viking. (Captain H.E. Dunsford DFC)

the seats reserved for government priority or official passengers. Conditions at Northolt were initially quite primitive, with some of the airline staff having to work from tents or covered lorries on the airfield perimeter. However, BEA soon erected temporary buildings on the south side, adjacent to Western Avenue, to house the operational staff, and took over old barrack blocks on the north side for administrative and training purposes.

On 7 August 1946 BEA lost Dakota G-AHCS. It was operating a Northolt-Olso schedule with three crew and eleven passengers when it flew into trees on the eastern face of the 2182 ft Mistberget Mountain whilst some twelve miles north of Oslo Airport. The three crew members were killed, but all the passengers survived.

New Dakota services to Prague and to Rome were inaugurated on 7 and 9 August 1946. On 20 August BEA operated a proving flight to Stavanger and Oslo with Vickers Viking G-AGRU 'Vagrant', as a prelude to the introduction of that type on scheduled services. These commenced on 1 September 1946, with the first Viking revenue service being operated from Northolt to Copenhagen by G-AHOP 'Valerie' under the command of Captain L.G. James. This service operated four-times weekly, and was speedily followed by the introduction of Vikings onto the Amsterdam route (twelve-times weekly), and the run to Stavanger and Oslo (three-times weekly) on the following day. Vikings also entered service on the route to Gothenburg and Stockholm on 6 October, and on schedules to Lisbon, Madrid, Gibraltar and Prague on 1 November. The Dakotas were also kept busy, opening new routes to Berlin via Hamburg on 1 September 1946, and to Vienna via Frankfurt on the following day. Also inaugurated on 2 September was a

Viking 1B G-AJDK in an early livery at Northolt. (Air-Britain)

Northolt-Prestwick service using the Dakotas of Scottish Airlines. The new Vikings were serviced in hangars on the north side of Northolt, but BEA Dakotas had to make the journey to Renfrew Airport, Glasgow for maintenance.

On 8 December 1946 BEA was forced to withdraw all its Vikings from service because of icing problems. The Vikings cruised at higher altitudes than their predeccessors, and the accretion of ice on the the leading edges of their tailplanes was leading to overbalanced elevators and consequent instability. BEA and Vickers co-operated on finding the cure, which included increasing the volume of icing fluid carried and improving its distribution over the tailplane leading edges. However, it was to be springtime before the Vikings re-entered service, and in the meantime the Dakota fleet had to keep the schedules operating. After a proving flight to Geneva on 18 April 1947, the modified Vikings returned to the schedules on 21 April, in time for the commencement of the summer timetable. On that date G-AHPA operated to Oslo, and G-AHPF flew to Prague. By the end of May 1947 all the Vikings were back in service.

BEA operated several variants of the Viking. The initial series 1A had a hybrid stressed-skin/geodetic wing and tail construction. Most of these were later converted to series 1S, of standard stressed-skin construction. They were operated in a twenty-one-seat configuration, with a double row of seats down one side of the aisle and a single row on the other side. Each seat was equipped with a reading lamp, cold air vent, book rack, and a steward call-button. The Viking 1B had an additional 28 inches added to its forward fuselage, allowing the passenger capacity to be increased to twenty-four (and, in later years, to twenty-seven and then thirty-six). The Viking was unpressurised, noisy and rather slow, but gave BEA sterling service.

On 19 May 1947 BEA introduced a new route to Geneva, and also a six-times weekly Dakota service from Northolt to Edinburgh, Aberdeen and Shetland. By the summer of 1947, Northolt Airport was attracting large numbers of spectators as well as passengers, and on 23 July a new public enclosure was opened on the eastern boundary. Quick to see the sales possibilities, BEA erected a marquee there, which it used to promote its services from the airport.

On 11 August 1947 BEA used Vikings on its domestic schedules for the first time, flying to Prestwick and to Renfrew Airport, Glasgow. An onward leg from Renfrew to Copenhagen was inaugurated the following day, but was withdrawn again on 1 December because of poor loads. The first Viking service to Prestwick was operated by G-AHPK 'Veracity', but this aircraft was to be lost in a landing accident a few months later. On 6 January 1948 G-AHPK took off from Renfrew at 1820 hrs on the daily BEA service S200B to Northolt. In command was Captain W. Morton. Also on board were fourteen passengers and three other crew members. At 2030 hrs Captain Morton was advised that he was five miles north-west of Northolt and was given clearance to land. At the time the cloudbase was 400 ft and it was raining. Between 2015 hrs and 2045 hrs the visibility dropped from 2000 yards to 650 yards. After making two unsuccessful landing attempts using the Standard Beam Approach system, Captain Morton requested that flares should be fired when he was next on final approach. However, a few minutes after 2100 hrs the aircraft struck 65 ft high trees bordering Breakspear Road North, on the outskirts of Ruislip. It struggled across Finebush Lane before crashing into a field. There was no fire, but Captain Morton was killed and the other crew members and six of the passengers were injured.

On 5 April 1948 Viking G-AIVP was also lost, but this time the aircraft and its occupants were casualties of what came to be known as the 'cold war'. The Viking was on approach to Berlin's Gatow Airport with ten passengers and four crew aboard, at the conclusion of BEA service 630 from Northolt via Hamburg. This was at the time of the Berlin Airlift, a period of great political tension. It was not uncommon for Soviet aircraft to fly dangerously close to Allied transports, which were restricted to allocated airspace 'corridors' on their way into and out of Berlin. The BEA aircraft collided head-on with a Soviet Yak 3 fighter that was performing aerobatics, and all on board both machines were

Former South-African Airways Viking G-AMGG. (Air-Britain)

Viking 1A G-AHOP 'Valerie' operated BEA's inaugural Viking service on 1 September 1946. (via Mr. F. Mennim)

lost. Soviet troops were first at the crash site and quickly cordoned off the area, denying access to British troops for several days, although on the following day the Soviet Union apologised for the incident and agreed to relax its patrol flights in the vicinity.

By the summer of 1948 BEA departures from Northolt had increased from the dozen or so each day in 1946 to sixty-six daily services. New seasonal routes included a daily Dakota flight to the Isle of Man and a Viking service to Nice, and on 17 October 1948 BEA carried its millionth passenger. To attract even more customers, an off-peak 'night fare' of £10 return to Paris was introduced for the summer of 1949. This compared favourably with the daytime fare of £14.40 return, and over the next few years this type of promotional fare was extended to cover many more destinations.

Accidents and technical problems were a fairly frequent occurrence in those days, and the danger of collision was always present. Dakota G-AHCW was *en route* from Northolt to Renfrew on 19 February 1949, and was in the vicinity of Exhall at 4500 ft when it collided with an RAF Avro Anson on a training flight. All six passengers and four crew on the Dakota were lost. On 19 December 1949 Captain Ramsden took off from Northolt for Brussels, but the undercarriage on his Viking G-AHPS failed to retract properly. He flew to the Vickers airfield at Wisley for advice and assistance, and after three hours in the circuit there he carried out a successful belly landing.

By 1950 Northolt was by far the busiest airport in Britain, and probably in Europe. In January 1950, it handled over 25 per cent of the total UK movements. BEA's engineering staff there were kept very busy, and in early 1950 the staff of the Certificate of Airworthiness Hangar managed to carry out major overhauls on two Vikings in the space of four days. Then, in September 1950, they surpassed their own record by overhauling three Vikings in only five days. Other BEA staff were sometimes called upon to perform unusual duties; a story in the September 1950 edition of the *BEA Magazine* recounts the experiences of BEA costs accountant Mr E. E. Pell. He checked in as a passenger for a business trip from Northolt to Zurich and ended up acting as steward on the flight. The aircraft had flown into Northolt from Vienna with a steward who was unwell, and Mr Pell was coerced by the station superintendent into taking over his duties for the next leg to Zurich. Aided by the Captain, Mr Pell handed out lunch trays and coffee, but was not entrusted with the aircraft's bar!

On 16 April 1950 BEA operated its first scheduled service from the new London Airport at Heathrow. This was a twice-daily Viking schedule to Paris, but the vast majority of BEA's flights were to continue to use Northolt for some years to come. During 1950 only 21,000 BEA passengers passed through London Airport, compared with 542,000 through Northolt, and on 27 May 1950 the Northolt-Paris route was upgraded to an hourly frequency.

On 13 April 1950 passengers on a service from Northolt to Paris had a very lucky escape. Captain Ian Harvey was in command of Viking G-AIVL, and was flying in thunderstorm conditions when an explosion in the passenger cabin caused the cockpit door to fly off its hinges and strike the First Officer. The galley and toilet were wrecked, and the stewardess Sue Cramsie was severely injured, with one arm almost severed. The Viking's rudder and elevator controls were found to be ineffective, but the ailerons still functioned. Captain Harvey turned back to Northolt and managed to land safely on his second attempt. On examination, it was found that an explosion in the toilet had ripped a hole almost eight feet square in the fuselage. All that was holding the tail on was a strip of roof structure and the cabin floor. Amazingly, none of the passengers had been injured; twenty of them elected to resume their journey to Paris on another flight leaving within the hour. In recognition of his airmanship, Captain Harvey was awarded the George Medal, to accompany the DFC he had already earned in Bomber Command during the war. Captain Harvey went on to fly Viscounts with BEA. He later became a captain on the Comet flight and a Training Captain on Tridents before retiring in June 1975.

During the summer of 1950, BEA introduced two seasonal holiday routes to France, a Dakota service from Northolt to Le Touquet, which was inaugurated by G-ALLI on 26 May and operated until 30 September, and from 16 July a twice-weekly service to Bordeaux with a coach connection to Biarritz.

On 29 July 1950 the airline pioneered services by a new form of propulsion. The prototype Vickers Viscount, srs V630 G-AHRF, was borrowed from the manufacturers and used to operate the world's first scheduled passenger service by a gas turbine-powered airliner. On that date flight BE329X2, under the command of Captain R. Rymer, flew from Northolt to Le Bourget, Paris, with fourteen revenue passengers and twelve BEA guests in an elapsed time of fifty-seven minutes. The Viscount completed thirty-six round trips to Paris in the period to 14 August, building up experience of turboprop operations for BEA. From 15-23 August it was switched to the Northolt-Edinburgh route for the 1950 Edinburgh Festival. The Edinburgh flights were the first UK domestic passenger services to be operated by a turbine-engined airliner.

Viking 1B G-AJDI in the last BEA livery to be worn by the type, plus two Dakotas. (The A.J. Jackson Collection)

Another Dakota was lost on 17 October 1950. G-AGIW departed Northolt for Glasgow (Renfrew) with twenty-four passengers and five crew aboard, but shortly after take-off the crew had to shut down one engine. They attempted to return to Northolt and requested a Ground Controlled Approach for landing. However, near Mill Hill the Dakota struck some trees and crashed, with the loss of all on board.

The first commercial operation of the 'Pionair' conversion of the BEA Dakota was flown on 24 January 1951, a charter flight from Northolt to Dublin for Smiths Instruments by G-ALYF. The Pionair conversion programme originated as a private venture project by Scottish Aviation. G-ALYF was the first Dakota to be so modified by the company. It was demonstrated to BEA, who purchased that particular machine and gave Scottish Aviation an order for the conversion of all the Dakotas they had in service, plus further examples as they aquired them. The Pionair conversion featured a new two-person cockpit layout,

Rapide G-AGUR, seen here in an early livery, was operated by BEA from 1947 to 1953. (Leslie Jones)

A winter scene at Northolt, featuring some 19 Vikings plus several Dakotas. (BEA photo-copyright British Airways, via Brian A.L. Jones)

A view of Northolt looking North-west. (BEA photo-copyright British Airways via Brian AL Jones)

A wintry view of Rapide G-AGLP in the first BEA livery. (BEA photo-copyright British Airways, via Brian A.L. Jones)

The prototype Viscount G-AHRF was borrowed from Vickers-Armstrong in 1950 for the world's first turboprop services. (The A.J. Jackson Collection)

Interior of the Northolt hangar with Viking G-AHPR. (BEA photo-copyright British Airways, via Brian A.L. Jones)

with the radio officer's position deleted. New British instrumentation replaced the original American instruments, which were considered difficult to read. A new single door with built-in airstairs was fitted to the passenger cabin, and new seating enabled the passenger capacity to be increased to thirty-two. Additional passenger windows were fitted, and the galley, washroom and toilet facilities were upgraded. The passenger cabin modifications were carried out by Scottish Aviation at Prestwick, but the flight deck rework was the responsibility of Field Aircraft Services at Tollerton.

Thirty-eight BEA Dakotas were eventually converted to Pionair standard, and a further ten were modified as the Pionair Leopard class for freight work. These retained the original double cabin doors. All the converted Dakotas were named after aviation pioneers, and BEA originally wanted to use the class name 'Pioneer'. However, Scottish Aviation was at that time manufacturing and marketing its own Pioneer short take-off and landing transport aircraft, and would not allow BEA to use the name, so the class name 'Pionair' was settled on. The Pionair entered scheduled passenger service with BEA on 21 March 1951, on the routes from Northolt to the Channel Islands.

Meanwhile, the Viking fleet had been used to continue the expansion of BEA's services out of Northolt. On 22 October 1950 a three-times weekly schedule to Barcelona was introduced, and on the 7/8 January 1951 Viking G-AJBV 'Sir Henry Morgan' inaugurated

View of Northolt, looking southwest. Keyline House is in the foreground, between the railway line and the end of the runway. (BEA photo-copyright British Airways, via Brian A.L. Jones)

a multi-stop service to Cairo, flown in association with Malta Airlines. This called at Nice, Rome, Malta, Tripoli and Benghazi *en route*, with a night-stop in Malta. On 12 February 1951 a three-times weekly service to Milan commenced, being upgraded to a daily basis from 9 April. After a gap of four years, services to Manchester were reintroduced on 1 April 1952, the Viking used then continuing onwards to to Zurich. A new routeing from Northolt to Basle was introduced on 2 May 1952, and on 11 July 1952 Viking G-AMGH inaugurated a service to Helsinki, which operated for the duration of the 1952 Olympic Games being held there.

In 1951 BEA made the decision to provide Tourist Class services on its international routes for the first time. For this purpose, Vikings were to be converted to thirty-six-seat 'Admiral' class layout, with most of the work being carried out (as with the Pionairs) by Scottish Aviation. The cost of each conversion was in the region of £10,000. The process included the upgrading of the cockpit instrumentation and radios, once again dispensing with the need for a radio officer. The first converted example was re-delivered to BEA on 15 July 1952.

Expansion at Northolt continued in 1953, with a new holiday route to Palma being opened on 14 May. This was twice-weekly, and was operated by Vikings with a technical stop at Bordeaux in each direction. Flight BE100 departed Northolt on Thursdays and Sundays, and the return leg BE101 set off from Palma on Fridays and Mondays. Including the technical stop, the journey took 6 hrs 10 mins, outbound and 6 hrs 30 mins inbound. For the summer season there were nine 'Admiral' class Viking services each day between Northolt and Le Bourget and two daily between Northolt and Brussels. The type also operated off-peak night flights to Basle/Mulhouse Airport on four nights each week and shared with Pionairs the operation of services to Dinard. Pionairs operated a busy schedule to both Jersey and Guernsey, a daily round trip to Manchester, and a weekday round trip from Birmingham to Northolt. The type was also used on daily service BE483/482 from Düsseldorf to Northolt and back. During 1953, a total of 1.3 million passengers used BEA's services through Northolt.

The January 1954 BEA timetable showed both 'Admiral' class Vikings and Dakotas in use on the domestic network. 'Admiral' class flights BE904/BE903 operated daily between Northolt and Renfrew, with an extra service on weekdays, and a Pionair-operated flight on Sundays. On weekdays Pionairs operated Northolt-Manchester-Renfrew, Northolt-Birmingham-Edinburgh-Aberdeen, and Northolt-Edinburgh-Renfrew. 'Admiral' class Vikings flew on every day except Sundays between Northolt and Belfast (Nutts Corner), and on Thursdays and Sundays Pionairs operated over the same route but via the Isle of Man. On weekdays Pionairs flew the Northolt-Manchester-Isle of Man service.

A rail strike in 1954 led to BEA organising an airlift of newspapers to Wales and the West Country. During the period 18 to 29 May 1954 a nightly service was maintained

'Admiral' class Viking seat layout from January 1954 timetable. (via Author)

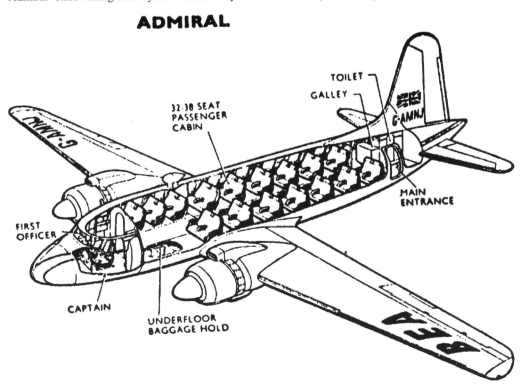

PIONAIR

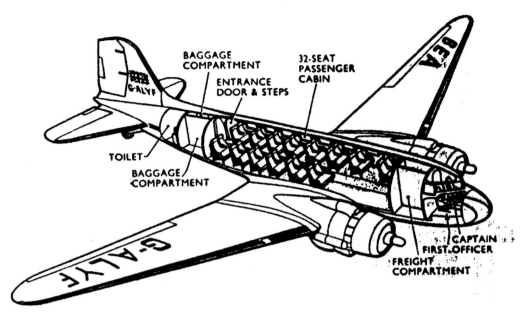

BAGGAGE COMPARTMENT

32-SEAT PASSENGER CABIN

ENTRANCE DOOR & STEPS

G-ALYF

TOILET

BAGGAGE COMPARTMENT

CAPTAIN

FIRST OFFICER

FREIGHT COMPARTMENT

'Pionair' class Dakota seat layout from January 1954 timetable. (via Author).

Viking G-AIVL at Northolt, with an unusual variation of the BEA badge under the cockpit window. (BEA photo, copyright British airways, via Brian AL Jones)

between Northolt and Cardiff and Exeter. A total of 531 tons was carried on 170 flights. Some 97 of these flights used BEA aircraft, and the others were operated by aircraft of the independent airlines Airwork, Eagle Aviation, Hunting-Clan, Silver City and Transair.

On 28 May 1954 BEA Viking G-AJBP opened a twice-weekly summer holiday service direct from Northolt to Biarritz. Additional services served Biarritz via Bordeaux. However, the Viking's days with BEA were numbered by then, and this was to be the last BEA international route to be inaugurated by the type. During the summer of 1954 BEA's cargo services and international passenger services were gradually transferred to the new London Airport at Heathrow. By October only the domestic routes were still using Northolt. On 30 October 1954 BEA's last scheduled passenger service out of Northolt was operated to Jersey as flight BE684 by Dakota G-AHCZ. All BEA operations were then transferred to London Airport. The airline had carried 3,777,000 passengers from and to Northolt, and at one period it was generating 83 per cent of the total movements at that airport. On the last day, two special local flights were operated from Northolt by Vikings G-AIVK and G-AIVI. The following day the Vikings were withdrawn from BEA scheduled services, although examples were still occasionally used that winter to operate extra legs or as back-up aircraft for more modern types. The last BEA aircraft to leave Northolt was a Viking on a positioning flight on 31 October 1954 to London Airport, where a number of examples were cocooned pending sale. Many were bought by UK independent airlines, with whom they provided useful service for many years.

CHAPTER FOUR

The Heathrow Years – Mainline Operations by Aircraft Type

Dakota Operations

By the time BEA transferred operations from Northolt to London Airport, its 'Pionair' class Dakota operations were mainly confined to regional passenger services to Scotland and the Channel Islands, and all-cargo services. (Those operations are covered elsewhere in this book.) However, the type was still to be found on the London-Belfast, London-Manchester and London-Birmingham routes, and on 22 April 1955 G-AGJZ opened a

Dakota G-ALCC was later passed on to BEA subsidiary Cambrian Airways. (The A.J. Jackson Collection)

Dakota G-AMFV went on to serve with Cambrian Airways. (The A.J. Jackson Collection)

Dakota G-AMDZ at London Airport, with the original spectators enclosure in the background. (BEA photo-copyright British Airways, via Brian A.L. Jones)

new BEA route from London to Salzburg. This was to be the last BEA route out of London to be inaugurated by a Pionair and was operated by the type until late 1959. During the summer of 1956, Pionairs were still operating out of London to Bordeaux on Mondays and Thursdays, and to Biarritz on four days each week, but by the following summer they had been replaced by Elizabethans except for a Biarritz service on a few Wednesdays, this continuing onwards to Gibraltar. Pionairs still flew alongside Viscounts on mainline services to Scotland and Manchester, with three flights to Renfrew, Edinburgh and Manchester on most days. They also still maintained a daily London-Dinard service (weekend flights out of Blackbushe Airport with Vickers Vikings were also available from Eagle Aviation), flew on a daily basis London-Cologne/Bonn-Hanover, and operated between Gibraltar and Madrid to connect with Viscount services to London. However, their days as international passenger carriers for BEA were drawing to a close. The final service on the London-Salzburg-London route on 29 October 1959 was the last BEA international scheduled Pionair service.

Pionair services between London and Belfast ended with a Belfast-London flight on 28 September 1956, and on 31 October 1960 G-AGZB operated the final Pionair scheduled passenger service out of London Airport. The aircraft took off for Birmingham under the command of Captain Peter Griffin, but was damaged whilst landing at Birmingham in fog and the return leg was cancelled. The outbound leg was the last BEA scheduled service to be operated out of London by a piston-engined type, the Pionair having outlived the later Airspeed Ambassador in BEA service.

Dakota G-ALLI landing at London Airport, with the new BEA engineering base in the background. (BEA photo-copyright British Airways, via Brian A.L. Jones)

Elizabethan Operations

On 22 September 1948 BEA placed an order valued at £3 million for twenty Airspeed AS 57 Ambassadors, a high-wing airliner powered by two Bristol Centaurus piston engines and capable of a cruising speed of 245 mph. After Queen Elizabeth II's accession to the throne in 1952, BEA renamed its fleet the 'Elizabethan' class. Each individual aircraft was named after a famous person of the time of Queen Elizabeth I, each aircraft carrying a reproduction of the signature of its namesake inside the passenger cabin. The prototype had made its first flight on 10 July 1947, but technical problems caused the development programme to be protracted. The 'Elizabethan' class was originally meant to enter service in time for the summer 1951 schedules, but none of the fleet were delivered in time.

To enable BEA to gain some operating experience with the aircraft, the flagship of the eventual fleet, G-ALZN 'Elizabethan', was furnished with forty-seven seats and loaned to the airline from 22 August 1951. During September 1951 it replaced Vikings on an ad hoc basis on some services between Northolt and Paris. It was then returned to Airspeed for inspection and rectification of minor snags, but during the next six months various other examples were loaned to BEA for the same purpose. The late delivery of the Elizabethans caused BEA many headaches, as they were advertised in the timetable as operating from London Airport. When a Viking (or two if neccessary) was substituted, the passengers had to be transported by bus to Northolt, where they were based.

The Elizabethan finally entered scheduled service on 13th March 1952, when G-ALZS inaugurated twice-daily flights between London Airport and Paris. The aircraft was furnished to carry forty-seven passengers, looked after by two pilots, a radio operator and two stewardesses. The passenger cabin featured an unusual 'Pullman-style' compartment in the centre section under the wing. The seats there faced each other across tables, with two seats on each side of the table on the starboard side and three on the port side. Elsewhere, the first eighteen seats were arranged in rearward-facing rows and the remainder of the seats were forward-facing. BEA passengers were quick to appreciate the fine views offered by the Elizabethan's high-wing layout and large windows. By the end of March 1952, BEA had taken delivery of six aircraft, and carried out proving flights to most of the capital cities of Europe. Aviation journalists were carried on some of these

Airspeed Ambassador G-ALZO was badly damaged in a training accident in 1953, but was returned to service. (The A.J. Jackson Collection)

Airspeed Ambassador G-ALZU flying the BEA flag above the cockpit. (The A.J. Jackson Collection)

flights, including a memorable one in severe weather conditions, with lightning on both legs of the journey, and an air-conditioning system failure.

On 20 April 1952 London-Milan services were inaugurated by G-ALZV, and London-Vienna services by G-ALZR. Compared with the previous Vikings, the Elizabethans offered substantial time savings of nearly two hours to Milan, and one hour twenty minutes to Vienna. Perhaps the most famous Elizabethan service was the 'Silver Wing' service to Paris, which was a revival of the pre-war Imperial Airways luxury lunchtime flights. After an inaugural flight for invited guests a week earlier, the first Silver Wing

Ambassador G-AMAC and Dakota G-ALCC at London Airport. (The A.J. Jackson Collection)

service for fare-paying passengers took place on 16 June 1952. Only forty passengers were accommodated in the all-First Class cabin, and the flight was deliberately slowed down to a one hour twenty minute schedule so that they could have time to enjoy a leisurely lunch of Scotch salmon, lamb cutlets, Cape pears in port wine, and champagne, served by an augmented cabin crew of head steward, bar steward and stewardess.

The passengers were transported from Kensington Air Station to London Airport by a special Silver Wing coach, and as the Elizabethan departed the ramp at London it received a personal salute from the BEA senior traffic officer. The fare was £15.19.0 return, compared with the £11.14.0 Tourist Class return fare.

Further Elizabethan routes were introduced in the autumn of 1952, with G-AMAD inaugurating London-Copenhagen-Stockholm services on 26 October. On 26 November 1952 BEA carried out its first Royal flight with an Elizabethan when HRH the Duke of Edinburgh flew London-Malta in G-AMAB (Captains W. Baillie, E.L.R. Poole, and J.W.W. Cooke). On 2 December 1952 the same aircraft carried him back from Malta to London, calling *en route* at Rome to pick up HRH the Duchess of Kent.

BEA's final Elizabethan was delivered on 6 March 1953. At the time, BEA's managing director, Peter Masefield, was reported as saying, 'Operating costs of the Elizabethan are coming down steadily. I wish we had thirty instead of twenty. We could use them all'. A few weeks later, on 17 April 1953 G-AMAC inaugurated Elizabethan services on the London-Manchester route. Two days later the type entered service on routes from London to Amsterdam, Düsseldorf via Brussels, Hanover via Amsterdam, Hamburg via Amsterdam, and Frankfurt. In the summer 1953 timetable Elizabethans were scheduled to operate a daily service from London to Vienna via Zurich, and Night Tourist services to Geneva on five nights each week. Utilisation of the fleet was, however, curtailed on 10 July 1953 when G-ALZO was severely damaged in a heavy landing at Blackbushe Airport during a training sortie. The aircraft was dismantled and taken by road to London Airport, where 26,000 man-hours of work restored it to service once more. Despite this setback, more routes were operated by Elizabethans during October 1953. The London-Brussels-Cologne service came on line on 4 October, Manchester-Birmingham-Paris on the 5th, Manchester-Amsterdam-Düsseldorf on the 6th and London-Nice-Malta on the 7th.

The January 1954 timetable featured Silver Wing services to Paris and to Nice for fares of £16 return and £40.14.0 return respectively. A Silver Wing service to Brussels was also to be introduced, but this was to be relatively short-lived. On 15 January 1954 a BEA Elizabethan set a new record by carrying thirty-four passengers from London to Paris in only forty-six minutes. Elizabethan services in the April 1954 schedules included both daytime and Night Tourist flights to Malta via Naples, daily daytime services London-Hamburg-Berlin and London-Düsseldorf-Berlin, and Night Tourist flights between London and Hamburg.

During the second half of 1954 the occupants of two Elizabethan flights were lucky to escape with their lives. In the first incident, Captain R.E. Gilman was in command of G-ALZN on a Silver Wing service from London to Paris on 11 August. He had just passed the Dieppe beacon and had been cleared to descend from 11,000 ft to 5000 ft when he felt a bump that he thought was caused by a near miss with another aircraft. After landing safely, he discovered that a two-foot piece of his port wing tip was missing. On investigation, it was found that the Elizabethan had been struck a glancing blow by Air France DC-4 flight AF424, which also landed safely.

Then, in November 1954 G-ALZR, commanded by Captain James Cooke lost both nosewheels shortly after taking off from London for Amsterdam with forty passengers on board. After moving all the luggage from the interior front baggage compartment to the rear toilet area, and flying around for two hours to burn off fuel, Captain Cooke landed safely on runway 10R at London on the main wheels and the nosewheel undercarriage leg. For this feat of airmanship he was awarded the Queen's Commendation for Valuable Services in the Air. Three years later he was on approach to Rome when he again lost both nosewheels and again landed safely. These two incidents were the only recorded cases of this problem affecting Elizabethan aircraft.

On 5 April 1955 G-AMAB, under the command of Captain A. Bates, took off from Düsseldorf with a full load of forty-seven passengers and six crew aboard. Some six minutes into the climb, at an altitude of around 6000 ft, the propeller on the port engine went into reverse pitch and could not be feathered. A very steep dive in cloud ensued before control was regained at 2500 ft. The decision was taken to return to Düsseldorf, but very low cloud conditions there, coupled with the fact that the glidescope of the ILS installation inside the Ambassador was unserviceable, caused the approach to be abandoned. The missed approach procedure was put into effect, but the Elizabethan began to lose altitude. High-tension power cables directly ahead forced the captain to take evasive action, during which the aircraft stalled and crashed some nine miles south-west of Düsseldorf. Fortunately, again there were no fatalities.

On 23 April 1955 BEA inaugurated a weekly London-Ajaccio (Corsica)-Malta service in association with The Malta Airlines. This was BEA's first service to Corsica, but on the outbound leg of the inaugural flight Elizabethan G-ALZZ had to make an unscheduled en-route stop at Paris with a suspected engine problem. BEA's Annual Report for 1955/6 revealed that of its fleet of 101 fixed-wing aircraft, only the turboprop Viscounts had made an operating profit, and that the Elizabethan fleet had incurred losses of £558,721. In the June 1956 BEA timetable the Silver Wing service BE432 was shown as operating daily from London to Brussels with Elizabethans, but there was no Silver Wing service in the reverse direction. Instead, the Belgian airline SABENA operated its 'Royal Sabena' all First-

'Elizabethan' class Airspeed Ambassador G-ALZS 'Sir William Shakespeare' in flight. (BEA photo-copyright British Airways)

Advertisment for the new Silver Wing service to Paris. (via Author)

Class service from Brussels to London with Convair equipment. During the peak season, some BEA London-Malta flights connected with onward services to Catania and to Cairo via Tripoli, these onward legs being operated in association with The Malta Airlines.

On 5 November 1956 BEA carried its two-millionth Elizabethan passenger. However, in 1957 the decision was taken to gradually phase out the type in favour of more Viscounts. Accordingly, on 1 June 1957 Viscounts replaced Elizabethans on the London-Brussels route, followed by the London-Nice service from 1 July.

As the Elizabethans were retired from front-line scheduled service, they became available for charter work, and in 1958 one was sadly destroyed in what became known as the Munich Air Disaster. On 6 February 1958 chartered BEA Elizabethan G-ALZU, under the command of Captain Thain, was at Belgrade Airport, ready to fly home the world-famous Manchester United football team, after they had competed in a match there. Also on the flight were the team's manager Matt Busby, club officials and sports journalists.

Flight BE609 flew from Belgrade to Munich for a refuelling stop, arriving there in snowy conditions at 1417 hrs. At 1531 hrs the aircraft began its take-off run at Munich, but the captain was unhappy with the rate of increase in power and the take-off was aborted. A second attempt was also abandoned due to fluctuations in power output, and the Elizabethan returned to its parking stand. After discussions between the crew, it was decided to make another attempt, this time opening the throttles more slowly so as to avoid the problem of 'boost surging'. Although fresh snow had fallen, it was thought that most of it would have been blown off the aircraft during the first two take-off attempts. There were a few centimetres of snow and slush on the runway, but this was not classed as a serious hazard by the Munich airport authorities.

At around 1600 hrs G-ALZU was again cleared to taxi out and take off from runway 25. As the throttles were advanced for take-off, surging was again experienced with No. 1 engine. It was throttled back and then opened up more slowly. Before take-off speed was reached, the aircraft entered an area of uneven slush on the runway and the speed dropped to 105 knots. By then there was insufficient runway left for the Elizabethan to be brought to a halt. It ran off the runway and went through the boundary fence. After crossing a small road it struck a house and a tree, skidding for a further 100 yards before hitting a wooden garage containing a truck. The garage burst into flames and the forward section of the aircraft slid on for another 70 yards before finally coming to rest. Of the

Elizabethan seating plan from January 1954 timetable. (via Author)

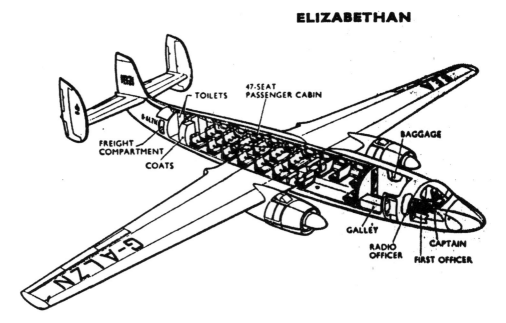

thirty-eight passengers and six crew aboard, twenty-one passengers and two crew members were killed.

Among the survivors was Captain Thain; the subsequent German inquiry into the accident blamed him for not ensuring that the upper wing surfaces were clear of ice before taxiing out. The UK authorities did not accept that wing icing was the primary cause, and the inquiry was finally reopened in 1965. Again, icing was put forward as the main cause of the accident, but slush on the runway was also considered to be a 'further cause'. Then, in 1968, a new British inquiry concluded that the accident was caused by drag, resulting from the nosewheel re-entering slush on the runway after the aircraft had passed the point where it could be safely stopped. The lowering of the nosewheel was in its turn caused by slush on the runway increasing the drag on the main wheels. Captain Thain was finally exonerated, but he did not return to airline flying.

BEA's final Elizabethan scheduled service was flight BE467 from Cologne to London, operated by G-AMAF under the command of Captain J.W.Cooke on 30 June 1958.

By the end of the financial year 1958/9, seven of the surviving fleet members had been sold to Butler Air Transport, BKS Air Transport, and Shell Aviation. During its service with BEA, the Elizabethan fleet had carried 2,430,000 passengers and flown 31 million miles.

The Elizabethan fleet was also partly responsible for BEA's purchase of Bristol 170 G-AICS. This aircraft was the only example to be delivered to BEA (in August 1950) out of an original order for fourteen aircraft. It was intended for use both as a carrier of bulky loads and as a means of transporting replacement Centaurus engines to Elizabethans stranded away from base. When it was delivered, none of the Elizabethans had entered service yet, and during the financial year 1950/1 it flew just 204 hours. It was never called upon to ferry a spare engine, and early in 1952 it went on long-term lease to Silver City Airways.

Viscount Operations

In 1946 two prototypes of a new airliner, the Vickers-Armstrong V609, were ordered by the Ministry of Supply to meet specification 8/46. The aircraft was intended for service with BEA, and in order to comply with the airlines requirement for a thirty-two-seat transport, it was to have a longer fuselage and an increased all-up weight of 38,170 lb. In its initial form it was to have been powered by Armstrong Siddeley Mamba engines. However, in August 1946 Vickers was instructed to change the powerplants to four Rolls-Royce Dart turboprops, an earlier version of which had previously been rejected by BEA. The new airliner was originally going to be called the Vickers Viceroy, but the granting of independence to India and its partition in 1947 rendered that name inappropriate, so it was renamed the Viscount. BEA was initially still unconvinced of the attractiveness of the Viscount, and its original order was cancelled in favour of the Airspeed Ambassador. However, Rolls-Royce then put forward proposals for an uprated version of the Dart to power a 'stretched' version of the original Viscount design, and BEA publicly declared an interest in this new model.

On 15 September 1949 the Viscount was granted its Certificate of Airworthiness, the first to be issued to a turboprop powered airliner. After conducting trial services from Northolt with the prototype during July 1950 BEA signed a contract for twenty examples of the developed Viscount 701 on 3 August 1950. This version was to be powered by four

Viscount 701 G-ALWE, the flagship of the 'Discovery' Class. (The A.J. Jackson Collection)

Rolls-Royce Dart 505 engines, enabling it to carry forty-seven passengers at cruising speeds of around 300 mph.

The first production Viscount 701, G-ALWE, made its maiden flight on 20 August 1952. From 25 August the Vickers-owned prototype Viscount 700 G-AMAV was loaned to BEA for route-proving flights, commencing with a London-Rome-Athens-Nicosia flight on that date and the aircraft was returned to Vickers in February 1953. The aircraft was delivered on 3 January 1953, and in the course of route-proving flights it set up new airline course records of 1 hr 10 min 17 sec for London-Cologne and 1 hr 15 min 41 sec for Cologne-London on 22 January. It was formally named 'RMA Discovery', the flagship of BEA's 'Discovery' class, by Lady Douglas at Wisley on 11 February 1953.

On the same day BEA announced an order for twelve examples of the proposed Viscount 801 development, for operation on high-density routes in an eighty-six-seat configuration. This order was replaced on 14 April by one for twelve of the new Viscount 802 version, which was to have a higher performance but to carry a reduced payload of seventy-one passengers. The main distinguishing feature of the Viscount 802 was the lengthening of the fuselage by 46 inches, and the moving rearwards of the rear cabin

Viscount 701 G-AMAV was entered in the London-Christchurch (NZ) Air Race in 1953. (The A.J. Jackson Collection)

bulkhead to accommodate extra seat rows. The cabin was to be furnished in a colour scheme of light grey, rose and maroon, and all interior fittings were to be removable, to allow rapid conversion to freighter configuration.

On 18 April 1953 BEA inaugurated the world's first sustained passenger services by a turboprop-engined airliner. Viscount 701 G-AMNY 'Sir Edward Shackleton', under the command of Captains A.S. Johnson and A. Wilson, operated the London-Rome- Athens-Nicosia flight, with the final leg being under charter to Cyprus Airways. The following day G-ALWE opened the London-Rome-Athens-Istanbul Viscount service, and on 25 April the same aircraft commenced Viscount services on the London-Zurich route. Viscount flights to Geneva were inaugurated on a daily basis by G-AMNY on 1 June 1953, and by July Viscounts were operating nightly Night Tourist services between London and Zurich. On 1 July G-ALWE carried out the first Viscount operation of daily flights BE210/211 from London to Stockholm via Copenhagen and return. All daytime Viscount services were initially operated in a forty-seat all-First Class configuration. Travellers were soon commenting favourably on the Viscount's smooth flight characteristics, the quiet cabin, and the view from the largest windows to be fitted to any turboprop airliner. At the time of the Viscount's operational debut, and for some five years afterwards, there was no other turbine-powered airliner available for short and medium-haul routes. In its first year of Viscount operations, BEA made a nett profit of £301,000 after absorbing all introductory costs.

From 17 July 1953 Viscounts began to appear on an ad hoc basis on the London-Glasgow route, and on 2 October the 'Clansman' all-First Class service was inaugurated. This was followed by the similar 'Chieftain' service to Edinburgh, and on 4 October Viscounts entered service on Tourist Class services to Glasgow. In January 1954 the BEA timetable featured the daily 'Clansman' flight BE901 departing Renfrew at 0800 hrs, and the return service BE912 leaving London at 1905 hrs. A 'Clansman' eight-day excursion fare was on offer at £10 return, compared with £8 return on Tourist services. Following the successful introduction of all-First Class flights to Scotland, BEA launched the similar 'Ulster Flyer' service to Belfast on 16 November 1953. The service operated daily, with

Air-to-air view of Viscount 701 G-AMOG. (The A.J. Jackson Collection)

Viscount 701 G-AMOP was sold to Cambrian Airways in 1962. (The A.J. Jackson Collection)

a morning departure from Nutts Corner airport at Belfast and a return leg from London in the evening. By January 1954 an eight-day excursion fare of £11 return was available. By the summer of 1956 the service had been upgraded to twice-daily, but by 1960 the service had ceased operating, along with the 'Clansman' and 'Chieftain' flights to Scotland.

October 1953 was also the month of the London-Christchurch (New Zealand) Air Race.

To publicise the performance of its Viscounts, BEA entered the prototype Viscount 700 in the Transport Handicap Section of the race. It was flown by Captains W. Baillie, A.S. Johnson and S.E. Jones. Also on board were Peter Masefield as team manager, and Raymond Baxter from the BBC. Additional fuel tankage was fitted in the main cabin to give the Viscount a range in excess of 3000 miles. During the period 8 to 10 October it was flown from London to Christchurch in a total elapsed time of 40 hr 43 min. Only four brief technical stops were made *en route*, at Bahrain for 14 minutes, Colombo (19 minutes), the Cocos Islands (22 minutes) and Melbourne (15 minutes).

Expansion of Viscount operations continued throughout 1954. On 2 January G-AMOL inaugurated the Viscount service to Madrid, and on 10 January G-AMOF launched a non-stop London-Palma service. On 21 February they replaced Elizabethans on the London-Nice-Rome route, and in April they opened non-stop services from London to Oslo and Stockholm. The Viscounts were also making their mark on BEA's operations from Manchester and Birmingham. On 11 April 1954 the type was introduced on daily services from both Manchester and Birmingham to London, and on the route from Manchester to Paris via Birmingham. Two days later, they commenced Manchester-Amsterdam-Düsseldorf operations, and on 17 December they inaugurated direct Manchester-Zurich weekend flights for winter sports enthusiasts. It was also during 1954 that BEA launched another all-First Class service, the 'Lisbon Flyer'. Flights BE150/151 operated between London and Lisbon on Mondays and Fridays at a fare of £65.14.0 return.

During the winter of 1954/5 several BEA Viscounts were involved in incidents that caused damage but fortunately no fatalities. On 24 October 1954 G-AMOG took off from Rome for Athens, but the port undercarriage failed to retract. After circling for two hours to burn off fuel, the crew landed the Viscount back at Rome. The undercarriage collapsed

Viscount 701 G-AMOK in the Central Area at London Airport after its take-off incident of 16 January 1955. (M.Wall)

on landing, but there were no serious injuries to the thirty-one passengers and six crew. In December 1954 two Viscounts were involved in accidents in the course of training flights on successive days. G-ALWF suffered an undercarriage collapse on landing at Blackbushe on 12 December. On the following day G-AMOB overan the Blackbushe runway after a take-off attempt that was aborted when the control column became jammed.

On 16 January 1955 G-AMOK was rostered to operate a scheduled London-Rome-Athens-Istanbul service. After a delay caused by poor visibility at London Airport, the aircraft was cleared to taxi along runway 1 (now runway 27R) to the holding point for runway 6 (now runway 15R). Because of the visibility problems, the Viscount was actually turned onto the disused runway 3, and began its take-off run. This runway had been out of service for some years and was being used for the storage of building equipment. The aircraft ran into a collection of contractors' equipment and stores, and ploughed through a steel barrier, huts and a pile of cast iron. In the course of this it shed its undercarriage and both port engines, and ruptured its fuel tanks. In spite of this there was no fire, and only the captain and one passenger were injured. Had the Viscount become airborne before reaching the obstructions it would have collided with the new Central Area buildings and control tower under construction. Despite the damage, G-AMOK was rebuilt by Marshalls at Cambridge and eventually returned to service wth BEA in 1958 as a Viscount 701X, with a high-density sixty-seat passenger cabin, airstairs, and a new two-man flight deck.

On 17 April 1955 the new Central Area terminal complex at London Airport came into operation, and the first departure from there was the 0730 hrs BEA service to Amsterdam, operated by Viscount 701 G-AMOA. Expansion of Viscount services continued, with London-Munich-Athens services being inaugurated by G-ALWE on 20 April 1955. From 17 August this service was extended to Cairo on a twice-weekly basis, becoming the longest route on the BEA network. Manchester-Milan night services began on 16/17 June, and on 4 October G-ANHB opened a twice-weekly schedule from London to Vienna.

Air-to-air view of BEA's first Viscount 802 G-AOJA. (The A.J. Jackson Collection)

On 18 January 1956 BEA carried its one-millionth Viscount passenger, and on 15 February the type replaced Elizabethans on the London-Frankfurt run. A twice-weekly London-Venice service was inaugurated on 11 April 1956. On 23 April Viscounts replaced Pionairs on the Manchester-Düsseldorf route, with a new intermediate stop at Birmingham.

As always, there was the occasional technical hitch. During April 1956 Mr R.C. Humphries was waiting to board a BEA flight from London to Zurich when the passengers were informed that they would be travelling on a Viscount instead of the rostered Elizabethan. About thirty minutes before take-off time, they were further advised that due to technical problems with the Viscount an Elizabethan would in fact be used. Finally, about fifteen minutes later, they were informed that the Viscount was now serviceable and would be used after all.

On 18 June 1956 Her Majesty Queen Elizabeth II made her first flight in a Viscount. Accompanied by Her Royal Highness Princess Margaret and Their Royal Highnesses the Duke and Duchess of Gloucester, she flew from London to Stockholm in Viscount 701 G-ANHC under the command of Captain W. Baillie. During 1956, BEA operated a daily Viscount service between London and Copenhagen and on every day except Saturday it was possible to continue onwards to Moscow (Vnukovo) by taking a Finnair Convair aircraft to Helsinki and then an Aeroflot Ilyushin Il-12 to Moscow. The First Class 'Lisbon Flyer' service was still operating on a Friday-only basis, and similar services operated to Madrid and Palma. The 'Madrid Flyer' service BE114/115 flew on Mondays and Fridays, and the 'Majorca Flyer' (flights BE108/109) operated on Saturdays and Sundays. On 7 October 1956 BEA extended its London-Nicosia Viscount service onwards to Tel Aviv, with the onward leg being operated under charter to Cyprus Airways.

BEA's first Viscount 802, G-AOJA, was named 'RMA Sir Samuel White Baker' by Lady Douglas of Kirtleside in a ceremony at Wisley on 27 November 1956. By then, the

Viscount 701 fleet had earned profits of £1,138,000 for BEA, and earlier that year the airline had signed a contract for sixteen Viscount 806 aircraft. These were to be powered by uprated Dart 520 engines. They would be faster than the Viscount 802s, although their dimensions were identical and their operating weights similar. BEA had specified a fifty-eight-seat layout for the Viscount 806s, and originally planned to promote both the 802s and 806s under the marketing name of 'Viscount Major', but this plan came to nothing. The first Viscount 806 to be delivered was G-AOJD on 11 January 1957, and it was this aircraft that operated the first service by the type on 13 February, flying from London to Glasgow with forty-seven passengers. The first international route to be served by the Viscount 806 was London-Amsterdam, the inaugural flight taking place on 15 February. Three days later Viscount 802s replaced Elizabethans on the London-Paris route, with G-AOJF operating the first service, with forty-six passengers aboard.

On 14 March 1957 BEA's first Viscount 701, G-ALWE, was approaching Manchester from Amsterdam on flight BE411. On board were fifteen passengers and five crew members. After an initial Ground Controlled Approach the Viscount broke cloud and the crew were cleared to continue the approach visually. At about one mile from the runway the Viscount entered a shallow descending right turn, with a steepening bank angle. The right wing tip touched the ground and the aircraft crashed into houses some eighty-five yards further on. All those aboard were killed, plus two people on the ground. The accident investigation concluded that the probable cause was 'the fracture, due to fatigue, of the 9/16 inch bolt holding the bottom of no. 2 starboard flap unit'. This had

Viscount 802 G-AORD at London Airport, with a Lufthansa Viscount in the background. (The A.J. Jackson Collection)

caused the aileron to become locked when the flap unit moved away from the trailing edge member.

BEA carried its two-millionth Viscount passenger on 22 April 1957, and in the spring of that year Viscount 802s supplanted Elizabethans on the Silver Wing First Class service to Paris. The May 1957 timetable showed flights BE333 and BE328 departing London and Le Bourget respectively at 1300 hrs. The luxury service finally came to an end on 30 April 1958, when Viscount 802 G-AOHU operated the last flight. From that date onwards London-Paris services were flown by Viscount 806 aircraft in a mixed First/Tourist Class configuration. On 1 June 1957 Viscount 802s replaced Elizabethans on services to Brussels and Düsseldorf. On 1 July they also appeared on the Copenhagen route, but the Viscount 701s were also making their debut on other international routes. They were introduced onto London-Hamburg-Berlin operations on 1 July, and on 7 October they reinstated BEA services to Prague, after an absence of six years.

BEA's first Viscount 806, G-AOYH, was delivered on 23 December 1957 and operated the first service by the type on 27 January 1958, from London to Amsterdam. On the previous day BEA had reached an agreement with Cyprus Airways, whereby BEA would operate all their flights on their behalf, using Viscounts based at Nicosia. This meant that BEA Viscounts would be seen as far afield as Kuwait, Bahrain and Doha, until they were replaced by Comet 4Bs in October 1961. The first BEA aircraft to visit Moscow was Viscount 802 G-AOHO, which landed at Vnukovo Airport on 18 February 1958 on a proving flight under the command of Captain W. Baillie. A formal agreement on air services to Moscow was reached with Aeroflot on 26 February 1958, but it was not until 14 May 1959 that scheduled Viscount 806 flights via Copenhagen commenced. To assist the crew with operations into Moscow, an interpreter was carried on every flight. Twice-weekly services to Warsaw with Viscount 701s commenced on 8 April 1958.

From 1 May 1958 BEA's Viscount 806s began operating in a two-class configuration, with sixteen seats in First Class and forty-two in Tourist. On BEA flights between London and West German cities, and on the Manchester-Düsseldorf route, reduced-rate Forces

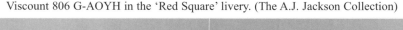

Viscount 806 G-AOYH in the 'Red Square' livery. (The A.J. Jackson Collection)

Fares were on offer to service personnel travelling home on leave and to their dependants flying out to spend time with them in Germany. A return ticket to London cost £25.4.0. from West Berlin, or £14.5.0 from Düsseldorf or Cologne.

As in most years, 1958 brought its share of accidents. On 28 April Viscount 802 G-AORC was flown empty to Prestwick on charter to BOAC. It was on its way to pick up some stranded London-bound BOAC passengers, but on approach to Prestwick it struck high ground and was written off. All five crew members survived and the accident was later deemed to have been caused by misreading of the altimeter.

Not so fortunate were the occupants of Viscount 701 G-ANHC on 22 October. The aircraft was *en route* from London to Naples operating flight BE142 when its flight path deviated away from airway Amber 1. In the vicinity of Anzio it encountered a flight of four Italian Air Force F-86E fighters, which were practising dive and climb attack manoeuvres. The Viscount was struck by the leading F-86E and both aircraft crashed. All twenty-six passengers and five crew aboard the Viscount perished.

The winter of 1958/9 brought the worst flying weather for ten years to the London area. On Christmas Eve 1958 Viscount 701 G-AOFX was diverted from London Airport to Bournemouth because of the weather conditions. Even at Bournemouth the weather was only just flyable, and the Viscount crew missed the runway and landed on the grass alongside. Nobody was hurt, and the Viscount was only slightly damaged.

From 2 April 1959 BEA Viscount 701s replaced Pionairs on the Gibraltar-Tangiers route operated on behalf of Gibraltar Airways. The first Viscount service was carried out by G-AMOE.

In 1953 Viscount 701 G-AMNY had pioneered turboprop airline operations, but on 5 January 1960 it was written off in a freak accident. After landing at Malta, it was taxiing along the runway when hydraulic pressure was lost. The wheel brakes and nosewheel steering became inoperative and the Viscount left the runway and rolled down a sloping area towards the control tower. Attempts to retract the undercarriage failed and the aircraft came to rest when it gently collided with the control tower. There were no fatalities among the forty-six passengers and five crew members.

Viscount 802 G-AOHO in its original livery. (The A.J. Jackson Collection)

The April 1960 BEA timetable listed many services operated in the Middle East for Cyprus Airways. The Viscounts flew as far as Rome or Athens under BEA flight numbers. They then continued onwards to Nicosia, Tel Aviv, Istanbul, Ankara, Beirut and Damascus as Cyprus Airways flights. There was also an operating agreement in place with Olympic Airways for a Saturday night London-Rome-Athens-Nicosia service under an Olympic flight number. On 5 June 1960 BEA began serving Sardinia, with a once-weekly call at Alghero as part of a London-Malta flight. The inaugural service into Alghero was operated by Viscount 701 G-AMNZ.

During 1960 BEA experienced aircraft shortages caused by the delayed delivery of its Vickers Vanguards. Two Viscount 779s, G-APZP and G-ARBW, were therefore leased from the Norwegian airline Fred Olsen Airtransport. These aircraft had a different flight-deck layout to BEA's Viscounts, and as there was no spare capacity on the Viscount training programme for conversion courses, it was decided to restrict their use to the London-Paris route and to use pilots who were waiting to fly Vanguards. The Viscounts were returned to their owner in the spring of 1961.

Viscounts were also helping to develop domestic services in 1960. On 1 August they were introduced onto Gatwick-Guernsey flights, and thanks to their operating economics BEA was able that year to announce the introduction of the world's lowest air fare in terms of cost per mile. On the London-Glasgow and London-Edinburgh routes the one-way fare was £3.3.0, which equated to around 2.25 d per mile. By November 1961, Vickers Vanguards had entered service on peak-hour flights to Scotland, but Viscounts were still rostered to operate a Friday evening round trip to Glasgow and two daily

Viscount 701 seating plan from January 1954 timetable. (via Author)

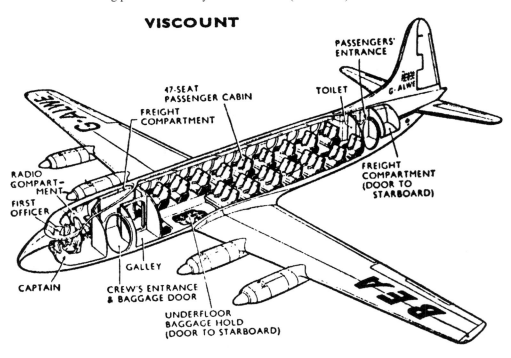

VISCOUNT

services between London and Edinburgh. They also operated a daily round trip from Birmingham to London, two daytime and one off-peak night service from London to Belfast each day, and eight weekday round trips between London and Manchester. The Viscounts also still had a limited role to play on international routes, flying twice-daily between London and Paris (Le Bourget) and also operating Tourist Class services to Malta for BEA before continuing onwards to Tripoli on behalf of Malta Airlines.

On 31 March 1963 BEA operated its final Viscount 701 revenue service, but the larger Viscount 802s and 806s still had a useful role to play. On 26 September 1963 a BEA Viscount service from Manchester landed at Aldergrove airport at 0205 hrs to inaugurate scheduled airline flights into Belfast's new airport, and on 1 November 1964 a Viscount flew BEA's first non-stop service between London and Berlin, the flights being on a daily basis. In October 1965 two Viscount 806s went on lease to Cyprus Airways for operation on their regional routes from Nicosia to Beirut, Tel Aviv, Jerusalem and Cairo. They were returned to BEA in late 1969/early 1970 when Cyprus Airways took delivery of Trident 2Es. During the summer of 1969 the Viscount fleet was still being kept busy, especially on domestic and Irish Sea routes. The type was operating a daily round trip from Birmingham to London and Birmingham-Glasgow, Birmingham-Edinburgh, Manchester-Belfast, Manchester-Edinburgh, Glasgow-Belfast, Birmingham-Dublin and Manchester-Dublin weekday services. There was also a Night Tourist service from Heathrow to Dublin on five nights each week. As late as the summer of 1971, BEA Viscounts were still to be seen on international schedules, operating flights BE706/707 on Sundays from Heathrow to Salzburg and return, as well as weekday services between Birmingham and Düsseldorf and a weekend Birmingham-Amsterdam rotation. A solitary Viscount was still detached to Gibraltar to operate flights to Tangier on behalf of Gibraltar Airways. Also, according to the BEA summer 1971 timetable, twenty-four Viscounts were still in service, configured to carry either seventy-two or seventy-four Tourist Class passengers.

Many of the Viscount 806s were transferred to the BEA subsidiaries BKS Air Transport and Cambrian Airways, and many Viscount 802s were absorbed into the British Airways fleet at the time of the amalgamation in 1974.

Comet 4B Operations
At the end of the 1950s BEA began to lose traffic share on key routes such as London-Paris and London-Nice to Air France, which had introduced the revolutionary Caravelle jet airliner. Air France Caravelles could fly from Nice to London in 1 hr 55 min, and from London to Paris in 45 min, compared with BEA's Viscount journey times of 2 hr 45 min and 1 hr 5 min respectively. BEA had on order the de Havilland Trident, originally intended to enter service in the early 1960s. However, its development had been protracted by many delays, some of them political, and the airline was obliged to look for an interim jet to cover its short-term requirements. At that time de Havilland had on its drawing boards the short-range Comet 4A, which had been ordered by Capital Airlines in the USA, but the order had been subsequently cancelled. By extending the fuselage length of this design by 3 ft 2 in de Havilland produced the Comet 4B, which was ideal for BEA's route network.

On 28 March 1958 BEA signed a contract for six Comet 4Bs for delivery in early 1960. These were to be powered by four Rolls Royce Avons, giving a cruising speed of around 500 mph. They were to be configured to carry twenty-two First Class passengers seated

Air-to-air view of Comet 4B G-APMA. (The A.J. Jackson Collection)

four-abreast and sixty-five Tourist Class passengers seated five abreast, or alternatively, 102 passengers in an all-Tourist layout. It was calculated that, based on an annual utilisation of 2400 hrs each, the six Comets would produce the same number of seat-miles as twenty-five Viscounts.

At the time of the Comet order BEA made the decision to dispense with flight engineers on the flight decks of the jets. BEA had built up an extensive network of ground engineers at its bases throughout Europe, and all Comet co-pilots were to be trained to carry out flight engineer duties in addition to their piloting role. This meant adding extra subjects such as refuelling techniques, and electrical and hydraulic systems to the curriculum for their ARB pilots' exams. To form the nucleus of its instructional staff for the flying training programme, BEA chose nine senior Viscount captains, because of their existing theoretical and practical knowledge of gas-turbine operations. Captain G.T. Greenhalgh was appointed head of BEA's Comet Flight. In order to gain Comet operating experience ahead of delivery of the Comet 4Bs, BEA sent its training captains to fly the Comet 3B, a Comet 4 that had been partially modified to Comet 4B standard, and to fly as observers aboard the Comet 2s of No. 216 Squadron, RAF Transport Command on their sorties to Africa and the Far East. The BEA pilots also flew as supernumery crew on BOAC Comet 4 services.

The first Comet 4B, G-APMA, made its maiden flight from Hatfield on 27 June 1959, and during that month BEA and the Greek airline Olympic Airways signed an agreement to operate integrated schedules between Europe and the Middle East via Athens. On the strength of this agreement, Olympic Airways purchased two Comet 4Bs, which were technically identical to BEA's. The maintenance of the Olympic Comets was to be carried out by BEA, and under the agreement it was possible for an Olympic crew to operate a BEA aircraft on their own services, and vice versa. It was then realised that the combined total of eight Comets was still very tight and left no standby capacity, so in August 1959 BEA purchased a ninth example. This allowed one Comet to be based at London as a standby aircraft for either airline. Cyprus Airways also joined the consortium, integrating its services via Nicosia with those of BEA and Olympic Airways.

Comet 4B G-APMA took part in the 1959 London–Paris Air Race. (The A.J. Jackson Collection)

In July 1959 the *Daily Mail* newspaper organised a London-Paris Air Race to celebrate the 50th anniversary of Blériot's cross-Channel flight. BEA entered a 'BEAline' team of thirteen executives, who made the journey suitably attired in bowler hats and carrying briefcases and umbrellas. Comet 4B G-APMA was loaned by de Havilland for the cross-Channel leg, and other modes of transport used included the London Underground, a London Transport bus and French taxis. The fastest competitor in the race used an RAF jet fighter and turned in the best overall time of 40 mins 44 sec, but the BEA team won the team prize plus a special prize of £1000 for travelling from Marble Arch to the Arc de Triomphe in sixty-one minutes.

BEA's first Comet 4B was flown to the Comet Base Training Flight at Stansted on 9 November 1959. Two Comets, G-APMB and G-APMC, were handed over in a ceremony at Hatfield on 16 November 1959, nearly two months ahead of the contractual delivery date. At that time BEA had only three captains with Comet licences, but proving flights commenced immediately, and on 5 December 1959 G-APMB made the first visit to Moscow by a BEA Comet. During the course of its programme of proving flights, BEA was involved in a protracted dispute with its pilots over pay. The pilots wanted a special pay award for operating jets, with the senior captains seeking an increase in their salary from £3500 per annum to £4200 per annum and a two-hour reduction in their working day. The pilots were refusing to operate revenue-earning flights until their demands were met, but the dispute was eventually resolved by conciliation, and on 1 April 1960 BEA inaugurated scheduled Comet 4B services. On that date G-APMB, commanded by Captain A.N. Werner, departed Tel Aviv at 0800 hrs GMT to fly to Athens, Rome and

Comet 3B G-ANLO, used for crew training prior to delivery of the Comet 4B fleet. (Kev Darling)

London. On the same day BEA began scheduled Comet services to Moscow, the first flight out of London being commanded by Captain W. Baillie in G-APMD. Jet services to the Middle East in collaboration with Olympic Airways and Cyprus Airways also commenced that day. The April 1960 BEA timetable listed a daily BEA daytime schedule from London to Rome and Athens, which continued onwards to Tel Aviv three times each week. There was also an overnight service on Tuesdays and Thursdays, which flew London-Munich-Athens under a BEA flight number and then continued onwards to Nicosia and Tel Aviv as a Cyprus Airways flight. Under the same arrangement Cyprus Airways also flew Athens-Istanbul three times weekly, Athens-Nicosia-Beirut once weekly, and Athens-Nicosia twice weekly, all as extensions of BEA London-Athens services. Olympic Airways also operated Comets from London to Athens and onwards to the Middle East, although until mid-July it was still possible to make the trip in an Olympic Airways piston-powered DC-6B!

The Comets were configured to carry twenty-two passengers in First Class, marketed under the revived name Silver Wing. The sixty-four-seat Tourist Class accommodation was divided into two cabins, a fifteen-seat compartment and the main cabin, with an adjustable bulkhead in between. The interior decor included seats in 'tomato and charcoal' coloured fabrics.

During 1960 the BEA Comets entered service on a number of the shorter European routes, to Warsaw and Zurich in May, to Copenhagen in June, to Stockholm via Oslo in July, and to Frankfurt on 1 August. During the period 1 May to 31 October 1960, the fleet of six aircraft achieved a daily utilisation of six hours per machine at a load factor of 66 per cent, and carried 15 per cent of BEA's summer traffic. To fly these services, BEA had trained about ninety pilots during the preceeding six months. This process was greatly aided by the use of the airline's Comet simulators, based at Heston. They cost £180,000 each and were also used by Olympic Airways.

During 1960 two incidents resulted in the temporary grounding of some Comet 4Bs. On 29 October the nosewheel axle of one of BEA's aircraft fractured during taxiing at London Airport. The Comet slid forward for some yards, but was not badly damaged. All the BEA Comets were, however, grounded for some twelve hours while their nosewheel legs were inspected. Then, on 6 November, a BEA Comet 4B was taxying out at Zurich when it

Comet 4B, G-APMG at Manchester, with a Dan-Air Ambassador and an Aer Lingus Viscount in the background. (Kev Darling)

suffered a fracture of the nosewheel leg axle, which resulted in the loss of both nosewheels. After this second incident all BEA's Comet nosewheel axles were replaced as a precautionary measure. The problem was attributed to the extra stresses imposed on the undercarriage during intensive short-haul operations, and a special axle sleeve was fitted to all the Comet 4Bs to strengthen the axle.

During 1961 Comet 4B equipment was introduced onto BEA's services to Geneva (from 1 April), and Düsseldorf (from 1 May). The jets were to be graced by royal personages many times that year. On 29 April the Queen and Prince Philip flew to Alghero, the aircraft then returning to London with the Queen Mother on the following day. As part of the same trip the royal couple, accompanied by the Duke and Duchess of Gloucester, were transported onwards from Alghero to Ancona on 5 May. They returned to London from Turin on 9 May, while the Duke and Duchess of Gloucester eventually flew home to London from Crete on 25 May.

At the end of 1961 disaster struck the Comet fleet. On 21 December G-ARJM was at Esenboga Airport, Ankara, on a scheduled service from London to Tel Aviv via Rome, Athens, Istanbul, Ankara and Nicosia. The Comet took off from Ankara with twenty-seven passengers and seven crew aboard, but a second or two after leaving the ground, it was seen to assume an excessively steep climb angle. There were also reports of wing

Landing shot of Comet 4B G-ARCP, later sold to BEA Airtours. (Kev Darling)

drop and fluctuations in engine noise during the initial climb. At a height of about 450 ft the aircraft entered a stalled situation, with the left wing down. It sank to the ground in a relatively flat attitude and crashed about 1600 m from the airport. All the occupants were killed. The accident investigation found the probable cause to be 'obstruction of the pitch pointer in the Captain's director horizon, which led him to make an excessively steep climb immediately following unstick'.

By April 1962, BEA had sixty captains and ninety-five first officers on its Comet Flight, and the expansion of jet services continued. On 1 April a four times weekly service to Helsinki via Stockholm was inaugurated, and 28 October marked the first Comet 4B service between London and Paris. Accidents still caused disruption to operations, however. On 2 August 1963 G-ARJN made a heavy landing in bad weather at Milan. Two people were injured and the aircraft was damaged.

In 1964 Trident jets finally began to be phased into BEA service. The workload on the Comets began to decrease, but they were still called upon to open new routes, such as a nonstop London-Tel Aviv schedule from 1 April 1964. Another Comet was involved in a

Comet 3B G-ANLO in BEA livery at the Farnborough Air Show. (Kev Darling)

landing incident on 5 November 1964, when G-APMD skidded off the runway at Malaga in heavy rain and gale force winds and sustained considerable damage.

On 3 April 1966 Comets were used to inaugurate non-stop flights between London and Tangier, and it was in that year that the type first entered service on UK domestic routes. Until then, BEA had been operating Vickers Vanguard turboprops on peak-hour services to Glasgow and Edinburgh, supplemented by Viscounts on off-peak flights. However, in 1966 BAC One-Eleven jets were scheduled to these cities by British Eagle from Heathrow and by British United Airways from Gatwick. In order to remain competitive BEA placed Comet 4Bs onto their peak-hour flights to Glasgow from 2 May, but the airline claimed to be doing so reluctantly, as it made little profit on the route with Vanguards and would actually lose money with jets. BEA even claimed to have offered to ban jets from its domestic routes to reduce noise pollution if its competitors would agree to follow suit.

Since April 1960 the Comets had been flying to Moscow with interpreters as part of their crew complement, and in June 1966 G.M.N. Usher, Russian Interpreter, Comet Flight, completed his two-hundredth round trip between London and Moscow. Since his first trip on 11 May 1964, he had accumulated a total of 1400 flying hours on the route.

The Comets began to appear on regional international services in 1967 when BEA commenced direct Manchester-Malta operations, but the airline suffered another fatal Comet crash that year. On 12 October G-ARCO departed Athens for Nicosia at 0241 hrs on flight CY284, operated for Cyprus Airways. Some 185 km off Ródhos, Greece, and at an altitude of 29,000 ft, a bomb exploded under a seat in the rear of the Tourist cabin. At

Air-to-air view of Comet 4B G-APMA. (Kev Darling)

Comet 4B G-APMA, with shiny silver fuselage undersides. (Kev Darling)

15,000 ft the Comet broke up and crashed into the sea. There were no survivors among the fifty-nine passengers and seven crew.

The Comets began to be phased out of front-line service in 1968, and the year began badly. On 4 February G-ARGM was commencing its approach to Nicosia when the undercarriage failed to lock down correctly. The flight was diverted to RAF Akrotiri where better emergency facilities were available, and made an emergency landing there on a bed of foam. Seventeen people were injured and the Comet sustained considerable damage.

Comets were introduced onto London-Hanover-Bremen services on 1 April 1968, and onto the London-Berlin (Templehof) route on 31 July, but these were stop-gap measures and they were withdrawn again once sufficient Super One-Elevens were available to replace them. During the period 1968-70 the Comets were gradually withdrawn and placed into storage, but in the summer 1969 BEA timetable seven Comet 4Bs were still shown as in service, operating in a ninety-six-seat Tourist Class layout. The type was rostered to operate a daily round trip between Glasgow and Birmingham and two weekday rotations between Manchester and Glasgow until 30 June, and four weekday trips from London to Dublin and back until 31 May. By the summer of 1970, no Comets were rostered for scheduled services, but G-APMA was retained as a standby aircraft for other types. During the winter of 1970/1 it was pressed into service to cover for aircraft shortages, and flew London-Dublin five times weekly, London-Bergen twice-weekly, and once-weekly London-Malta and London-Paris. Comets that had been passed on to BEA Airtours were also leased back at various times during that winter.

The summer of 1971 saw G-APMA still carrying out its back-up duties, operating a total of six round trips from London each week. On Mondays it flew to Glasgow and back

BEA Comet 4B G-ARJN at Manchester. (Kev Darling)

Comet 4B G-ARJK surrounded by servicing vehicles during turnround. (Kev Darling)

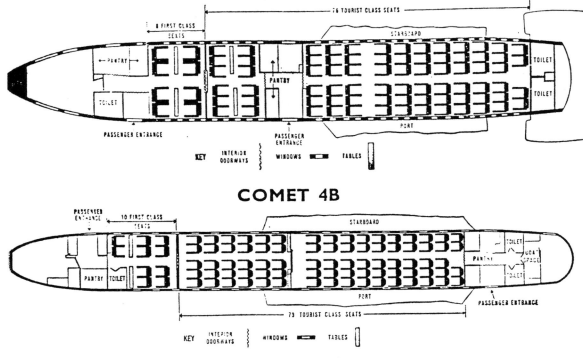

COMET 4B

Alternative seating layouts for the Comet 4B. (via Author)

Proposed BEA Britannia srs 323 route network. (via Author)

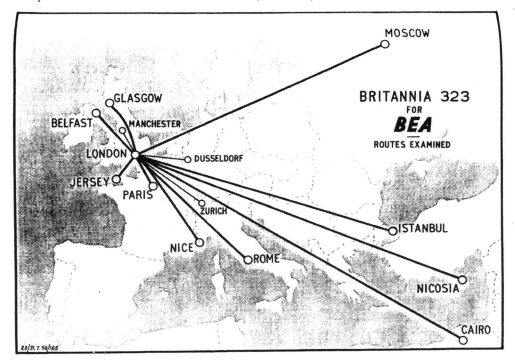

BRISTOL BRITANNIA 323

for

BRITISH EUROPEAN AIRWAYS

August 1956

Cover of 1956 Bristol brochure on proposed Britannia srs 323 for BEA. (via Author)

as flights BE5054/5063 and to Helsinki and return as BE770/771. On Tuesdays, Wednesdays and Thursdays it visited Malaga as BE130/131, and on Saturdays it operated flights BE712/713 to Dubrovnik and back. The aircraft's final service for BEA was flight BE131 from Malaga to Heathrow on 31 October 1971. In BEA scheduled service the Comet 4B fleet had carried some seven million passengers, and many of the Comets continued to fly for BEA's charter subsidiary BEA Airtours on package holiday charters.

Vanguard Operations

BEA issued an outline requirement for a Viscount replacement as far back as 1953. This aircraft was to carry sixty passengers on non-stop flights to the farthest points on the route network, and to enter service in 1959. In 1956 Bristol Aircraft produced a brochure on their proposed Britannia srs 323, which was specifically tailored to meet BEA's needs. It was to be powered by four Bristol Proteus 755 turboprops, conferring a cruising speed of 400 mph at an altitude of 23,000 ft. Bristol claimed that the external noise level on take-off would be less than that of the Dakota, which was still in widespread service with BEA at the time. Delivery was promised for September 1958, or possibly as early as July 1957 if existing Britannia options were not taken up by customers. A range of seating options was offered, including a five-abreast eighty-seven-seat Tourist Class layout and a mixed-class configuration with eighteen First Class seats and eighty-four Tourist Class seats arranged six-abreast. Bristol's figures showed a break-even load factor on the London-Paris route of 63 per cent in First Class and 70 per cent in Tourist. On the longer London-Rome route, these figures would be reduced to 34 per cent in First Class and 39 per cent in Tourist. The Britannia 323 was also claimed to be very suitable for domestic routes such as London-Manchester and London-Belfast. It was offered to BEA at a price of £1,613,000 per example, including spares. However, all Bristol's efforts were to no avail, as on 20 July 1956 BEA signed a contract with Vicker-Armstrong (Aircraft) Ltd for twenty Vanguard aircraft intended for service entry in 1960.

At first, BEA wanted the design to have a high-set wing to give passengers the best possible view, but then fell into line with Trans-Canada Airlines, the only other airline to order the Vanguard. The design was finalised as the Vickers V950 Vanguard, capable of accommodating up to 100 passengers and powered by four Rolls-Royce Tyne turboprop engines. Notable features of the Vanguard design were its large cargo holds and capacious 'double-bubble' fuselage, which were to provide it with a 'second career' as a freighter once its passenger-carrying days were over. In 1958 BEA realised that on shorter routes, where maximum fuel was not required, the weight thus saved could be traded for extra payload in order to utilise fully the Vanguard's total gross weight of 63,958 kg. To meet this scenario, in July 1958 Vickers-Armstrong announced the V953 Vanguard variant, with a payload of 13,154 kg. BEA promptly tried to amend its order so that all of its aircraft were this model, but by then the first six Vanguards were in an advanced state of construction as V951s and so the BEA order was amended to comprise six V951s and

Vanguard 951 G-APEC broke up in mid-air near Ghent in October 1971. (The A.J. Jackson Collection)

Vanguard 951 G-APED was finally scrapped at Heathrow in 1973. (The A.J. Jackson Collection)

fourteen V953s. The prototype Vanguard, V950 G-AOYW, made its maiden flight on 20 January 1959, from Weybridge to Wisley under the command of Captain G.R. Bryce.

BEA's Vanguards were intended to enter commercial service on 1 July 1960, and early that year G-APED carried out a programme of route-proving flights to cities such as Paris and Brussels. However, the new Tyne engines ran into technical problems during bench-testing and Rolls-Royce recommended that the Vanguards be grounded until the faults were cured. This took until almost the end of the year, and it was not until 2 December 1960 that the V951 Vanguard was granted its Certificate of Airworthiness and BEA took

Vanguard 951 G-APEE on final approach, prior to its crash at Heathrow in October 1965. (The A.J. Jackson Collection)

Vanguard 953 G-APEI at Heathrow surrounded by service vehicles. (The A.J. Jackson Collection)

delivery of its first example, G-APEE, at Wisley. During that month the type began to be used on an ad hoc basis on some scheduled services, commencing with a flight from London to Paris by G-APEF under the command of Captain A.S. Johnson on 17 December 1960. This was thus the first passenger-carrying service by a Vanguard, and the V951s subsequently made further ad hoc appearances in place of the advertised type on other routes. On 19 December G-APEE flew London-Zurich and back and then operated a service to Geneva on the following day. It then positioned to Düsseldorf and flew a Düsseldorf-London service on 21 December. Meanwhile G-APEF had appeared on a London-Glasgow schedule on the 20th.

The V951 Vanguard entered regular BEA scheduled service on 1 March 1961, but during the spring and summer of that year a shortage of Vanguard and Comet capacity led to BEA leasing aircraft from BOAC for use on European routes. BOAC Britannia 312s were mainly employed on services to Copenhagen, Frankfurt and Nice, while Douglas DC-7Cs operated four daily round trips to Paris (Le Bourget) and also flew to Zurich and Frankfurt. On 18 May 1961 the V953 Vanguard entered scheduled service with BEA, the inaugural flight being operated from London to Paris by G-APEG.

The November 1961 BEA timetable showed the Vanguard fleet heavily committed to domestic mainline routes. Six London-Glasgow round trips, each offering First and Tourist Class accommodation, were operated each weekday. On the London-Edinburgh route morning and evening Vanguard services operated on weekdays, and the type was also used at weekends. The Vanguards also operated a London-Glasgow-Edinburgh-Glasgow-London Off-Peak Night service every day except Saturdays, and three round trips between London and Belfast each day. A single London-Manchester-London service was operated by Vanguards on weekdays. The big turboprops were also utilised on a few round trips each day between London and Paris. At that time, BEA's Vanguards and Viscounts had competition on the route from the Caravelles and Super Constellations of Air France, as well as the Comet 4Bs of Olympic Airways, with daily round trips. Both of these airlines operated into Orly Airport at Paris. On the BEA flights, complementary meals or refreshments were served to First Class passengers, but Tourist Class passengers had to purchase food packs before boarding at Heathrow or Le Bourget. Vanguards were also used for services to Malta. On Sundays a Vanguard operated the London-Palermo-Malta service under a BEA flight number and then continued onwards to Tripoli as a Malta Airlines flight. There was also a BEA flight from London to Malta via Naples on Thursdays. Competition for traffic to Malta came from the UK independent airline Skyways of London, which operated a weekly overnight flight from London to Tunis and Malta using venerable Handley Page Hermes aircraft in all-Tourist configuration.

On 11 April 1962 BEA Vanguard G-APEF flew into a large flock of seagulls shortly after taking off from Edinburgh. Two engines failed immediately and the Vanguard returned to Edinburgh for an emergency landing. Shortly after touchdown a third engine failed.

During 1962 Vanguards were introduced onto the routes from London to Barcelona, Dublin, Gibraltar and Palma. By the summer they were responsible for nearly half of the services on the domestic trunk routes from London to Belfast, Edinburgh and Glasgow. Their introduction resulted in traffic growth of 21 per cent on the Scottish routes and 16 per cent on the Belfast service. During the early 1960s BEA slashed the check-in period at Glasgow (Renfrew) to ten minutes for London-bound passengers with hand baggage only. The scheduled flying time to Heathrow was one hour and ten minutes, and a BEA coach would be waiting to convey them onwards to the town terminal in Cromwell Road. The average total journey time between the city centres was around two and a half hours, compared with about eight hours by train. In October 1962 the new terminal building at Manchester Airport was officially opened by the Duke of Edinburgh; the first BEA aircraft to use the new facilities was a Vanguard on flight BE4010 from London, under the command of Captain Ron Burrows.

During 1962 Watney's Draught Red Barrel beer was introduced on Gibraltar, and proved so popular that supplies ran dry that summer. BEA was contracted to fly over

Vanguard 953 G-APEN on final approach in the last BEA livery. (The A.J. Jackson Collection)

Final approach view of Vanguard 953 G-APET. (The A.J. Jackson Collection)

twenty 10-gallon kegs of the brew in the cargo hold of its Vanguard service, the first airlift of beer into Gibraltar.

On 29 March 1963 Vanguard G-APEJ landed at Dublin in a nose-down attitude and its nosewheel collapsed on touchdown. Later that year G-APEF had the distinction of operating what was scheduled to be the last service from Heathrow to Nutts Corner airport at Belfast. The aircraft performing flight BE6062 departed Heathrow at 2140 hrs on 25 September 1963 for Nutts Corner, but crosswinds there resulted in the Vanguard being diverted to the new Belfast airport at Aldergrove. The last BEA scheduled service out of Nutts Corner was flight BE6074, a Vanguard departure at 2245 hrs on 25 September, and BEA's Vanguard G-APEH operated the first passenger-carrying service out of Aldergrove the following day. Another Vanguard to suffer the indignity of a heavy landing was G-APEE, whose nosewheel collapsed as a result at Glasgow on 6 October 1964. Serious as this was, a worse fate was in store for this aircraft and its occupants the following year.

At 0015 hrs on 27 October 1965 G-APEE began its approach to runway 28R at Heathrow at the conclusion of a Night Tourist service from Edinburgh. The weather at Heathrow was foggy, with a Runway Visual Range of 350 m. At 0023 hrs an overshoot was initiated, and the decision was taken to attempt a landing on runway 28L, where the Runway Visual Range was 500 m. The Instrument Landing System (IAS) on this runway was not fully functional, so a full talkdown service was provided by air traffic control. At 0035 hrs, however, this approach was also abandoned. The Vanguard then proceeded to the holding point at Garston and circled there for thirty minutes or so. During this period another Vanguard landed successfully on runway 28R, but a further one was forced to overshoot. At 0118 hrs, without any improvement in the weather, the crew of G-APEE commenced another monitored approach, this time to runway 28R. At 0122 hrs the Precision Approach Radar controller informed them that they were three-quarters of a mile from touchdown and lined up with the runway centreline. Twenty-two seconds later the pilot in command announced that he was once more overshooting. The aircraft climbed to between 400 and 500 ft, then the climb changed to a steep dive and the

Vanguard crashed onto the runway about 2600 ft from the threshold. All thirty passengers and six crew were killed. The inquiry into the accident attributed the probable cause to a combination of factors, including the pilot's lack of experience of overshooting in fog, position error in the pressure-driven instruments and the crew's over-reliance on them, and incorrect flap selection.

In early 1966 the authorities at London Zoo decided to fly their female Panda Chi-Chi to Moscow for mating with the Moscow Zoo's Panda, An-An. On 10 March 1966 BEA Vanguard V953 G-APEO was taken out of service and moved to the BEA Engineering Base at Heathrow for the neccessary modifications for the trip. The Vanguard's 132-seat all-Tourist cabin was reduced to sixteen First and seventy-one Tourist configuration, the bulkheads and catering were repositioned, and the forward airstairs were removed. The journey to Moscow, with the Panda and thirty passengers, including many press representatives, took four and a half hours. All the effort was to no avail, however, as the mating attempts were unsuccessful, and Chi-Chi was returned to London the following summer.

During the summer of 1966 BEA's Vanguard schedules were thrown into disarray by a series of failures in their Tyne engines, which reached its height in May and June. Aircraft sat idle for days whilst awaiting the spare parts necessary to re-engine them. For the summer of 1967 BEA introduced a new destination, Gerona in Spain. Daytime services were operated by Comets but Vanguards were responsible for five night-time flights each week. They were also used to open a new weekly service from Glasgow to Palma. The end of the 1968 summer season also saw the end of BEA operations to Klagenfurt in Austria, with a Vanguard departure from Klagenfurt at 1720 hrs on 13th October 1968 to Munich and London.

BEA still had thirteen Vanguards in passenger service in the summer of 1969. Five were V951s configured for eighteen First Class and 108 Tourist Class passengers; the remainder were V953s with 135 Tourist Class seats. Twice a week they operated a morning flight from Birmingham to London, returning in the late evening. They were also used for a limited number of Manchester-London services, and in mid-summer they flew five-times daily between Belfast and London. On this route a small number of seats in the quieter rear compartment of the cabin were pre-bookable for a supplement of £1. The type was still used exclusively on the Edinburgh-London route, operating nine round trips on weekdays. Apart from one Night Tourist service, these flights all offered First and Tourist Class seating. The Glasgow-London route was shared with Tridents, but even so the Vanguards still made eight round trips every weekday, with all but three of them offering First and Tourist Class accommodation. The fare from London to Glasgow or Edinburgh was £9.13.0 for a Tourist single ticket, £13.1.0 for a First single, £7.9.0 for a Night Tourist single, or £7.10.0 for a Tourist Standby single ticket. Vanguards also operated a daily Night Tourist service from London to Dublin, and a round trip between London and Shannon on Saturdays and Sundays.

In 1970 BEA operated daily Vanguard flights to Leipzig for the duration of the twice-yearly Leipzig Trade Fair. However, at the end of the summer season it ceased operations to Gerona, the last Gerona-London service being flown by a Vanguard on 31 October 1970.

For the summer of 1971 the Vanguards were again kept busy on the BEA domestic schedules. Seven round trips each day were operated between London and Belfast; there were eight flights each way on the London-Edinburgh route on weekdays; four daily round trips beween London and Glasgow; and daily services from London to Jersey and from London to Manchester. In addition, there was one flight each weekday from Manchester to Belfast and return, and on Wednesdays only there was a London-Guernsey-London service. The big turboprops were still to be seen occasionally on international schedules, flying London-Salzburg-London on Wednesdays and Saturdays. They also operated to Gibraltar, with a direct daytime service on four days each week, a Night Tourist flight on Tuesdays and Saturdays, and an indirect routeing via Madrid that flew out from London on Mondays and returned on Thursdays. There were also Vanguard flights between Heathrow and Malta, operated in conjunction with Malta Airlines. Night Tourist services operated on a daily basis, and there was also a daytime operation on Saturdays.

On 2 October 1971 V951 Vanguard G-APEC was operating flight BE706 from London to Salzburg. It was in the vicinity of Aarsele in Belgium when a structural failure of the rear pressure bulkhead occurred. The Vanguard started to break up, spiralled down out of control, and crashed in a field next to a highway. All fifty-five passengers and eight crew members perished.

During 1973 the remaining Vanguards began to be phased out of passenger service, but during the summer of that year they were still operating to Salzburg three times each week. They also flew to Gibraltar on a weekly basis, as well as on some domestic schedules to Belfast, Jersey and Edinburgh from London, and from Birmingham to Jersey. They were also to be seen operating passenger charter flights to Munich from Bristol, Exeter, Liverpool and Tees-Side airports. By the time the winter schedules commenced on 1 November 1973, only four Vanguards remained in BEA passenger service. The remainder had been sold or scrapped, or were undergoing conversion to Merchantman freighters. The four survivors, G-APEH, G-APEI, G-APER and G-APEU, were rostered to operate only three scheduled flights each week, one to Gibraltar and two to Edinburgh. For the rest of the time they acted as back-up aircraft for the Trident fleet, or operated charter flights. The airline's final Vanguard passenger service actually took place after BEA had been amalgamated into British Airways, when G-APEU flew a round trip between Heathrow and Jersey on 16 June 1974.

Trident Operations

In response to an announced requirement for a jet airliner capable of carrying over a hundred passengers on short/medium-haul routes, and with the ability to land in poor visibility, BEA was approached by three aircraft manufacturers. Bristol offered its Model 200, with three engines and a 'T-Tail', while Avro offered its Avro 740 design, again with three engines but with a 'V-Tail' configuration. The design selected by BEA in January 1958, however, was the DH 121, to be built by the Airco consortium. This aircraft had three Rolls-Royce Medway engines clustered around the tail unit. Its 35-degree swept wing was aerodynamically clean and gave the design a high cruising speed of over 600 mph. An unusual feature was the offset nosewheel, which retracted sideways. The DH 121 had a gross weight of 150,000 lb, a range of 2070 miles, and could carry up to 111 passengers.

On 1 March 1958 the government approved BEA's intention to order twenty-four DH 121s. By 1959, however, BEA had developed reservations about the aircraft, considering

VANGUARD NINE FIVE THREE

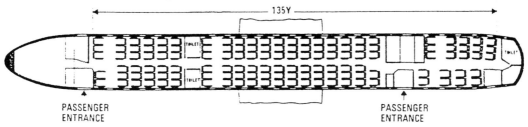

Vanguard 953 seating plan (all-Economy layout). (via Author)

it to be too big for its needs. The original design was shelved and replaced by one for a shorter aircraft with three of the less powerful Rolls-Royce Spey engines, a 'T-Tail', a gross weight of 105,000 lb, and a range of 930 miles. Interestingly, as the design was tailored to BEA's specification for a short-range aircraft with very low operating costs, no provision was made for the serving of hot meals and the seats were non-reclining. The design was finalised, work on systems and structures commenced, and on 12 August 1959 BEA signed a £28 million contract for twenty-four DH 121s, with an option on a further twelve.

The new airliner needed a name, and in May 1960 BEA Chairman Lord Douglas of Kirtleside offered a prize of £100 to the staff member of BEA or one of the three companies, de Havilland, Fairey Aviation and Hunting, which made up the Airco consortium, who suggested the best name. Some 1075 entries were submitted, twenty-five of them proposing the name Trident. On 8 August 1960 the DH 121 was officially named Trident, after deliberations by a panel of judges headed by Lord Douglas, who said the name reflected 'a natural allusion to the new formula of this advanced aircraft with its triplex arrangement for engines, controls and systems. This constitutes a fundamental feature for reliable automatic landing'. The first Trident, G-ARPA, was rolled out in the full BEA colour scheme at Hatfield on 4 August 1961, on the same day that BEA's final Comet 4B was handed over to the airline. The Trident made its maiden flight on 9 January 1962, and during its development so many enhancements were made that BEA's initial model was renamed Trident 1C. Among the improvements were the addition of an extra centre-section fuel tank to increase the range to 1400 miles, and the installation of reclining seats and a hot meal galley after all.

BEA pilot training on the Trident commenced in October 1963. The first example to be delivered was G-ARPF on 13 December 1963. It was immediately put to work on crew training sorties from Stansted, and it was during this period that a Trident was flown by HRH the Duke of Edinburgh. He took the controls of G-ARPH on 3 April 1964 during a 90-minute training sortie out of Stansted. He carried out two landings, becoming the first member of the Royal family to fly in the type

When first delivered to BEA, the Trident 1Cs were fitted out in either an eighty-seat-mixed-class configuration, with four-abreast seating in First Class and six-abreast in Economy, or with ninety-three Economy seats arranged six-abreast. The Trident cabin was unusual in that it included a couple of aft-facing rows of seats in the forward cabin and three similar rows in the main cabin. The Trident was officially christened by Lady

BEA's first Trident, srs 1C G-ARPA. (The A.J. Jackson Collection)

Douglas at Heathrow on 28 February 1964, when she poured a bottle of champagne over the nose of G-ARPG. This aircraft operated BEA's first Trident revenue service on the morning of 11 March 1964, when it replaced a Comet on a London-Copenhagen morning schedule. Tridents were substituted for other types on an ad hoc basis, chiefly on schedules to Geneva and Nice, on about four flights each week until 1 April 1964, when the Trident entered regular scheduled service with BEA. Once again G-ARPG was used, the inaugural service being the 0950 hrs flight BE564 from London to Zurich. From that date Tridents operated daily to Zurich and Nice. By the end of the year, they were also in service on routes from London to Helsinki, Stockholm, Copenhagen, Rome, Frankfurt, Geneva, Valencia, Brussels, Barcelona, Munich, Prague, Venice and Vienna.

One notable Trident passenger in 1964 was BEA's outgoing Chairman, Lord Douglas of Kirtleside. On the Thursday before Easter he made his farewell flight with BEA in this capacity, on the inaugural Trident service to Vienna. To mark the occasion he was piped aboard G-ARPG by a Scots piper. Lord Douglas was succeeded by Anthony Milward, who said at his first press conference: 'On the London to Frankfurt route, the hottest and most competitive, on which there are eighteen jet flights a day, we could not hold our own with the Viscount, but with the Trident we have increased our load factor by 10 per cent since June.'

The Trident had many outstanding virtues, but it was never renowned for its short-field performance. It soon aquired the nickname 'Gripper' because of its long take-off run, and it was said that it only left the ground because of the curvature of the earth! A more serious shortcoming was discovered after the Trident 1C had been in service for some months. It became apparent that it could not carry a full payload on certain routes, either because of runway limitations or because of the high ambient temperatures at some destination

Air-to-air shot of Trident 1C G-ARPB. (The A.J. Jackson Collection)

airports. The London-Athens service could not be operated non-stop, and Comet 4Bs still had to be used on some of the longer sectors. These long stage-lengths had not been envisaged when the original BEA specification was issued. The Trident 1C's shortcomings resulted in a proposal from Hawker Siddeley for a Trident 1F, with Rolls-Royce Spey 511 engines, up to 128 seats in a five-abreast configuration and the ability to fly non-stop from London to Athens, Beirut and Tel Aviv.

On 5 August 1965 BEA announced a £30 million order for fifteen Trident 1Fs for delivery from 1968, plus options on a further ten examples. The contract was officially signed on 26 August 1965. As the design evolved, the type name was changed, firstly to Trident 2ER and then to Trident 2E. This model had a sealed tail fin incorporating an additional 350 imp. gallon fuel tank and Spey 25-512 engines of increased thrust. In 1966 it was announced that the Trident 1Cs were to be re-engined with the Spey 1A, producing 5 per cent more power. Meanwhile the Trident 1Cs continued to be introduced onto more routes, and by 31 March 1965 fourteen examples had been delivered. On the following day BEA inaugurated a new 'Quicksilver' service between London and Paris. Thirteen flights a day were scheduled to make the trip in a flying time of fifty-five minutes, although it usually only took in the region of forty minutes to get from Heathrow to Le Bourget. Other journey times were being slashed too. On 17 May 1965 Captain R.E. Bell flew a Trident from London to Oslo in ninety minutes. In May 1946 the same journey by Dakota aircraft had been scheduled at 4 hrs 48 mins.

The Trident was designed from the outset for eventual fully automatic landings in bad weather. A milestone was passed on 10 June 1965 when Trident 1C G-ARPR made the world's first autoflare touchdown (albeit in good weather) with fare-paying passengers aboard at the conclusion of flight BE343 from Le Bourget (Paris) to London. In command

Take-off shot of Trident 1C G-ARPC. (The A.J. Jackson Collection)

was BEA's Flight Manager, Development, Captain Eric Poole, and to mark the occasion each passenger was presented with a certificate. On 1 July 1965 BEA inaugurated jet services from Manchester, when Tridents replaced Viscounts on the Manchester-Paris route, the inaugural service being operated by Trident 1C G-ARPO. By the following summer, BEA was using Trident equipment on services from Manchester to Copenhagen, Brussels, Amsterdam, Düsseldorf, Zurich and Paris.

Meanwhile, back at Heathrow, BEA had introduced 'airbridges' at the Europa Terminal (now Terminal Two). These allowed passengers to be 'trickle-loaded' as they checked in for their flights, and they were introduced on services to Paris from 15 November 1965. By March 1966 twenty-one Tridents had been delivered, and on 1 April the type entered service on the London-Cologne route, followed by London-Basle on the following day. For the summer of 1966 a modified exterior paint scheme was applied to the fleet, with the fuselage undersides being painted grey in place of the previous polished metal. Later, the name 'Trident' was to be applied to each side of the centre engine air intake. On 16 January 1967 G-ARPC inaugurated Trident operations to Belfast. These were two-class services, featuring an eight-seat First Class cabin.

Progress towards fully automated landings continued, and on 19 April 1967 the Smiths Autoland system was certified at duplex level for Category 1 operations. Then, on 16 May 1967, Trident 1C G-ARPP made the world's first fully automated landing by an airliner on a commercial service when it arrived at London from Nice. The passengers were given a commemorative tie or neck-scarf. This landing signalled the commencement of 'Operation Automatic', which was to involve G-ARPP in a programme of twenty-seven duplex automatic landings during the course of a week, at fifteen airports in nine countries. The programme terminated on 23 May when G-ARPP arrived at London from Frankfurt. Some 1400 passengers had been landed automatically during 34 hrs 30 mins of flying time. On average, only forty seconds out of each flying hour was under manual control, mainly during the take-off phase.

This year ended on an unfortunate note for the Trident fleet. On 3 December G-ARPU landed short of the runway at Copenhagen and struck a pipe. Six people were injured and the aircraft suffered substantial damage.

On 7 February 1968 the Trident 1Cs were cleared for full Category 2 duplex autoland, and this was followed by clearance for triplex Category 2 autoland in September of that year. In the intervening period, G-ARPD had demonstrated the Trident's speed by flying from Paris to London on 7 March in a 'block to block' time of twenty-seven minutes.

BEA's first Trident 2E, G-AVFC, was handed over to the airline on 15 February 1968, on a special category Certificate of Airworthiness for crew training and route-proving flights. On the following day it was christened by Lady Milward, the wife of BEA's Chairman, with a cup of British cider instead of the usual champagne. As with the Trident 1C this variant first entered BEA service on an ad hoc basis, being substituted for other types on scheduled flights. Its first appearance in this capacity was on 17 April 1968, when it replaced a Trident 1C, on a London-Milan service. Regular scheduled services

Trident 1C G-ARPJ on take-off. (The A.J. Jackson Collection)

Air-to-air view of Trident 1C G-ARPL. (The A.J. Jackson Collection)

commenced on 1 June 1968, the initial destinations being Madrid, Stockholm, Dublin and Milan. Three cabin layouts were available: eighty-five Tourist Class seats plus eight First Class; seventy-three Tourist Class seats plus sixteen First Class; or ninety-seven seats in an all-Tourist configuration. BEA marketed the aircraft as the 'Trident Two', and took full-page magazine advertisments to promote it as 'the fastest, most advanced jetliner in Europe'. In another advertising campaign in 1969, it was described as 'Triumphant Trident Two. The Number 1 plane for Number 1 people'.

Later in 1968 Trident 2Es replaced Comet 4Bs on routes from London to Moscow, Athens, Beirut, Nicosia and Tel Aviv, and on 3 November 1968 they inaugurated London-Gothenburg services. Before that, however, the BEA Trident fleet was to be depleted in an accident in which the BEA aircraft just happened to be in the wrong place at the wrong time. On 3 July 1968 an ex-BEA Elizabethan (Ambassador), G-AMAD, was landing at Heathrow on a racehorse charter flight for its new owners, BKS Air Transport. Just before touchdown, the hinge mechanism on one of its flaps failed. In an asymmetric flap condition, the aircraft veered off the runway centreline and crashed into two empty BEA Trident 1Cs that were parked in the Central Area. Its wing clipped the tail fin of G-ARPI and sliced completely through the rear fuselage of G-ARPT. The tail of G-ARPI was smashed off above the centre engine air intake 'S' duct, but the aircraft was repaired and eventually returned to service in February 1969. However, G-ARPT was damaged beyond repair and was broken up.

During 1968 BEA came close to entering Trident aircraft for the *Daily Mail* Transatlantic Air Race. On 20 April the newspaper announced the race, which was to celebrate the fiftieth anniversary of Alcock and Brown's pioneering flight across the Atlantic. BEA proposed using three Tridents in relay to carry its 'runner' from London to New York. A Trident 1C would fly from London to Shannon, where a Trident 2E would take over for the Shannon-Gander leg. Then another Trident 2E would carry out the final leg from Gander to New York. In the event, BEA had to withdraw for financial reasons when hoped-for sponsorship from Castrol and the loan of a Trident 2E from Hawker Siddeley failed to materialise.

Non-stop Trident services to Athens were inaugurated on 2 January 1969. On 1 July Tridents were introduced onto the London-Stuttgart route. The summer 1969 timetable featured Trident operations on many UK domestic services. On weekdays two daily round trips were operated between London and Belfast, and four between London and Glasgow. There was also a twice-weekly Trident round trip between Manchester and Glasgow, and daily services between London and Dublin and London and Shannon. On 29 July 1969 another Trident was lost, fortunately without casualties. Trident 1C G-ARPS was destroyed by fire whilst parked at Heathrow. Arson was suspected but never definitely established as the cause.

In April 1970 BEA's pioneering work with the development of autoland techniques was recognised when the airline received the Queen's Award to Industry for Technological Achievement. Throughout that year Trident 2Es appeared on more routes, including new services to eastern Europe. On 3 April a twice-weekly London-Budapest-Bucharest route was inaugurated, and on 2 June another twice-weekly service commenced, this time to Sofia via Belgrade. By the summer of 1970 Trident 2Es had completely replaced Comet 4Bs on international scheduled services, and on 7 November they were used to open a weekly schedule from London to Marrakesh via Gibraltar.

Trident 1C G-ARPN at Heathrow with two other Tridents and a Vanguard. (The A.J. Jackson Collection)

BEA's first Trident 2E G-AVFC in the 'Red Square' livery. (The A.J. Jackson Collection)

Back in 1965, when Anthony Milward had ordered Trident 2Es for BEA, he had announced a future requirement for thirty-six 'Airbus-type' aircraft for delivery from 1970. He was anticipating the aquisition of the 300-seat European Airbus in the mid-1970s, but wanted to order a mixed fleet of Boeing 727s and 737s as an interim measure. Failing to secure government approval for the dollar purchase of these aircraft, he then set his sights on the proposed BAC Two-Eleven, but this project was not proceeded with. Another 'paper' contender was a 200-plus seat version of the BAC VC-10, but this was rejected by the airline.

What BEA was looking for was an aircraft with extra range and improved 'hot and high' take-off performance for its Mediterranean routes. To meet the requirement, Hawker Siddeley offered the Trident 3B (Boost), with three Rolls-Royce Spey 512s plus an additional RB.162-86 engine mounted above the central Spey, just below the rudder. This engine was intended for use only during take-offs and noise abatement procedure climb-outs, in conditions where the runway length and ambient temperatures would otherwise have prevented operation with a full payload. It offered 15 per cent extra thrust on take-off, for a 5 per cent weight penalty. The Trident 3B was also fitted with an AirResearch auxiliary power unit, and had a fuselage 16 ft 5 in longer than the 1C and 2E models. The wingspan was the same, but an increase in the wing chord resulted in an additional 32 square feet of wing area. The wing and engine enhancements made the Trident 3B capable of operating from the same runway field lengths as the 2E, despite a 12,500 lb increase in weight. The new variant offered around twice the payload of a Trident 1C and a range midway between those of the earlier two earlier models. The government agreed to support the development of the Trident 3B to the tune of £15 million, and a £83 million

BEA order for twenty-six examples plus options on a further ten was announced in the House of Commons on 13th March 1968 by the President of the Board of Trade, Anthony Crossland. The contract was formally signed on 16 August 1968, with the installation of the Smiths Autoland system at triplex level being stipulated.

BEA's first Trident 3B, G-AWZA, was handed over at Hatfield on 7 December 1970, and the variant received its Certificate of Airworthiness on 8 February 1971. The inaugural service of the Trident 3B (or 'Trident Three', as it was referred to in BEA advertising), took place on 11 March 1971. On this date G-AWZC, under the command of Captain J. Turner, operated a London-Madrid flight in 1 hr 58 mins. The new variant commenced regular scheduled services on 1 April 1971, the initial routes being to Paris and Lisbon from London. Two passenger cabin configurations were possible. In an all-Tourist layout, the aircraft could accommodate 140 passengers, or it could be furnished with eighteen First Class seats four-abreast plus 119 Tourist Class seats six-abreast. The cabin decor featured burgundy seats with beige base cushions, pigskin armrests, and cork-patterned pull down tables.

Despite the introduction of the Trident 3Bs, the Trident 2Es were still being used to inaugurate new routes. On 1 April 1971 G-AVFF opened a new BEA service from London to Reykjavik, Iceland. Captain M. Channing was in charge of the first flight, which took 3 hrs 9 mins. The service operated twice-weekly throughout the summer, reducing to a weekly basis during the winter. For those who preferred propeller-power it was still possible that summer to fly from Heathrow to Glasgow on Fridays aboard a BEA Vanguard, then transfer to an Icelandair Douglas DC-6B for the rest of the journey.

Trident 3B G-AWZK on final approach and in the final BEA livery. (The A.J. Jackson Collection)

BEA's schedules for the summer of 1971 included Trident-operated Night Tourist services to Nicosia, with Satuday night flight BE446 operating via Rhodes at a return fare of £105. On Friday nights, flight BE450 operated to the same destination, but via Heraklion. Services to Tel Aviv were scheduled for five days each week at a Tourist Class return fare of £90.95. There was also a Friday night flight, BE330, from London to Palermo at a Weekend Night Tourist fare of £63.60 return. A daytime service to Gibraltar and Marrakesh operated on Saturdays, whilst on Sundays it was possible to fly on a daytime service to Tangier. Tridents also flew services to the USSR, operating to Moscow on Mondays, Fridays and Saturdays and to Leningrad on Sundays.

During the summer of 1971 a BEA Trident opened the Wycombe Park Air Display on 11 July. Operating as special flight NOP 401, the aircraft made three low runs over the airfield with a full load of staff passengers, before returning to its base at Heathrow. Trident 2E G-AVFE carried HM the Queen from London to Ankara for a State Visit on 18 October 1971, and on 31 October a Trident operated BEA's final service out of Le Bourget airport at Paris. After flight BE057 had departed to Heathrow, the airline's staff were transferred to Orly airport, their new Paris operating base.

By November 1971 Trident 3Bs were in operation on routes out of London to Dublin, Palma, Glasgow, Oslo, Milan, Amsterdam, Madrid, Brussels, Rome, Pisa, Zurich, Nice,

A Trident performing an autoland landing in fog in 1971. (via Mrs Angela Poole)

Geneva, Copenhagen, Naples and Malta, and were also in use on some Birmingham-Malta services.

On a foggy day at the end of November 1971, BEA Trident 3B G-AWZK became the only aircraft that morning to land at fog-bound Schiphol Airport at Amsterdam, at the end of the 0745 hrs service from Heathrow with thirty passengers aboard. In command of the autoland landing was Captain Eric Poole, BEA's General Manager, Flight Development. The Trident broke through the fog 100 ft above the runway, with 400 m visibility, putting the landing at the bottom end of the Category 2 bracket.

In December of 1971 BEA aquired Trident 1E G-AVYB from Channel Airways, followed by G-AVYE in January 1972. G-AVYB was transferred to BEA subsidiary Northeast Airlines, while G-AVYE was operated by BEA's Channel Islands Division, based at Birmingham. It operated in a 123-seat all-Tourist configuration on the Glasgow-Birmingham-Paris route, on some Birmingham-Düsseldorf flights, and on inclusive-tour charters out of Birmingham.

On 1 April 1972 BEA inaugurated Trident services between London and Marseilles. In May 1972 the Trident 3B was granted full Category 3A autoland clearance. The various categories of autoland were defined thus:

Category 1. Operations down to a Decision Height of 200 ft, with visibility of more than 2600 ft.

Category 2. Operations down to a Decision Height of between 200 ft and 100 ft, with visibility of between 2600 ft and 1200 ft.

Category 3A. Operations to and along the runway with external visibility during the final stages of landing down to 700 ft. Decision Height 65 ft.

Category 3B. Operations to and along the runway with visibility of 150 ft (sufficient only for taxiing). Decision Height 12 ft.

Category 3C. Operations to and along the runway with no external visibility. No Decision Height.

On 18 June 1972 Trident 1C G-ARPI, which had survived being struck by the BKS Ambassador at Heathrow in July 1968, took off from runway 28R there at 1608 hrs as

Seating configuration plans for Tridents One, Two and Three. (via Author)

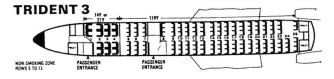

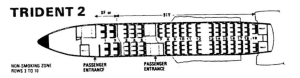

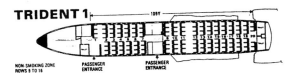

flight BE548 to Brussels. In command was Captain Stanley Key. The Heathrow weather at the time was rainy with some turbulence. Fifty seconds after leaving the runway, as the Trident was passing through 1770 ft at an airspeed of 162 kt, the droops (leading edge wing slats) were retracted, even though the specified minimum speed for this action was 225 kt. The aircraft entered a deep stall condition and started to lose height. At 1611 hrs, with an airspeed of only 54kts, the Trident crashed into a field next to the A30 road near Staines. All 109 passengers and nine crew members were killed. The investigation into the accident listed the probable causes as:

Failure by the pilot in charge to achieve and maintain adequate speed after noise abatement procedures.
Droop retraction at 60 kt below the minimum speed.
Failure to monitor speed error and to observe droop lever movement.
Failure to diagnose the reason for stick-pusher operation and warnings.
Operation of the stall recovery overide lever.

At the post-mortem it was discovered that Captain Key had an undetected abnormal heart condition, and it was suggested that this might have been a possible contributory factor. The condition might have been aggravated by an argument that took place in the crewroom before the flight over a long-standing dispute between BEA and the pilots' union BALPA. Crash investigators discovered graffiti referring to Captain Key scribbled on the third pilot's table, but no positive evidence was found to link Captain Key's heart condition to the crash.

From 2 April 1973 BEA began operating to Casablanca. Flight BE228 was routed via Gibraltar, and the inaugural service was operated by Trident 2E G-AVFF with Captain P. Lyons in command. During the summer of 1973 the Trident fleet was utilised for an extensive programme of holiday charter flights, in addition to its scheduled service commitments. As well as many charters from Heathrow, flights were operated from Belfast to Venice and Tunis; from Birmingham to Alicante, Gerona, Ibiza, Munich and Palma; from Glasgow to Ibiza and Munich; and from Newcastle to Munich. However, it was Manchester that had the largest charter flight programme, with Trident flights to Gerona, Ibiza, Milan (Malpensa), Munich, Naples, Palma, Paris (Orly), Oporto, Rimini, Rome, Tunis and Venice.

Super One-Eleven Operations
In response to its requirement for a jet-powered successor to the Viscount, BEA was offered the initial short-fuselage version of the British Aircraft Corporation (BAC) One-Eleven. However, BEA was not overly impressed, as its passenger capacity was only about the same as the srs 800 Viscounts. BAC first proposed a stretched One-Eleven in 1963, but was unwilling to proceed further without firm orders. BEA began to study the concept in early 1966, and by September it had finalised its specification for such an aircraft. On 27 January 1967 a contract was signed for eighteen One-Eleven srs 510EDs, with options on a further six. This version featured a 13 ft 6 in fuselage stretch, more powerful Rolls-Royce Spey-25 mk 512-14 engines, extended wing tips and a strengthened structure. An AIResearch gas turbine auxiliary power unit was to be fitted in the rear fuselage, to be used for engine start-ups and to heat or cool the cabin during

turnrounds. The maximum cruising speed was to be 550 mph at a normal cruising altitude of 30,000 ft. The development costs of some £10 million were to be paid for initially by the government and recouped by a levy on each aircraft sold. BEA's total investment in the srs 510EDs was in the region of £32 million. The option on the six further aircraft was directly connected at the time with the question as to whether the runways at Jersey and Guernsey could be lengthened to accept the type as a replacement for the Viscounts used on Channel Island services.

Although it could carry a maximum of ninety-nine passengers, in BEA service the aircraft was to be furnished with ninety-seven seats in a single class cabin. The seats were arranged five-abreast, apart from the rearmost row, which had two seats on one side of the aisle and an extra bar unit opposite. The passengers were to be provided with a 'Tiffin Tray Service', consisting of cold meals, hot beverages and a bar service. It would have been possible to provide a hot meal service by replacing three seats with an additional pantry unit, but BEA declined this option. The aircraft was fitted with an outward opening door on the forward port side and a ventral stairway with airstairs at the rear of the fuselage. Unlike other customer airlines, BEA declined the optional forward airstairs, largely because of the nose docking arrangements it used at Heathrow, instead opting for a manually operated set of steps. All BEA's examples were to be fitted with the non-standard Smiths Industries SF5 flight director and compass system, and the instrument panel was designed around that of the Trident, to ensure some degree of commonality between the two types.

Super One-Eleven G-AVMI in the final BEA colour scheme, but with 'Super One-Eleven' titles on the tail. (The A.J. Jackson Collection)

Super One-Eleven G-AVMX carries a banner proclaiming '150th BAC One-Eleven to be delivered'. (The A.J. Jackson Collection)

The optimum payload of ninety-seven passengers, 970 kg of baggage and 1700 kg of mail and freight was achievable over stages of up to 380 statute miles, except where airfield limitations such as those at Berlin (Templehof) reduced the payload or take-off fuel. In practice, this meant that the aircraft was ideally suited to the following BEA sectors:

Birmingham-Dublin, Manchester-Dublin, Manchester-Glasgow, Manchester-London, Cologne-Berlin, Düsseldorf-Berlin, Frankfurt-Berlin, Hamburg-Berlin and Hanover-Berlin. Those legs between German cities formed part of BEA's Internal German System, which is described in chapter five.

On 7 February 1968 the prototype One-Eleven srs 500, G-ASYD, was joined on the Wisley-based flight development programme by the first production example, G-AVMH. This aircraft was mainly used to develop features peculiar to the BEA order, and was principally involved in development of the Elliott-Automation autoland system. Through the summer months of 1968, it was a frequent user of the ILS facilities at Bedford, Gatwick and Liverpool airports in this context. The second production aircraft, G-AVMI, was handed over to BEA on 8 July 1968, and crew training began. Base training was carried out at Wisley, with Bournemouth and Tees-Side airports being used for circuit training and night flying. Route training was conducted from Manchester Airport, which had been designated as the main base for the fleet once it was in service. BEA took delivery of G-AVMJ, the first of its fleet, at Hurn, Bournemouth on 29 August 1968, more

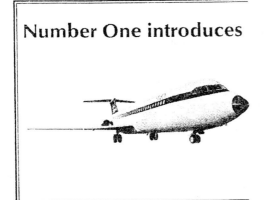

Number One introduces

the Super One-Eleven

The light, bright, spacious interior of the Super One-Eleven helps make it a brilliant new addition to BEA's jetliner fleet. And now you can fly the Super One-Eleven on many BEA routes, such as those from London to Berlin, Munich and Dusseldorf. And on flights from Manchester to Paris, Amsterdam and Brussels. You can also fly the Super One-Eleven on nearly all our German Internal Services.

 No. 1 in Europe

1969 advertisement for the new Super One-Eleven. (via Author)

than a month ahead of the contract delivery date. In September 1968, BEA aircraft G-AVML took part in the flying programme at the Farnborough Air Show, and it was at Farnborough on 18 September that another example, G-AVMK, was officially named by Lady Freda Milward as 'Super One-Eleven'. This was the fleet name chosen for the srs 510EDs in a joint BEA/BAC staff competition.

After negotiations with the British Airports Authority had brought about reduced landing fees at Stansted and Prestwick, the latter airport was selected as BEA's main training base for the Super One-Eleven fleet. A programme of 10,000 landings was scheduled for the period 1 November 1968 to 31 July 1969, and there were to be three aircraft and six training captains allocated to training duties at any one time. Each trainee was to log an average of fourteen hours flying time on the type during his/her two-week stay at Prestwick. Having obtained a type endorsement, the trainee then progressed to line training, where around thirty legs were to be flown. During the programme, 250 BEA pilots were converted onto the Super One-Eleven.

On 17 November 1968 the aircraft commenced scheduled operations on German internal services and on the Manchester-London route, where it had already made appearances on an ad hoc basis. The decision to base the Super One-Eleven Division at Manchester, and to carry out servicing and overhauls on the type there, gave a major boost to the morale of the staff there, as the airport had been somewhat overshadowed during the 1950s by BEA's main northern base at Liverpool. Now all that was to change. BEA had been losing traffic on the Manchester-London route to the new electrified train services, and the new jets were to be a major weapon in the fight to win back passengers. The interior decor had been designed by Charles Butler Associates of New York to give a brighter feel to the cabin interiors. The selection of an American company was in itself a break with tradition, as BEA had until then always preferred to use British interior designers. The interior of the cabin was furnished in various shades of turquoise, light blue and white, with a bold combination of red and gold on the ninety-seven passenger seats. In later years, the extra bar unit at the rear of the cabin was to be removed, to increase the passenger capacity to ninety-nine. The first examples had been delivered in

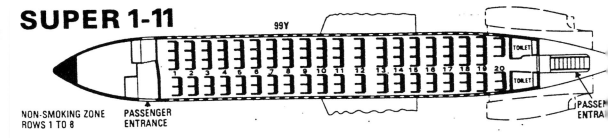

Super One-Eleven seat layout. (via Author)

the 'red square' external livery, but in 1968 BEA adopted a new colour scheme, and subsequent aircraft were delivered in the new markings.

By the end of 1968 seven Super One-Elevens had been delivered, and the type was in service on the London-Munich route. It soon proved itself to be very reliable for a new type, and was rostered to operate as many as twelve sectors in a day, with only a twenty-minute turnround between some legs. During the winter of 1968/9, it replaced Tridents on services from Manchester to Brussels, Copenhagen, Glasgow, Paris via Birmingham, Zurich, Dublin and Munich. The first royal Super One-Eleven flight took place in May 1969, when HM the Queen, Prince Philip and Princess Anne began a State Visit to Austria with a flight to Vienna in G-AVMP.

For the summer of 1969, the type was scheduled to operate six daily round trips between Manchester and London, a daily Birmingham-London rotation, a daily Birmingham-Dublin-Birmingham service, and two daily round trips between Birmingham and Glasgow. On weekdays only, there were two services between Manchester and Glasgow, five round trips between London and Dublin, and two between Manchester and Dublin. The aircraft was also used on some Glasgow-Birmingham-Paris services, and on some flights from London to German cities. By the summer of 1970, Super One-Elevens were operating new routes out of Glasgow, flying to Düsseldorf via Manchester and to Palma via Manchester. From Manchester, the type also operated four round trips to Amsterdam each week, adding to the comprehensive list of European destinations served from that city.

As part of a general BEA reorganisation, on 1 April 1971 the Super One-Eleven Division took over responsibility for all international routes out of Manchester, all domestic services from there apart from those to the Channel Islands, and the German internal route network, which was operated by Manchester-based Super One-Elevens. The summer 1971 timetable featured still more new Super One-Eleven services. There was a daily Manchester-Belfast round trip, and two flights each day between London and Shannon. On services to Germany, there were two daily flights from London to Düsseldorf, a daily Manchester-Düsseldorf-Berlin service, and a weekday round trip from Glasgow to Düsseldorf. For holidaymakers, there was a Saturday service from London to Alghero at a Tourist Class fare of £41.15 each way.

Expansion of Super One-Eleven operated services continued in 1972. On 1 April new services from Manchester to Geneva and to Munich were inaugurated on a three-times weekly basis, followed by a weekly London-Cagliari service on 3 May. This service was actually the responsibility of BEA's Mainline Division, although operated by a Super

One-Eleven. On 2 April 1973 the type was introduced onto some London-Aberdeen services, reducing the flight time by thirty-five minutes, but the majority of flights continued to be Viscount-operated. On the same date a four-times weekly Manchester-Milan service was inaugurated. During the summer of 1973, the aircraft was also utilised on holiday charter flights out of Manchester to Barcelona, Gerona, Ibiza, Mahón, Munich, Oporto and Palma.

The Super One-Eleven's service with BEA was characterised by reliable, unspectacular operation, free of major accident or incident. All eighteen of BEA's examples continued to serve with British Airways after the merger in 1974.

The BAC Two-Eleven and Three-Eleven
In the early 1960s BEA foresaw a requirement for a new short/medium-range type for entry into service in the 1970s, initially as a replacement for the high-capacity Vanguards. Among the proposals considered, but not proceeded with, was the Vickers VC-11, a short-range version of the VC-10 with 136 seats and powered by four Rolls-Royce Spey engines. As time progressed, BEA's requirement grew from a 100–150 seat aircraft to one with around 200 seats, and to meet this new specification put forward its new Two-Eleven project. This was to be powered by Rolls-Royce Conway engines and utilise scaled-up One-Eleven components, but would feature a six-abreast cabin layout. It appeared to be ideal for BEA's requirements, and the airline was keen to place an order. However, on 15 December 1967 it was announced in the House of Commons that the government would not be financing the project, preferring to opt for British participation in the European Airbus. As an interim measure, BEA then placed an order for Trident 3Bs in March 1968.

Even while the Two-Eleven was still alive, BAC had been considering wide-bodied designs, and in mid-1968 it commenced work on the BAC Three-Eleven. This was an entirely new project, designed to fill the size gap between the Boeing 727-200 and the Lockheed Tri-Star. On European scheduled services it would carry 245 passengers in an eight-abreast one class layout over a distance of 1450 miles. It would be powered by two rear-mounted Rolls-Royce RB211-41 turbofan engines.

In May 1969 the British government decided to withdraw from further financial participation in the European Airbus, as its conditions (exclusive use of Rolls-Royce engines and orders for at least seventy-five examples at time of launch) had not been met. BEA was firmly behind the Three-Eleven project, but refrained from placing an order until the government gave the go-ahead for the programme and it was officially launched. Meanwhile, BAC was waiting for BEA to place an order, which would bring the company closer to its required figure of fifty sales before going ahead with the project. All that was needed was the go-ahead from the Treasury. Unfortunately, two factors intervened to frustrate the hopes of both BAC and BEA. At the June 1970 General Election the existing Labour government was replaced by a Conservative administration which was not so committed to the British aviation industry, and in the autumn of that year Rolls-Royce suffered a financial crisis and had to appeal to the government for state aid to save the company. On 3 December 1970 the Ministry of Aviation announced that owing to the continued government funding of Rolls-Royce, there were no funds available for the Three-Eleven project or for re-entry into the European Airbus programme. The Three-Eleven project was then abandoned.

With the collapse of the Three-Eleven project, BEA was permitted funds to buy aircraft from the USA. On 26 September 1972 an order was placed with Lockheed for six Tri-Stars, with options on a further twelve. The total cost of the order was £60 million for the aircraft, plus £20 million for spares and equipment. The Tri-Stars were to be configured for eighteen First Class and 336 Economy Class passengers, and were to be equipped for autoland. This proved to be the last aircraft order placed by BEA, and although a Tri-Star gave demonstration flights in the UK in partial BEA markings, the fleet was actually delivered to British Airways after the merger with BOAC.

CHAPTER FIVE

German Internal Services

At the end of World War Two Germany was divided in political and social terms into two sectors: communist East Germany was controlled by the occupying Soviet Union, and democratic West Germany was controlled by the Western allies. Although geographically deep inside the eastern sector, the pre-war capital Berlin was also split for administrative purposes into East Berlin and West Berlin. The East German authorities refused to allow West German airlines to operate domestic flights into West Berlin through their airspace. These services were therefore operated by the airlines of the 'occupying powers', namely BEA, Air France and American Overseas Airlines. BEA's first German internal service probably took place on 9 September 1946, when a Dakota under the command of Captain John Liver flew from Hamburg to West Berlin.

In 1948 the Soviet authorities blockaded road, rail and canal access to West Berlin, and the decision was taken to supply the population with food and fuel by air. On 4 August 1948 BEA's Charter Department was tasked with managing the British civil airline participation in the Berlin Airlift. BEA did not use any of its own aircraft, but by September 1948 it was co-ordinating the activities of seventeen British charter airlines. In order to release its Charter Department for other duties, on 1 April 1949 BEA formed its

Super One-Eleven G-AVMN on final approach. (The A.J. Jackson Collection)

Civil Airlift Division, which functioned until the termination of the Civil Airlift in September 1949.

On 1 December 1949 BEA commenced Viking services between Berlin (Gatow) and Düsseldorf, and on 12 June 1950 Dakota services between Berlin and Hanover were inaugurated. In 1950 American Overseas Airlines was taken over by Pan American Airways, which continued to operate the German Internal Services, using four-engined Douglas DC-4s in competition with BEA's Dakotas and Vikings. On 1 January 1951 BEA commenced a major expansion of its own internal network, beginning with a Dakota service from Berlin to Cologne on 28 January. This service continued onwards to London, giving Cologne a direct link with London for the first time.

Berlin-Düsseldorf and Berlin-Munich Dakota operations began on 15 April 1951. The Vikings were withdrawn from the internal routes, and the operations entrusted to a fleet of six Dakotas, although Vikings still flew between Düsseldorf and Berlin as part of a through service to London. On 8 May 1951 the Dakotas were transferred to BEA's new Berlin terminus at Templehof Airport, and for the first time twelve German nationals were recruited to operate out of there as cabin staff.

The July 1953 BEA timetable featured six daily services between Berlin and Hanover, four daily round trips between Berlin and Hamburg, daily Berlin-Cologne and Berlin-Munich services, and two flights each day between Berlin and Düsseldorf. These services continued through the winter of 1953/4 without significant cutbacks, and the Berlin-Hanover frequency was even increased to seven flights a day. During 1954 BEA Elizabethans made limited appearances on the German domestic routes, commencing with a Berlin-Düsseldorf flight on 2 March, followed by first appearances on Berlin-Cologne and Berlin-Hanover services on 11 April, Berlin-Munich service on 14 June, and the Berlin-Frankfurt service on 14 November.

By 1956 many of BEA's internal services were being operated on its behalf by aircraft of Air Charter Ltd under the flight prefix BEG. DC-4s operated the Hanover-Berlin service three times each weekday, while Dakotas flew the twice-daily Düsseldorf-Berlin service, the daily Hamburg-Berlin service and the daily Cologne-Berlin service. BEA Elizabethans were utilised once-daily on the Hamburg-Berlin route, and there was a daily BEA Pionair flight from Cologne to Hanover, which connected with an Air Charter-operated schedule to Berlin.

In the late 1950s BEA began to feel the effects of competition from Pan American Airways, which had introduced larger and more comfortable Douglas DC-6B equipment on its German domestic network. To counter this threat BEA placed Viscount 701s onto its Internal German Services from 1 November 1958. Seven Viscounts had been converted for high-density operations on the network, being fitted with sixty-three seats and built-in airstairs. In 1960 the remaining Viscount 701s were also modified in this way and placed onto the German domestic routes. Viscount services between Bremen and Berlin via Hanover commenced on a twice-daily basis on 1 April 1964. That year BEA recorded 19,376 aircraft movements at Berlin alone, with the total on the Internal German Services exceeding 40,000.

On 1 June 1965 Viscount services between Berlin and Stuttgart were introduced. At that time the Internal German Services were operated almost exclusively by crews of the Viscount Flight, based at Heathrow. Night-stopping pilots were accommodated in a variety of hotels in Berlin, Frankfurt and Hamburg, and they enjoyed block membership (courtesy of BEA) at the British Officers' Club, the Marlborough. They were also enrolled in the American Officers' Club at Templehof, although they had to pay their own membership subscriptions there.

BEA was making an annual profit from the German domestic network of around £1 million, but it now faced the threat of the jet aircraft used by its rivals. Air France had been the first to introduce jets, but the absence of thrust-reversers on its Caravelles restricted their operation at Berlin to Tegel Airport, which was some way outside the city. Pan American then introduced Boeing 727-100s, just managing to get them into Templehof Airport by means of some 'interesting' approaches between the surrounding apartment blocks. BEA's initial response was to refit the cabins of its Viscounts to 'Silver Star' service standards, with upgraded catering and greatly increased legroom, made possible by replacing the existing seating with just fifty-three seats of the type used in Comet 4B First Class cabins. Silver Star services were inaugurated on 1 may 1966, initially on the Berlin-Düsseldorf route. However, the move did little to stem the Berliners' migration to the Boeing jets, and by 1967 BEA's market share had dropped from 40 per cent to 30 per cent.

As an interim measure to provide the routes with jet equipment, BEA began to use Comet 4Bs from 1 April 1968. On that date they entered service on flights from Berlin to Bremen and Hanover. On 1 August they made an appearance on Berlin-Cologne and Berlin-Düsseldorf schedules, and on 1 November they came into use on services to Munich, Nuremberg and Munster/Osnabruck. However, they were not particularly suited to operations along the narrow air corridors into and out of Berlin, where they were restricted to a service ceiling of 10,000 ft and had to land on Templehof's longest runway of only 5266 ft. Once Super One-Elevens became available, the Comets were gradually

Super One-Eleven G-AVMZ on final approach. (The A.J. Jackson Collection)

withdrawn. The last Comet service took place on 30 April 1969, with a flight from Berlin to Hamburg and onwards to London.

Super One-Elevens began to be used on an ad hoc basis from 1 September 1968, when G-AVMJ operated Berlin-Hamburg and Berlin-Bemen services. Full scheduled operations began on 17 November 1968. The type's performance and operating economics were specifically tailored to the internal German route network, where all the routes were under 400 miles. For the precise flying neccessary within the 20-mile wide Berlin air corridors, the Super One-Elevens were fitted with the latest Decca Omnitrac display, all flying being within the Decca coverage. From the beginning of 1969, super One-Elevens use was extended throughout the German network, making their first appearance on services from Berlin to Munich, Munster/Osnabruck and Nuremberg on 13 January; to Bremen, Hamburg and Frankfurt on 16 February; to Cologne and Düsseldorf on 2 March; and to Hanover and Stuttgart on 1 May. The Comets had been phased out of the network, but Viscounts were to continue to serve for a further two years or more before their eventual retirement.

On 24 September 1968 BEA signed a new route-pooling agreement with Air France. Under this arrangement, Air France ceased to operate its own flights within Germany, and certain BEA flights were henceforth operated as joint BEA/Air France services. By then, Air France's market share had fallen to only 4 per cent, due principally to the neccessity to operate its Caravelles into Berlin's Tegel Airport. On the Berlin-Frankfurt and Berlin-Munich routes joint BEA/Air France flight numbers would be used, and the cabin crews would consist of a mixture of BEA and Air France personnel. The Super One-Elevens used would have a new livery applied, in which BEA's fuselage titles would be reduced in size and made less prominent. The tail fins would bear the legend 'Super One-Eleven' in white on a dark blue background, in place of the BEA logo.

During 1970, and in the two subsequent years, some BEA flights on the network were operated by BAC One-Eleven srs 400s of the BEA subsidiary Cambrian Airways. These were leased with full crews, and wore BEA stickers. Viscounts still held a place in the summer 1971 schedules, although this was to be their last season on the routes. They operated between Berlin and Bremen three times a day, to Hamburg twice daily, and to Hanover no fewer than nine times each day. The last scheduled Viscount service on the network was flight BE1380 from Hanover to Berlin, operated by srs 802 G-AOJB on 31 October 1971. However, on the following day the same aircraft, under the command of Captain P.W. Hargreaves, operated an extra service, flight BE1351A, from Berlin to Hanover before positioning to London.

The summer 1971 timetable showed the Super One-Eleven fleet to be hard at work on the German services. Each day the aircraft operated two round trips from Berlin to Bremen, five to Cologne, four to Düsseldorf, eleven to Frankfurt, nine to Hamburg, three to Hanover (plus two operated by Cambrian Airways srs 400s), six to Munich, and four to Stuttgart. The Berlin-Frankfurt and Berlin-Munich services were operated under joint BEA/Air France flight numbers. There was also a daily round trip between Hanover and Bremen.

On 31 October 1972 the operating agreement with Air France came to an end, the last joint flight being BE/AF1856 from Frankfurt to Berlin. BEA then reverted to operating to Frankfurt and Munich in its own right, and the Super One-Elevens used were repainted into the full BEA colours as they became due for overhaul.

On 1 June 1973 a four-times weekly holiday service from Berlin to Sylt in the Frisian Islands was inaugurated.

CHAPTER SIX

The Scottish Network

When BEA was established on 1 August 1946 it was not yet in a position to operate its domestic services with its own aircraft and crews, and so until 1 February 1947 the routes continued to be flown by the various constituent airlines of the wartime Associated Airways Joint Committee. On the routes within Scotland the predominant aircraft was the de Havilland Rapide, but BEA had already laid plans for its replacement with more modern equipment. In late 1946 twenty-five Miles Marathons were ordered by the Ministry of Supply on behalf of the airline. They were intended to carry fourteen passengers plus freight on the Scottish routes, and were allocated the class name 'Clansman'. Individual machines were to be named after Scottish clans, with the flagship G-AMGW bearing the name 'Clansman'. The first production Marathon G-ALUB was painted in BEA livery as 'Rob Roy' and delivered to Northolt in 1951 for trials on the routes to the highlands and islands. However, the Marathon's comparatively high operating costs resulted in the order being reduced to twelve examples, then to seven, and then being cancelled completely in April 1952. Meanwhile, the Rapides soldiered on, supplemented by Dakotas on mainline routes to England.

Early in May 1947 BEA announced details of its new Scottish schedules, which included the long London-Edinburgh-Aberdeen-Shetland route. On the return leg the

Rapide G-AGPH, seen here in the original BEA livery, was written off at Barra in December 1951. (The A.J. Jackson Collection)

flying time from Aberdeen to Northolt was some three hours, plus the time spent on the ground at Edinburgh. The return fare from Aberdeen to Northolt was £15.5.0. From 2 August 1947 the timing was adjusted to allow southbound travellers to spend around six hours in London and still get back to Aberdeen the same day, but the service was suspended for the winter months. It resumed the following summer, and continued throughout that winter, but by then only three seats each day on the Shetland-London route were allocated to passengers joining at Aberdeen. In 1947 BEA's staff at Aberdeen handled some twenty aircraft movements each day.

In use on some Scottish services in 1947 were a few ex-*Luftwaffe* Junkers Ju 52/3m tri-motors. These were operated in twelve-passenger configuration as the 'Jupiter' class. By the end of the year they had all been withdrawn, but before this one of them had made news by dropping food, newspapers and cigarettes to the beleaguered crew of the lighthouse at Dubh Artach in the Hebrides, the first supplies these men had received in over two months.

On 1 July 1947 an 'almost Scottish' route from Belfast to Carlisle and onwards to Newcastle was introduced, operating on weekdays with Rapides. There was also a Carlisle-Isle of Man Rapide service, but they were both dropped at the end of the summer because of poor passenger loads.

During the first half of 1948 BEA began the regular carriage of mail on the services from Inverness to Stornoway, Glasgow to Stornoway, and Glasgow to Islay. The schedules for the summer of 1948 included two services each weekday between Glasgow and Islay, three from Glasgow to Campbeltown, and one round trip each weekday on the routes from Glasgow to Inverness, Benbecula, Shetland and Tiree. The flights to Inverness and Shetland were operated by Dakotas, but all the others were carried out by 'Islander' class Rapides. There was also an Edinburgh-Orkney round trip operated by Dakotas on weekdays only. From Aberdeen, Rapides operated on weekdays to Wick, and a Dakota performed a weekday Northolt-Aberdeen-Northolt rotation. However, development of BEA's mainline services into Aberdeen was hampered by the fact that the airline considered the runway there to be too short for use by its Vikings.

At the beginning of July 1950 a Glasgow-Perth Rapide service was inaugurated, only to be suspended on 31 August. On 28 July, Orkney-born Mrs Madeleine McLaren departed Glasgow (Renfrew) on one of her regular visits to Kirkwall. What made this event slightly unusual was the fact that she was ninety-six years old at the time, and this was her sixth such trip since her ninetieth birthday.

BEA's 'Islander' class Rapides were withdrawn from the Scottish routes and replaced by 'Pionair' class Dakotas on 30 September 1952. The only exception was the service to the beach airstrip at Barra. To service this route, and to operate air ambulance flights, three Rapides were retained at the Glasgow base. On 1 October 1952 Tiree was added as a stop on the Glasgow-Benbecula-Stornoway route, with the inaugural Pionair service being operated by G-ALXL. The Glasgow-Campbeltown and Glasgow-Islay routes were combined, and G-AGIU performed the first Pionair service over the new routeing.

Meanwhile, on the east coast, operations from Aberdeen were slowly expanding. During the winter of 1952/3 the Aberdeen-Edinburgh service was extended to Manchester. On the London route, Pionairs departed Northolt at 0830 hrs, called at Edinburgh *en route*, and arrived at Dyce Airport, Aberdeen at 1310 hrs. The price of an eight-day return ticket was £11.5.0. In 1952 BEA ran its own free bus service from Dyce into the city centre, but a charge of ten shillings was later introduced.

BEA opened its first ground radio station, at the beach airstrip at Barra, on 1 June 1953. The January 1954 timetable showed Rapide flights BE978/9 as operating between Glasgow and Barra 'on request, and subject to tides and weather' on Mondays and Fridays. Pionair flights BE948/9 operated the Glasgow-Tiree-Benbecula-Stornoway and back service on four days each week at a return fare of £7.15.0. On weekdays flight BE952/3 flew Glasgow-Inverness-Wick-Orkney (Grimsetter)-Shetland and return. On Mondays and Fridays there were direct flights between Aberdeen and Orkney which provided connections at Aberdeen to London, Birmingham and Edinburgh; on other days an Aberdeen-Wick-Orkney schedule offered onward connections to Shetland. The Aberdeen-Shetland monthly return fare was £7.10.0. Pionair aircraft operated weekday flights BE974/5 from Glasgow to Campbeltown and Islay and return, and on every day except Saturday there was a Pionair round trip between Glasgow and Belfast (Nutts Corner). For the summer of 1954 a new Aberdeen-Glasgow-Manchester-London routeing was introduced.

On 12 February 1955 BEA took delivery of its first 'Hebrides' class de Havilland Heron 1B, G-ANXB 'Sir James Simpson'. The aircraft was used initially for air ambulance flights, but on 1 April 1955 scheduled Heron services commenced over the Glasgow-Tiree-Barra-Tiree-Glasgow route, with the aircraft being configured for fourteen passengers. Landings at Barra were made on the Traigh Mohr beach, more commonly known as the Cockle Strand. The schedules were adjusted to take account of changing tide states, and new pilots were advised to make sure they could see the knees of the seagulls on the beach before they landed or took off. If they could not, the sand was too wet!

In the mid-1950s BEA used Herons to operate an early morning Stornoway-Inverness-Glasgow service, departing at 0700 hrs. The early start necessitated an overnight stop for the captain and second officer, no stewardess being carried on the small Heron aircraft. Former BEA station superintendent at Stornoway Robin Mackenzie recalls that in those days the local hotel was unable to provide staff at that early hour for breakfast duties, so a compromise was reached whereby the neccessary items were left out for the crew to cook their own breakfast. The airport bus departed the BEA town office at 0630 hrs, picking up the crew from the hotel *en route*. On arrival at the airport the one BEA traffic officer checked in any passengers joining there and completed the Ship's Papers. Then, with the help of the airport firemen, he pushed the Heron out of the hangar and loaded the baggage, while the flight crew checked the weather and completed the flight plan. The night-stopping crew usually arrived back at Stornoway at around 1830 hrs, to be met by the same traffic officer, so if they had any special requests for him, such as a box of Stornoway kippers, he could aquire these while they were away. After dinner in the hotel it was not unusual for the crew to visit a kipper house to watch the processing of a herring into a kipper and to sample one straight from the kiln.

For the summer of 1957 a seasonal holiday route from Aberdeen to Jersey via Edinburgh was inaugurated, with flights on Sundays. At that time this was the only Sunday movement at Aberdeen, and the airport had to be opened especially to accommodate the Pionair services. The steadily increasing costs involved in this led to the suspension of the service after the summer of 1960, but BEA still continued to try to expand its services from Aberdeen. In December 1959 the airline's first Handley Page Herald made a proving flight into the airport. The new turboprop was intended as a replacement for the Pionairs on local routes, with Viscounts eventually taking over on the London services. For the winter of 1961/2 a direct Aberdeen-Shetland Pionair service was introduced on weekdays. Pionair flights BE8192/8199 flew the Edinburgh- Aberdeen-Edinburgh route on every day except Sundays, connecting with morning and evening Vanguard services from London at Edinburgh. Viscount flights BE8064/8069 operated from Glasgow (Renfrew) to Aberdeen and back, and provided similar connections at Glasgow with Vanguard services from London.

During the period April to August 1961, Edinburgh's Turnhouse Airport had been closed to air traffic while the runway was lengthened and resurfaced, and other improvements were carried out to upgrade the airport to international status. While this work was being performed the airfield at East Fortune, about one and a quarter hour's drive from Edinburgh, had its main runway opened to accommodate airline movements. Prefabricated buildings were erected on one of the other runways to serve as a temporary passenger terminal, and the wartime control tower was refurbished. Some 99,800 passengers passed through East Fortune during the period in question, with aircraft as large as BEA Vanguards being accommodated.

On 16 April 1962 BEA's inaugural Herald service was operated over the route Glasgow-Aberdeen-Wick-Orkney-Shetland by G-APWB. Pionairs had been replaced by Viscounts on the Glasgow-Benbecula-Stornoway route on 1 April 1961, and with the arrival of BEA's third Herald the type was retired from the Scottish routes. The final Pionair service was flight BE8679 from Islay to Campbeltown and Glasgow on 19 May 1962. This was operated by G-ALTT, which was also the last Pionair to depart from Renfrew, being ferried to Wymeswold for a Check Four overhaul. From there it was flown out to Gibraltar for operation by Gibraltar Airways on the forty-two -mile route to Tangier. Since 1 August 1946 BEA's Dakotas/Pionairs had carried 8.5 million passengers and flown 97 million miles.

In 1965 the Heralds began operating their first route to a destination outside Scotland, a Glasgow-Belfast service. The longest sector they were used on was Glasgow-Jersey. This route was operated on a fortnightly basis during the peak summer weeks of 1965 and took 2 hrs 15 mins in each direction. BEA soon discovered the high cost associated with operating a fleet of just three examples, and made the decision to dispose of the Heralds once the runways at Kirkwall (Orkney), Islay and Sumburgh (Shetland) had been improved sufficiently to accept Viscounts. By the end of October 1966 these improvements had been made, and the Heralds were withdrawn and returned to the Ministry of Supply. Their final day of operations was 31 October 1966, and the last flight was BE8679, Islay-Campbeltown-Glasgow, operated by G-APWB.

A five times-weekly Manchester-Edinburgh Viscount schedule was introduced in 1968, and on 1 November 1968 a daily (except Sundays) Viscount service was inaugurated on the London-Aberdeen-Inverness route. For the summer of 1969 Viscounts were in use on all the Scottish internal services, except the Heron-operated routes to Tiree and Barra. These were flown in the morning on every day except Sunday. Until 14 June the Herons operated the Glasgow-Tiree-Barra service, but from that date separate flights were scheduled from Glasgow to each destination.

On 1 April 1970 a daily non-stop Viscount service from London to Inverness was introduced, the aircraft continuing onwards to Stornoway and Benbecula and then flying

Heron 1B G-ANXB undergoes preparation for flight at Glasgow. Attaching the battery lead to the nose is Thomas Young, Electrician. (via Les Young)

to Glasgow. In the meantime, a second Viscount was operating the reverse routeing. As most of BEA's more remote Scottish stations were not supplied with ground power units, the Viscounts used were fitted with extra batteries for starting their engines unaided.

The April 1971 BEA reorganisation resulted in the formation of the BEA Scottish Airways Division, based at Glasgow. This was responsible for all the routes within

The rudimentary terminal at Barra in the 1950s. (via Les Young)

Herald G-APWA, loaned from Handley Page prior to the type's introduction on Highlands and Islands routes. (The A.J. Jackson Collection)

Scotland, plus the Glasgow-Belfast route and the mainline services from Aberdeen and Inverness to London. These latter routes were no longer combined, and during the summer of 1971 there were three weekday Viscount round trips between Aberdeen and London and a single Viscount rotation on the Inverness-London route. The Aberdeen-London single fare was £14.9.0, and that from Inverness was £15.14.0.

Jet services came to Aberdeen on 15 September 1972 with the arrival of BEA's first Trident-operated service from London and the announcement that the airline had been granted permission to use Super One-Elevens on the route.

Tragedy struck on 19 January 1973, when Viscount 802 G-AOHI took off from Glasgow on a test flight that was intended to last about fifteen minutes. The crew planned to carry out the tests under visual flight rules, although the weather conditions were marginal, with rain, snow and strong winds. The Viscount had climbed to around 4000 ft when it crashed close to the peak of Ben More, about thirty-five miles north of Glasgow. All four crew members were killed.

During March and April 1973 BEA took delivery of two Short Skyliners as replacements for the Herons on internal scheduled services. The Skyliner was a nineteen-seat development of the Skyvan turboprop, and the two aircraft were based at Glasgow.

The last Heron-operated schedule was from Barra to Tiree and onwards to Glasgow, flown by G-ANXB on 30 March 1973, and on 2 April the first Skyliner entered BEA service. The inaugural flight was BE8746 from Glasgow to Tiree, and a Glasgow-Barra service was also operated later that day. Once the second example had been delivered, the type also took over the route from Glasgow to Campbeltown and Islay.

Viscount 806 G-AOYJ, seen here at Aberdeen in September 1970 still wearing its Cyprus Airways cheatline after return from lease. (Author)

On 2 April 1973 the Super One-Eleven was introduced on the Aberdeen-Heathrow route, and on 1 November that year a Short Skyliner service linking Glasgow and Aberdeen commenced. This was withdrawn in February 1974, only a month or so before the formal dissolution of BEA.

CHAPTER SEVEN

Scottish Air Ambulance Operations

The BEA Air Ambulance Unit was formed at Glasgow in April 1948, although BEA had been operating ambulance flights on an ad hoc basis since February 1947 and had completed 182 of these flights by March 1948. The Air Ambulance Unit was under the initial management of Captain David Barclay, and its first aircraft were two Rapides, manned by three pilots and three radio operators. On 12 February 1955 the first Heron aircraft was delivered to Glasgow, and this operated its first air ambulance flight on 4 March.

On average the Heron fleet operated some 250 ambulance flights each year. Patients from Orkney and Shetland were usually flown to Aberdeen, whereas those from the Western Isles were usually taken to Glasgow or sometimes Inverness. The annual

Heron 1B G-AOFY, which was lost at Islay during an air ambulance flight in 1957. (The A.J. Jackson Collection)

Symbols of all that is

best in air travel

B·O·A·C

BEA

1. Advertisement for BOAC and BEA, featuring the BEA coat of arms and the 'key' logo.

2. Cover of October 1950 BEA Continental Timetable, mentioning the Festival of Britain.

3. BEA leaflet promoting Forces Fares and the attractions of travel by Viscount.

4. Front cover of BEA international ticket issued in 1967.

0602   8403 737

BEA

Passenger ticket and baggage check

Issued by

BRITISH EUROPEAN AIRWAYS

Bealine House Ruislip Middlesex
Member of International Air Transport Association

Your attention is drawn to the conditions
of contract printed inside this ticket

Europe's finest Air Fleet

the *BEA* fleet

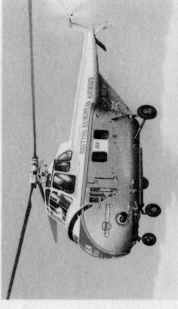

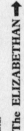
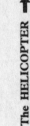

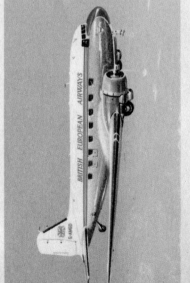

← The VISCOUNT

British European Airways Viscount 'Discovery Class.' World's first turbo-prop airliner : 47 passengers, five crew. Four Rolls Royce Dart propeller-turbines. Cruising speed 291 m.p.h. Designed and built by Vickers-Armstrong Ltd.

The ELIZABETHAN →

British European Airways Elizabethan Class. 47 passengers, five crew. Two 2,600 h.p. Bristol Centaurus engines. Cruising speed 245 m.p.h. Designed and built by Airspeed Division of the de Havilland Aircraft Co. Ltd.

← The PIONAIR

British European Airways 'Pionair' Class. 30/32 passengers. Three crew, two Pratt and Whitney Twin Wasp engines. Cruising speed 167 m.p.h. BEA version of the Douglas DC-3.

The HELICOPTER →

King Arthur Class Helicopter. Westland-Sikorsky S.55. Powered by one 600 h.p. Pratt and Whitney Wasp engine. Cruising speed 90 m.p.h. Length 42 feet. Rotor diameter 53 feet. It carries a crew of one and four to five passengers.

5. 1955 BEA advertisement showing the airline's front-line fixed-wing and helicopter types.

6. BEA Domestic Route Map 1953.

7. Viscount 802 G-AOHJ with Channel Islands titles at Manchester in 1971. *(Author)*

8. Viscount 802 G-AOHL with Scottish Airways titles at Gatwick in 1972. *(Author)*

9. Viscount 802 G-AOJF with BEA Channel Islands titles on a rainy day at Gatwick in December 1969. *(Steve Williams)*

10. Viscount 806 G-AOYS runs up its engines at Liverpool in November 1968, possibly after a weather diversion from Manchester.

(*Steve Williams*)

11. BEA Airtours Comet 4B G-ARGM taxying at Gatwick in May 1972. *(Steve Williams)*

12. The nose of Viscount 701, G-ALWF, seen at Duxford in the 1980s after restoration to its original BEA markings. *(Author)*

13. Comet 4B G-APMG at the BEA engineering base at Heathrow.   *(Kev Darling)*

14. Viscount 802 G-AOJC with BEA Scottish Airways titles, taxying at Heathrow in
    March 1973.   *(Steve Williams)*

15. Vanguard 953 G-APEO landing at Manchester in April 1968.

(*Steve Williams*)

16. Trident 2E G-AVFI in the final BEA livery, being demonstrated at the 1968 Farnborough Air Show.

(Steve Williams)

17. Super One-Eleven G-AVMI in the 'Red Square' livery at Munich-Riem in July 1968. *(Steve Williams)*

18. Trident 1C G-ARPE at Manchester in 1971. *(Author)*

19. Trident 2E G-AVFG at Liverpool in December 1972, possibly on a weather diversion from Manchester.

(Steve Williams)

20. Trident 1C G-ARPE at Manchester in 1971.   (Author)

21. Short Skyliner G-BAIT at Glasgow in 1973.   (Author)

22. Trident 1C G-ARPR taxying at Manchester in April 1968.   (*Steve Williams*)

23. Night-time shot of two Super One-Elevens at Liverpool in the final BEA livery during
   January 1973.   (*Steve Williams*)

24. BEA Routemaster buses of 1966/7 vintage outside Terminal 2 at Heathrow.
(Peter Dann)

25. A BEA Routemaster double-decker bus at Heathrow.
(Peter Dann)

26. A BEA Routemaster bus, baggage trailers and Land Rover in the final BEA livery at Heathrow.
(Peter Dann)

operating costs of around £12,000 were covered by the Scottish Health Service. Once both Herons were delivered, one aircraft was allocated to the scheduled services and the other was kept on one-hour standby for air ambulance flights. In ambulance configuration the Heron was equipped with two stretchers, oxygen equipment and cots for babies.

On 21 Febrauary 1956 Captain David Barclay carried out three medical rescue sorties in the space of eight hours. At 1100 hrs he took off from Renfrew Airport, Glasgow and flew through a snowstorm to Kirkwall to pick up a woman who needed to be taken to hospital in Aberdeen. On his way back to Glasgow, he responded to a call to fly to Barra and collect an 81-year-old woman who had fallen and broken her leg. On completion of

Interior view of a Rapide in air ambulance configuration. (via Robert Mitchell)

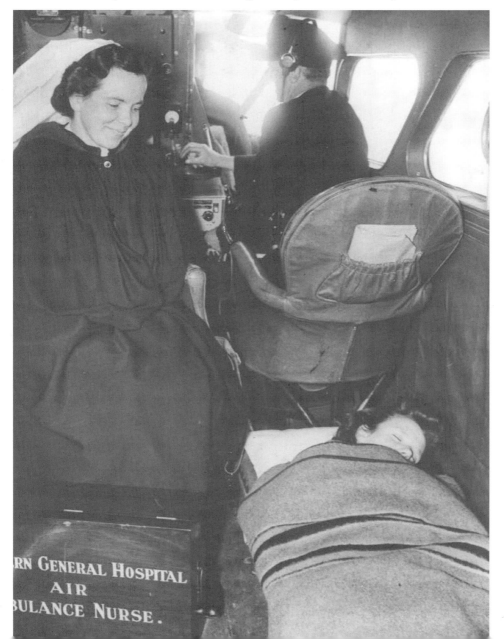

this mission he was sent to Benbecula, where a 74-year-old man needed transferring to Glasgow. By the time he finally landed back at Renfrew at 1900 hrs, he had flown a total of 740 miles.

On 20 February 1957 Heron G-ANXA was damaged while landing at Coll in strong crosswinds on an ambulance flight. Worse was to come before the year had ended. On 28 September G-AOFY was despatched to Glenegedale Airport on Islay to pick up a patient in urgent need of specialist attention on the mainland. On board the outbound flight were two pilots and a nurse, Sister Jean Kennedy. At Islay a let-down was carried out in conditions of low cloud and poor visibility. Whilst turning onto final approach the left wing of the Heron came into contact with the ground. The aircraft crashed, killing all three people on board.

Captain David Barclay received due recognition of his work with the Air Ambulance Unit. He was awarded the MBE, and on 29 February 1960 he was the subject of a 'This Is Your Life' television programme. Among those appearing to pay tribute was Jimmy Mitchell, who had been Captain Barclay's radio officer with Scottish Airways in pre-BEA days and had served with BEA at Renfrew as flight administration Officer since 1949. He was finally to retire from BEA in 1965.

During the financial year 1962/3 the Air Ambulance Unit transported 350 patients. These were looked after in the air by volunteer nurses from the Southern General Hospital in Glasgow, who had received additional training in aviation medicine, emergency proceedures and crash survival techniques. On the occasions when the regular Heron was not available, a BEA Herald was sometimes substituted on ambulance flights.

With the retirement of the Herons at the end of March 1973, BEA handed over responsibility for the Scottish Air Ambulance Unit flights to Loganair.

CHAPTER EIGHT

Channel Islands Operations

Although BEA officially took over the constituent airlines of the Associated Airways Joint Committee on 1 February 1947, there were some exceptions, and one of these was Channel Islands Airways. It was not until 1 April 1947 that this airline and its fleet of Rapides were absorbed into the state airline. On that date BEA sent over to Jersey a Junkers Ju 52/3m aircraft loaded with new BEA signs for the check-in desks, stationery, uniforms, and other items. The choice of aircraft, however, incensed many of the residents, as the last time they had seen a Ju 52/3m land it had been in *Luftwaffe* markings during the recent occupation of their islands.

Dakota services between Northolt and Jersey commenced on 21 April 1947, and during that summer the type also operated flights from Jersey to Paris (Le Bourget) and to Rennes, but the French routes were relatively short-lived. The Rennes service was dropped in 1949, followed by the Paris route the next year. During the summer of 1949 routes from London to Guernsey and Alderney, and inter-island services were also operated. On 1 November 1947 BEA operated its last scheduled service out of Croydon

Rapide G-AJXB was sold to Eagle Aviation in 1955. (The A.J. Jackson Collection)

Airport. On that day three Rapide trips to Guernsey were operated, with the final one flown by G-AGIF. From that date all BEA's Channel Islands services departed for the time being from Northolt. During 1947 BEA's Channel Islands Unit (which included the base at Southampton) carried 72,931 passengers.

For the summer of 1948 BEA scheduled three daily Dakota round trips between Southampton and Jersey, plus an additional one on four days of the week, and a daily Dakota service between Southampton and Guernsey. On 11 June 1949 a twice-daily Jersey-Dinard service was inaugurated, and during that summer sixty-one Dakota flights each week operated between Northolt and Jersey.

In 1950 BEA opened up its its first route out of Gatwick Airport, a twice-weekly summer Rapide service to Alderney. This was successful enough for it to be reinstated for the following two summer seasons. Another summer-only routeing introduced in 1950 was a Manchester-Birmingham-Jersey Dakota service, which commenced on 13 May and was upgraded to a daily frequency from 22 May. On 29 July 1950 the BEA staff at Jersey broke all records for the airport by handling 2086 BEA passengers and 118 aircraft movements in a single day.

In 1951 a direct Sunday service between Glasgow and Jersey was introduced, and during the period 4 August-2 September the prototype de Havilland Heron 1 G-ALZL appeared on services to Jersey from Northolt and Southampton. This aircraft was leased from the manufacturer to assess its suitability for the Channel Islands routes, and in the course of thirty-four flights it carried 481 passengers. It also flew into Alderney, becoming the largest BEA fixed-wing aircraft to have visited that airport.

On 17 June 1952 an air display was held at Jersey Airport to celebrate the completion of a 1400-yard tarmac runway at the end of the previous year. BEA sent over to the display Viking G-AMNJ and Elizabethan G-ALZV (both making the first visit of their respective types to the airport) plus the Rolls-Royce Dart-powered Dakota conversion G-ALXN 'Sir Henry Royce'.

The July 1953 BEA timetable featured expanded schedules between Jersey and Dinard, with daily morning and evening services, plus an extra flight on Tuesdays, Wednesdays and Thursdays. There was also a daily service from Guernsey to Dinard, again with extra midweek flights. The Southampton-Alderney route was operated three times daily during the peak season, with extra flights on Mondays, Fridays and Saturdays. All of these services were operated by 'Islander' class Rapides. On Saturdays an 'Admiral' class Viking made the round trip from Glasgow to Jersey and back, and on Sundays a 'Pionair' class Dakota flew Glasgow-Guernsey-Jersey and return. As might be expected, the winter 1953/4 timetable contained much reduced frequencies on the Channel Islands routes. There was a twice-daily Pionair service from London (Northolt) to Jersey, with one of these flights including a stop at Guernsey, and an additional flight on weekdays. Once a day, a Pionair flew Southampton-Jersey-Guernsey and back. The Southampton-Alderney route was served by a Rapide on three days each week, and the same type maintained a daily service between Guernsey and Alderney, with additional flights on weekdays. Rapide services to Dinard operated out of Jersey on Mondays, Wednesdays and Fridays, and out of Guernsey on Fridays only.

In 1955 BEA purchased a 25 per cent shareholding in Jersey Airlines. This was followed in 1956 by an agreement whereby BEA handed over its Guernsey-Southampton and Jersey-Dinard routes to this airline. On 9 March 1956 BEA's Rapides were withdrawn

Passengers boarding Dakota G-ALXM at Northolt for a service to Guernsey. (BEA photo-copyright British Airways)

from all Channel Islands routes except those to Alderney. On 20 April these too came to an end, when BEA transferred its Alderney services to Jersey Airlines as well. BEA's last service to Alderney was operated on this date by Rapide G-AKZB. Jersey Airlines also took over BEA's order for two Heron srs 2s, which had been intended as replacements for the Rapides. Not long afterwards, more Channel Islands routes were transferred, when BEA and Cambrian Airways announced on 9 May 1956 the signing of a ten-year agreement covering the operation of services between the UK mainland and the Channel Islands, as well as the development of services linking Wales and the west of England with London and Manchester. Under the agreement, all BEA services between Liverpool and the Channel Islands were handed over to Cambrian Airways.

During 1956 BEA began using Viscount equipment on its services to Jersey, and direct services from Edinburgh and from Belfast were introduced. Sunday services from Aberdeen via Edinburgh followed the next year.

On 9 June 1958 HM the Queen officially opened the rebuilt Gatwick Airport complex. The first official departure after the opening ceremony was a flight to the Channel Islands by BEA Pionair G-ALXK. The aircraft had been chartered by Surrey County Council and carried civic dignitaries and messages of goodwill to the states of Jersey and Guernsey.

During 1958 BEA transferred most of its Channel Islands services from London Airport to Gatwick, and these accounted for well over half of the total scheduled passenger figures at the airport that year. BEA's initial staff at Gatwick numbered 137. These personnel also handled weather diversions from London Airport and other new BEA services, such as the one to Paris that was opened in April 1961. By the spring of 1963, however, all of these other routes had either been withdrawn or transferred to Heathrow, and only BEA's Channel Islands services still operated out of Gatwick. One of these was a Gatwick-Guernsey Viscount service, which had been inaugurated by srs 701 G-AOFX on 1 August 1960.

The installation of a hard runway suitable for Viscounts at Guernsey meant that BEA could retire its Pionairs from the Channel Islands routes. This in turn brought about the withdrawal of BEA from Southampton Airport, as the grass runway there could not accept Viscounts. BEA's final service out of Southampton was flight BE754, operated by Pionair G-AHCX on 19 March 1961. From 20 to 31 March 1961, the Pionairs operated out of Bournemouth instead of Southampton until the Viscounts took over at the beginning of April. BEA's last scheduled Pionair Channel Islands service was operated by G-AGNK on 31 March 1961, but some examples were still retained at Jersey that summer for use as back-up aircraft or to fly extra legs if services were very heavily booked. BEA's first Viscount schedule out of Bournemouth was operated by srs 701 G-ANHF on 1 April 1961, and during that summer the type was rostered for up to twenty-three services each

Viscount 802 G-AOHT at Gatwick on a Channel Islands service. (Author)

week. In the November 1961 timetable two Viscount round trips each day were operated between Heathrow and Jersey.

In 1964 Vanguards began to be used on peak-hour extra legs between London and Jersey, but during the winter of 1965/6 the runway at Jersey had to be closed for strengthening. Viscount services still operated into Guernsey, and a Sikorsky S-61N helicopter was borrowed from BEA Helicopters and used to provide connecting flights between Guernsey and Jersey. The S-61N arrived in the Channel Islands on 1 November 1965, along with spares, three pilots and a licensed engineer. It departed again on 28 February 1966, having carried 4306 passengers. Once the improved runway at Jersey was back in service, heavier types such as the Vanguard could be accommodated on a regular basis, and for the summer of 1966 the big turboprops were regularly rostered onto London-Jersey and Manchester-Jersey services.

In 1969 Aurigny Air Services was formed to provide inter-island services, and as a result BEA ceased carrying local passengers between Jersey and Guernsey. In the summer 1969 schedules, Vanguards were used on two Heathrow-Jersey round trips each day plus an extra rotation on Fridays, with the rest of the services being Viscount-operated. The Vanguards also operated a once-daily Manchester-Jersey rotation, whilst Viscounts were utilised on flights to Jersey from Glasgow, Edinburgh and Southampton. The type also operated to Guernsey from Birmingham, Manchester, Glasgow, Gatwick and Heathrow.

The 1971 reorganisation of BEA resulted in the formation of BEA Channel Island Airways, based in Jersey. This division was responsible for all services from the mainland to the Channel islands, plus the airline's domestic and international services out of Birmingham, and also the operation of the single Viscount based at Gibraltar on lease to Gibair.

For the summer of 1972 a daily Amsterdam-Jersey round trip was introduced. This was the first direct BEA service between Jersey and continental Europe since the Jersey-Dinard route was transferred to Jersey Airlines in 1956.

CHAPTER NINE

Scilly Isles Operations

In 1946 BEA's services to the Scilly Isles were still being operated on its behalf by Great Western and Southern Air Lines, a situation that was to continue until 1 February 1947, when BEA began operating the route in its own right. The October 1946 BEA timetable included four round trips each weekday between Land's End and the Scillies, operated by Rapide aircraft at a fare of £1 one-way, or £1.15.0 for a 60-day return ticket. Train connections to Land's End were available via Penzance. By April 1949 the air fares had increased to £1.6.0 and £2.4.0 respectively. The frequency of the 20-minute flights had

Rapide G-AGSH was inherited from Channel Islands Airways. (BEA photo-copyright British Airways)

Sikorsky S-61N G-ATFM with a trolley-load of suitcases. (The A.J. Jackson Collection)

also increased, to six daily round trips plus four extra services on Fridays, Saturdays and Mondays. On weekdays it was possible to travel from London to the Scilly Isles in a single day by catching the Cornish Riviera Express train from Paddington at 1030 hrs, changing at Penzance for Land's End and then getting the BEA flight that arrived at the Scillies at 1850 hrs.

During August and September 1951 BEA leased the prototype Heron 1 G-ALZL from de Havilland to assess its suitability for services to the Channel Islands and the Scilly Isles. During the trials the Heron was operated between Land's End and St Mary's on the Scillies, becoming the largest BEA fixed-wing aircraft to visit these airports.

In January 1954 BEA 'Islander' class Rapides flew the 35-mile route twice-daily on weekdays, and from 1 March a third rotation was introduced. When maintenance was required, the Rapides were ferried to the BEA base on Jersey, and continued to appear there for this purpose long after the type had ceased to operate scheduled services to Jersey.

On 21 May 1959 Rapide G-AHLL overran the grass landing area at Land's End (St Just) on landing. One person was injured and the aircraft suffered substantial damage and was withdrawn. Another Rapide was lost on 12 December 1961, again at St Just. This time it was G-AKZB that overran the wet grass runway and was written off, fortunately without serious injuries.

For the summer of 1962 three Rapides (G-AGSH, G-AHKU and G-AJCL) were assigned to the Land's End-Scilly Isles route, along with four pilots, four traffic staff and five engineers. An hourly service was provided on Saturdays, and eight or nine round trips on weekdays. The twenty-fifth anniversary of the air link was marked in 1962, and BEA decided it was time to think about a possible replacement for the Rapides. There was no economically viable way of enlarging the airfield at St Just to take bigger aircraft, and no fixed-wing aircraft of similar capacity, performance and economics to the Rapide was on the horizon, so it was decided that helicopter operations were the answer. BEA evaluated the Boeing-Vertol 107, Bristol 192 and Sikorsky S-61, and on 1 August 1963 placed an order for two Sikorsky S-61Ns. One was to be used to maintain the services to the Scillies, while the other was to be used for charter work. During 1963, evaluation flights were carried out using BEA Westland-Sikorsky S-55s, and one of them, G-AOCF, was based at Land's End to assist in the setting up and testing of the Decca Flight Log that was to be used on the S-61N services.

On 1 May 1964 the last Rapide services on the route were all operated by one aircraft, G-AHKU. The final scheduled flight was under the command of Captain Ron Hurcombe, and had the distinction of being the very last UK scheduled service to be operated by a biplane. It was not, however, to be BEA's last Rapide operation out of the Scillies, as later that day G-AJCL was utilised for an air ambulance flight to the mainland.

On the same day that the Rapides were making their farewell appearances BEA Sikorsky S-61Ns G-ASNL and G-ASNM operated special inaugural flights to the Scilly Isles. On 2 May the type took over the scheduled services. Only one S-61N was needed to maintain the schedules, in place of three Rapides. The helicopter operated four round trips every day and five extra services on Saturdays and Sundays. The one-way fare was £2.3.0 on Tuesdays, Wednesdays and Thursdays, and £2.13.0 on the other days. On Mondays, Fridays and Sundays a day-return fare of £4.6.0 was available. By the end of 1964 36,334 passengers had been carried on the helicopter flights. The services were initially operated out of Land's End (St Just), but in September 1964 the mainland base was transferred to a new purpose-built heliport in Penzance. This had been constructed on the site of a former rubbish tip in an industrial development area, and was the first of its kind in Europe. It featured a completely self-contained passenger terminal and maintenance base. It was closer to surface transport links than St Just and had a better weather record.

For the summer of 1969 six daily round trips were rostered, with extra flights on certain days. The services were listed under the flight number prefix BV in the BEA timetable,

1969 Advertisement for the Scilly Isles helicopter service. (via Author)

Fly the fast comfortable route to the Scillies.

For full flight details see the timetable on these pages or contact: BEA Helicopters Ltd., Penzance Heliport. Tel: Penzance 3871/2

 Helicopters

and the S-61Ns seated twenty-five or twenty-six passengers. The one-way fare ranged from £3.2.0 to £3.12.0, depending on the time of day. There was also a Joyride Return fare of £3.17.0, for passengers who just wanted to experience the helicopter flight, and were willing to fly straight back on the next service.

In 1969 BEA had four S-61Ns in service, and the fleet was to grow further in the 1970s as North Sea oil operations expanded. While BEA was waiting for additional examples to be delivered, there were periods during the winters of the early 1970s when the Scilly Isles duty S-61N was temporarily 'borrowed' for use in the North Sea, and was replaced by a chartered Britten Norman Islander landplane operating out of Land's End.

CHAPTER TEN

Helicopter Operations

In 1947 the BEA Helicopter Experimental Unit was set up to enable the airline to explore the advantages and drawbacks of using helicopters for scheduled service operations. On 26 June the BEA Board made the decision to order three Sikorsky S-51s and two Bell 47 B3s for the Unit, these being the first helicopters to be operated by a British airline. On 1 July the Unit was officially formed at Yeovil, the location being chosen because it was also the home of Westland Helicopters. The first public appearance by a BEA helicopter was on 28 September 1947, when two Sikorsky S-51s, G-AJOR and G-AKCU, were demonstrated at Hampden Park, Glasgow.

On 27 January 1948 BEA began dummy mail-run services on a scheduled basis over the 115-mile routeing Yeovil-Sherborne-Gillingham-Blandford-Wimborne-Poole-Wareham-Dorchester-Weymouth-Bridgeport-Lyme Regis-Yeovil, using S-51s. No mail or dummy mail was carried on the circuit, which took 1hr 55min including stops. The operation continued until 7 March 1948, and out of 570 scheduled calls only twenty-three were missed, six because of a fault in the helicopter's fuel system, which resulted in precautionary landings, and seventeen because of bad weather. The timekeeping was within the five-minute tolerance demanded by the General Post Office. During the same period BEA also investigated the possibilities of using helicopters to deliver mail to rural areas, with a Bell 47 B3 being flown over a 22-mile route linking a number of villages to the north-east of Yeovil.

The success of these trial runs led to BEA inaugurating the first helicopter-operated public mail service in the UK. On 1 June 1948 the Deputy Mayor of Peterborough presented a Royal Mail pennant to Captain J. Theilmann, who then flew S-51 G-AKCU from Peterborough to King's Lynn, Wells, Sheringham, Cromer, Norwich, Thetford, Diss, Harleston, Great Yarmouth, Lowestoft, Beccles, Norwich again, and East Dereham before returning to Peterborough. This machine was followed by a second S-51 (G-AJOV, flown by Captain G.A. Ford), which flew as far as Norwich and back to Peterborough. On the first day of the operation 140 lb of mail was transported. The longer routeing was operated on weekdays, and the shorter one on Saturdays. The services continued until 25 September 1948, by which time 38,046 lb of mail had been carried, 95 per cent of the flights rostered had been completed, and 98.4 per cent of the scheduled calls had been accomplished. BEA calculated the costs of the services at £28.4.0 per flying hour, 8/6d per route-mile, and £1.5.0 per capacity ton-mile. In parallel with these daytime operations BEA also flew experimental night services on a four-times weekly basis between Peterborough and Downham Market, achieving 100 per cent regularity. More night trials followed in 1949, beginning with a flight with twenty-three bags of dummy mail from Peterborough to Norwich on 14 February, and regular S-51 night operations with more

Cover of timetable for the world's first regular passenger helicopter service. (via Author)

GWASANAETH AWYR CWYMRU
WELSH AIR SERVICE
CARDIFF — WREXHAM — LIVERPOOL   Y3

BEA

World's first regular
PASSENGER HELICOPTER SERVICE
TIMETABLE FROM 1 JUNE 1950 UNTIL FURTHER NOTICE

BEA

BRITISH EUROPEAN AIRWAYS

dummy mail during the period 21 February-18 March. Despite bad weather throughout the trials 75 per cent of the rostered flights were completed. In charge of the Helicopter Experimental Unit at this time was Wing Commander R.A.C. Brie. The Unit suffered a setback on 24 May 1949 when S-51 G-AKCU was caught in a downdraught coming off the mountains near Croesor Dam in North Wales, and was written off in the ensuing crash.

On 17 October 1949 BEA inaugurated the first night helicopter services in the UK to carry real mail. The first service was operated by S-51 G-AJOV, piloted by Captain J. Cameron, between Peterborough (Westwood Aerodrome) and Norwich. The flights continued until 15 March 1950. During this period around 95,000 lb of mail was carried, and 73.5 per cent of the services arrived within five minutes of the scheduled time. The total flying time involved was 220 hours, including eighty hours under Instrument Flight Rules (IFR).

A major landmark occurred on 1 June 1950, with the commencement of the world's first ever sustained and regular passenger services by helicopter. 'King Arthur' class S-51s were used on the route from Liverpool (Speke) Airport to Cardiff (Pengam Moors) Airport, with the inaugural service being flown by G-AJOV under the command of Captain Theilmann. On board the first service were BEA Chairman Lord Douglas of Kirtleside, Lady Douglas, and the Minister of Civil Aviation, Lord Pakenham. Other guests were transported over the route in S-51 G-AJOR, piloted by Captain Cameron. From 1 July 1950 an on-demand stop at Wrexham (Plas Coch Farm) was incorporated into the schedule. On weekdays only, flight E306A departed Cardiff at 0915 hrs and arrived at Liverpool at 1110 hrs. The evening service, E306T, left Cardiff at 1730 hrs and arrived Liverpool at 1925 hrs, or ten minutes later if the optional stop at Wrexham was included. In the reverse direction, flight E307A departed Liverpool at 0900 hrs and arrived at Cardiff at 1100 hrs (or ten minutes later if calling at Wrexham), and flight E307K left Liverpool at 1600 hrs and flew direct to Cardiff, arriving at 1800 hrs. The fare from Liverpool to Cardiff was £3.10.0 single, or £5.10.0 return. The service ran until 31 March 1951 and carried a total of 819 passengers. Some 1086 flying hours were completed, and a punctuality rate of 88 per cent was achieved.

On 1 June 1951 BEA commenced passenger helicopter operations between London and Birmingham. Once again, S-51s were used, flying from London Airport via Northolt to

Sikorsky S-51 G-AJOR, plus Vikings and Dakotas, at Northolt. (The A.J. Jackson Collection)

the Haymills Rotorstation in Birmingham. This was located at Hay Barn Recreation Ground, just off Coventry Road, on the route from Elmdon Airport into the city centre. On the inaugural service, Lord and Lady Douglas and the Parliamentary Secretary to the Minister of Civil Aviation flew from Northolt to Birmingham in G-AJOV, while Sir George Cribbett of the Ministry and Peter Masefield of BEA made the same journey in G-AJHW. Two flights carrying invited guests were made on 2 June, and the first public service was scheduled for 4 June. On that date, G-AJOV set off from Birmingham for London, but was forced by bad weather to land at Thame instead. The initial frequency of the service was set at three round trips on every day except Sundays, but a shortage of helicopters resulted in the route being operated only twice-daily between 28 June and 21 July. From 23 July the original frequency was reinstated, but on 9 April 1952 the passenger service was withdrawn and replaced by a freight-only service between London Airport and Birmingham, with an on-demand call at Northolt.

In September 1951 the Unit's base was relocated to Gatwick Airport. At that time the unit was equipped with three S-51s and two Bell 47 B3s, and during its early days at Gatwick it was to carry out much work on the evaluation of helicopter navigation and approach aids. In the 1950s Gatwick was to become the central servicing base for all the Unit's helicopters.

During October 1951 BEA issued a specification for a large, passenger-carrying helicopter, the first such requirement to be announced by any airline. In the short-term, however, another new helicopter type joined the fleet when Bristol 171 G-ALSR arrived on 9 November 1951. It was on loan from the Ministry of Supply, and carried the name 'Sir Gareth' during its time with BEA. The airline was suitably impressed by its evaluation of the machine, and on 18 July 1952 the Board decided to place an order for two Bristol 171 mk 3As. These were intended as eventual replacements for the S-51s, and were to accommodate up to four passengers. During July and August 1952 a series of experimental flights were made to the site of the proposed heliport on London's South

Bank. S-51s and Bristol 171s were used, with S-51 G-AJOR making the first such visit on 28 July 1952.

In February 1953 BEA's helicopters had the chance to demonstrate their usefulness in an emergency situation. Following severe flooding in Holland two BEA S-51s were flown out via Lympne and Antwerp to assist in the rescue work. Based near Eindhoven, and commanded by Captains Cameron and Crewdson they completed forty-five hours' flying time during the period 4 to 11 February, rescuing 76 people and transporting doctors, medical supplies, drinking water and food to twenty villages.

The two Bristol 171s on order were delivered in 1953. The first one commenced operations on 13 July, becoming the first British-made helicopter to enter BEA service. The initial operations consisted of a weekday freight-only service between London Airport and Birmingham (Elmdon) Airport, with an on-demand stop at Northolt. The inaugural flight was made by G-AMWH 'Sir Geraint' under the command of Captain Cameron. In the January 1954 BEA timetable flights BE045/6 were shown as operating on Mondays to Fridays, but the service was withdrawn on 14 January 1954. BEA still had ambitions for the Bristol 171 as a passenger carrier, however, and on 15 June 1954 the airline inaugurated passenger services between London Airport, Northolt, and Southampton (Eastleigh) Airport. The first public service was operated on the following day, when G-AMWH carried three passengers from London Airport to Southampton. No passengers joined at Northolt, but on the return leg two people were flown from Southampton to Northolt and two all the way to London Airport. The fare from London to Southampton was set at £1.10.0 one-way or £2.10.0 return.

Encouraged by its initial passenger-carrying services, BEA signed a contract on 6 October 1954 for another, larger, helicopter type. The contract with Westland Helicopters was for two Westland-Sikorsky WS-55s. These were to be powered by Pratt & Whitney

Bell 47B-3 G-AKFA during crop-spraying trials. (The A.J. Jackson Collection)

Wasp engines, giving a cruising speed of 90 mph, and the total price for the two machines was £54,000. They entered BEA operations on 22 December 1954 on a new Gatwick-London Airport-Southampton route, with Captain Cameron flying the inaugural service in G-ANFH 'Sir Ector'. On the first day three passengers were carried between Gatwick and London Airport, four flew from London Airport to Southampton, one (plus some freight) from Southampton to London Airport, and one from there to Gatwick.

The cost of the Helicopter Experimental Unit during the financial year 1954/5 was £92,070. Most of this was covered by a £80,561 grant from the Ministry of Aviation in respect of the Unit's experimental work, which included the calibration of various systems of heliport and helicopter cockpit lighting. The Unit also engaged in helicopter crop-spraying.

On 25 July 1955 BEA inaugurated scheduled passenger services between London Airport and the South Bank Heliport at Waterloo. The first service was operated by WS-55 G-ANUK 'Sir Kay'. The WS-55s were configured to carry four or five passengers, and eight round trips were operated each day, at a flying time of of just thirteen minutes and a one-way fare of £1.15.0. By the time the services were discontinued on 31 May 1956, 3822 passengers had been carried. A few weeks later another new passenger route was introduced, this time between Birmingham (Elmdon Airport), Leicester (Saffron Lane), and Nottingham (Trent Lane). From 3 July 1956 'King Arthur' class WS-55s operated over the route twice each weekday, using the BEH flight number prefix. This service was withdrawn on 10 November 1956, having transported 1829 passengers.

On 20 July 1956 the twin-engined, twin-rotor Bristol 173 Mk 2 G-AMJI landed in a field beside the BEA headquarters at Ruislip. It was on loan from the Bristol Aeroplane Company, and carried out trial flights for a short time, but did not carry passengers.

In 1957 Wing Commander Brie retired, and his place as head of the Helicopter Experimental Unit was taken by Captain J. Cameron. During 1958 a helicopter approach light installation, the first in the UK, was installed at Gatwick, and the Unit began testing a British-made helicopter autopilot, mounted in a WS-55.

During November 1957 the Fairey Rotodyne convertiplane had made its first flight. This was a fifty-four to sixty-five seat vertical take-off airliner, powered by two Rolls-

Bristol 171 Sycamore MK.3A G-ALSR was operated on loan from the Ministry of Supply 1951-4 (The A.J. Jackson Collection)

Westland-Sikorsky WS.55 G-ANFH inaugurated Gatwick-London Airport-Southampton helicopter passenger services in 1954 (The A.J. Jackson Collection)

Royce Tyne turboprops for forward flight, and with a rotor head for vertical take-off and landing. In 1956 the US helicopter operator New York Airways had issued a Letter of Intent for five examples, but Fairey needed up to £10 million to finance development of the revolutionary aircraft. It was offered 50 per cent of this by the British government in the form of a loan repayable by a levy on sales, provided BEA placed a firm order. The airline had ambitions of operating the Rotodyne on short city centre to city centre routes, such as London-Paris and London-Brussels. In 1959 BEA announced that it was going to issue a Letter of Intent for six examples of a developed version. However, concern over the environmental impact of the aircraft's high noise levels, and other factors, meant that BEA never placed a firm order. In 1960 the helicopter interests of Fairey Aviation were merged into Westland Helicopters, but no firm orders for the Rotodyne were received, and the project was cancelled in February 1962.

On 1 January 1964 BEA Helicopters Ltd was formed. Two twin-turbine Sikorsky S-61Ns had been ordered by BEA the previous summer, and the term Helicopter Experimental Unit was no longer considered appropriate for a division that had matured into a scheduled service operator, so the unit was entirely reorganised and the new BEA subsidiary created. The two S-61Ns entered service in May 1964, with one being allocated to the Scilly Isles services and the other being based at Gatwick for charter work. The new helicopters could each accommodate twenty-five passengers, in a cabin that was furnished in turquoise, cream and green, and every passenger had a window seat.

With the arrival of the S-61Ns BEA's fleet of smaller helicopters was reduced from five aircraft to just two, a four-seat Bell 47J and a seven-seat WS-55. These types, plus the Gatwick-based S-61N, were kept busy on police traffic patrols over the M6 motorway, television and film work, crop-spraying, and general charters.

With a view to diversifying into the new field of oil-rig support flights BEA joined with Vancouver-based Okanaghan Helicopters to form International Helicopters Ltd. Each company contributed one S-61N, and to maintain its fleet levels BEA Helicopters purchased a third example. The new joint company commenced operations on 9 July 1965, flying in support of Shell Oil out of a temporary heliport in Lowestoft Docks. From here, the S-61Ns flew to the North Sea drilling platform 'Neptune 1', some 48 miles north-east of Lowestoft. However, the partnership was short-lived, and late in 1965 BEA Helicopters bought out Okanaghan Helicopters' share and its S-61N and henceforth continued to operate the flights in its own right.

In March 1967 the oil tanker *Torry Canyon* went aground off Land's End and began leaking crude oil. As part of the attempts to refloat her, a BEA Helicopters S-61N was chartered by the Royal Navy and used to lower a three-ton compressor onto her deck. The efforts to refloat the stricken tanker were later abandoned, and she was broken up by bombs and rockets from Royal Navy Buccaneer strike aircraft.

In 1967 oil-rig support operations from Aberdeen commenced with an S-61N flight to the Shell rig 'Staflo'. A base was also established at Sumburgh on Shetland, where a single S-61N was stationed. By that time BEA Helicopters' fleet of S-61Ns had grown to eight aircraft, and during the first months of 1968 they were to be involved in rescue operations at sea. In January an S-61N saved the crew of the oil rig 'Sea Quest', which had broken loose from its moorings in a force ten gale whilst 110 miles off Flamborough Head. This operation was followed on 4 February 1968 by the company's first casualty evacuation flight from an oil platform to a hospital in Aberdeen.

One of the S-61Ns was lost on 15 November 1970, fortunately without any serious injuries being sustained. G-ASNM was *en route* from an oil platform to Aberdeen when it suffered a failure of its transmission system. As a precautionary measure the flotation-equipped helicopter was landed on the sea, and all its passengers and crew were safely taken off. An attempt was later made to tow the stricken helicopter to harbour, but during the tow the S-61N took on water and sank.

Augusta Bell 47J G-APTH in a revised version of the 'Red Square' livery. (The A.J. Jackson Collection)

By 1971 BEA Helicopters employed a total staff of 160, including twenty-eight pilots, and the fleet now included a four-seat Bell Jet Ranger for general charter work. One of the more unusual operations the company was engaged for that year involved the transportation of drilling equipment up a Scottish mountainside. Operating on behalf of Robertson Research International, S-61N G-ATFM made more than thirty lifts from the shores of Loch Lomond, completing the job in two days despite being hampered by strong winds. At the conclusion of the drilling work, the equipment was brought down again by S-61N G-ATBJ. Because of the nature of the terrain, the helicopters had been required to carry each underslung load up to a height of 1500 ft, over a distance of two miles.

On 20 May 1971 BEA Helicopters unveiled its plans for a new complex at Aberdeen Airport, and on 13 October the company announced its intention of transferring the bulk of its maintenance workload from Gatwick to Aberdeen. The new complex at Aberdeen was to cost £150,000 to construct, and was duly opened on 15 November 1972. In the meantime BEA Helicopters had secured a contract from the Department of Transport to provide a long-range search and rescue unit at Aberdeen, operating under HM Coastguard control. This became operational on 1 November 1971, and provided for a winch-equipped S-61N, manned by a specially trained crew recruited from the Royal Navy, to be on 24-hour standby.

In 1972 BEA Helicopters had six S-61Ns allocated to oil-rig support duties, and one operating the scheduled services to the Scilly Isles. The oil-related helicopters were based at Aberdeen, Sumburgh and Beccles, where a Bell 212 was also stationed. The Jet Ranger was also still available for general charters. The Aberdeen-based search and rescue unit was called into action on 6 December 1973, to save the crew of the trawler *Navena*, aground off Orkney. The helicopter crew were later to be decorated for their efforts.

On 1 April 1974 BEA and BOAC were amalgamated to form British Airways, and BEA Helicopters Ltd was consequently renamed British Airways Helicopters.

Sikorsky S-61N G-AYOY at the BEA Helicopters' base at Aberdeen Airport. (BEA photo-copyright British Airways)

CHAPTER ELEVEN

All-cargo Operations

BEA began scheduled all-cargo operations on 10 August 1947, when Dakota G-AGYZ inaugurated a daily Northolt-Brussels service. From October 1948 this service terminated at Brussels, but the Dakotas went on to open further new routes from Northolt in subsequent years. On 3 April 1949 a service to Malta via Nice and Rome was introduced. This was followed by services to Hanover on 3 February 1950 and to Paris (Le Bourget) on 1 March that year.

In August 1950 Bristol 170 G-AICS was delivered to BEA. This was the sole survivor of an original 1946 order for fourteen examples. Eight were to be the passenger-carrying Bristol Wayfarer version and the other six were intended for the carriage of bulky cargo

'Pionair-Leopard' class Dakota G-AHCX being loaded. (BEA photo-copyright British Airways, via Anthony Kelly)

SEND YOUR FREIGHT BY AIR

B.E.A. offers a speedy air cargo service to all ports of Europe and on its network within the British Isles. There are reduced rates for consignments of over 45kgs. and many special commodity rates. For full information ask for B.E.A. "Air Freight" booklet.

Air cargo advertisment from the January 1954 BEA timetable. (via Author)

loads and also for ferrying spare Bristol Centaurus engines to Elizabethan aircraft stranded away from base. However, adverse economic conditions resulted in the order being slashed to just the one example, and even this was destined never to transport a Centaurus engine. During the financial year 1950/1 G-AICS flew just 204 hours, and in early 1952 it went on long-term lease to Silver City Airways, who eventually purchased it in 1957.

In 1951 BEA began night mail services between Manchester and Belfast, and during that year two new versions of the Dakota entered service with the airline. The Pionair-Leopard class was the cargo equivalent of the Pionair conversion by Scottish Aviation, and featured the same two-man cockpit layout and updated instrumentation, but retained the original Dakota cabin double doors. The other Dakota conversion was more radical. G-ALXN and G-AMDB were fitted with Rolls-Royce Dart 505 turboprop engines and used on BEA cargo services to build up operating experience in anticipation of the delivery of the new Viscount airliner. The first Dart-Dakota, G-ALXN, was redelivered to BEA on 9 June 1951, and on 15 August it inaugurated the first regular cargo services to be operated by a turboprop aircraft, carrying 5500 lb of newspapers and mail from Northolt to Hanover (Bückeburg) on the inaugural flight. Occasionally, a stop at Brussels

Dakota G-AGIZ, here wearing BEA Freight Express titles, was later converted to Pionair-Leopard standard. (The A.J. Jackson Collection)

G-ALXN, one of two Dart-Dakotas used for BEA Express Air Freight Services. (The A.J. Jackson Collection)

was incorporated in this service, and on 20 April 1952 another route to Milan via Paris was introduced. Both Dart-Dakotas carried the legend 'BEA Express Air Freight' on their tail fins, and on the longer flight legs the high altitudes attained neccessitated the use of oxygen by the crews of these unpressurised aircraft. In the first half of 1953 both Dakotas were converted back to piston power and resumed their BEA careers as conventional Pionair-Leopard freighters.

In the April 1953 schedules BEA Pionair-Leopard aircraft operated freight services from Northolt to Paris, Malta via Nice, Rome (with an optional call at Marseilles), Istanbul via Rome and Athens, Copenhagen via Amsterdam, and Hanover via Brussels or Amsterdam. They also flew between Hamburg and Berlin and operated domestic services from Northolt to Manchester, Belfast and Glasgow. On 2 April 1953 Viscount turboprops began to be substituted for Pionair-Leopards on some cargo services to Nicosia via Rome and Athens as part of the new aircraft's programme of proving flights. BEA's Viking aircraft were also used on cargo services during January 1954, being rostered onto flight BE025 from Northolt to Nice and Malta on Sundays, returning on the following day as flight BE026.

By 1956 the Viscounts were seeing more use as freighters during the night hours, with a twice-weekly London-Milan service being inaugurated on 10 October. By June 1957 Viscounts were operating freighter services BEF21/22 from London to Paris (Le Bourget) and back in the early hours of every morning except Mondays. The bulk of the cargo schedules, however, still utilised the Pionair-Leopards, and the June 1957 timetable had them rostered to fly London-Nice-Rome on three nights each week. During the early hours of Tuesday and Friday, flights BEF02/03 operated London-Amsterdam-London,

Viscount 802 G-AOHL being loaded with a consignment of labour-saving gardening devices. (BEA photo-copyright British Airways)

Argosy 101 G-AOZZ at Heathrow. (BEA photo-copyright British Airways, via Anthony Kelly)

and there was also a nightly London-Copenhagen-Hamburg service. On 10 October 1957 the type inaugurated a twice-weekly London- Düsseldorf-Stuttgart operation.

A Viscount was lost while operating a cargo service on 10 October 1957. In the early hours of that day srs 802 G-AOHP took off from London for Copenhagen with a consignment of mail, freight and newspapers and a crew of two. At 0327 hrs the flight was cleared to descend to 7000 ft on approach to Copenhagen. A further descent to 3500 ft was authorised, and the propeller de-icing was switched on as the aircraft passed through 4000 ft. At 0346 hrs the crew were instructed to hold at the Bella beacon. The initial approach drills were completed and the undercarriage was lowered. After three minutes the crew commenced a procedural turn to intercept the Instrument Landing System (ILS), and at 0357 hrs the airframe de-icing was switched on. Immediately, the left current flow warning light came on, along with the central warning light, and the

Argosy 101 G-APRN at Heathrow, with two Comet 4Bs in the background. (BEA photo-copyright British Airways, via Anthony Kelly)

Viscount swung to the left. The no.1 engine rpm and jetpipe temperature were observed to be falling, and the fire drill for that engine was carried out. The aircraft's flight attitude was corrected and full power was applied to the other three engines. The Viscount started to lose height rapidly, and the captain retracted the undercarriage and flaps. A turn to the right to regain the ILS caused the aircraft to enter a 45-degree bank, at an airspeed of 135 knots and a high rate of descent. The crew then discovered that nos 3 and 4 engines had also failed. The propellers were feathered as the Viscount descended at 600 ft per minute, and an emergency landing without wheels or flaps was made some fourteen miles from Copenhagen Airport. Thankfully, both crew members survived, but the Viscount was a write-off. The investigation into the accident gave the probable cause as 'accumulation of ice on the engine cowlings, which, because of a malfunction of the de-icing system, was allowed to build up before being dislodged. The passage of lumps of ice through the engines caused a partial flame-out, which produced sufficient loss of power to initiate auto-feathering and thus stopped the engines'.

The three crew members of Dakota G-AGHP were not so lucky on 16 May 1958. They were operating a cargo service in storm conditions near Châtenoy in France, when the aircraft suffered a structural failure and crashed with the loss of all on board.

A shortage of freighter capacity in early 1960 led BEA to use chartered Avro York aircraft of Dan-Air for some of its cargo services. From 18 February 1960 they operated a twice-weekly London-Paris night service, and they were also utilised on some London-Manchester-Glasgow schedules. Viscounts were seeing increasing use on freight flights, but the Pionair-Leopards were still to be seen on some cargo services out of London. The longest service they operated that year was flight BEF06 from London to Rome via Nice. After a nightstop in Rome the aircraft returned to London, making an optional call at Milan if required.

Argosy 222 G-ASXM at the BEA engineering base at Heathrow. (The A.J. Jackson Collection)

On 27 April 1961 BEA ordered three Armstrong Whitworth Argosy srs 102 turboprops for its all-cargo network. These twin-boom aircraft featured large loading doors at the front and rear of the fuselage; palletised cargo could be transferred directly into them from lorries using special handling vehicles, which BEA also acquired. BEA's Argosy order specified the fitting of Rolamat conveyor systems and cargo lashing points, and the aircraft were scheduled for delivery in late 1961. The airline's first example, G-APRN, was delivered to London on 6 November 1961 and began earning its keep from 17 November, being rostered onto some London-Milan services on an ad hoc basis. The arrival of the other two examples shortly afterwards led to the Argosies taking over the route on a scheduled four flights-weekly basis from 19 December 1961. From 8 January 1962 they flew London-Manchester-Glasgow daily, and on 30 January they took over on daily services from London to Copenhagen, Düssledorf, Frankfurt and Paris. Their entry into full service led to the retirement of BEA's Pionair-Leopards and the termination of the Dan-Air Avro York charters.

The November 1961 BEA timetable included the following all-cargo schedules:

Flights BE392F/393F between London and Paris (Le Bourget), nightly except Mondays.

Flights BE500F/501F between London and Brussels on four nights each week.

Daytime services BE132F/133F between London and Milan (Linate) on four days each week.

Flights BE608F/609F between London and Frankfurt on every night except Mondays.

Daytime services BE3936F/3937F between London and Jersey on Tuesdays and Thursdays.

Rear view through the hold of Argosy 222 G-ASXO. (BEA photo-copyright British Airways, via Anthony Kelly)

Daytime services BE4940F/4941F between London and Manchester on five days each week, and continuing onwards to Glasgow (Renfrew) on Mondays, Wednesdays and Fridays.

Flights BE7916F/7915F between Manchester and Belfast on every night except Saturdays.

Services between London and Amsterdam on every night except Saturdays.

Joint BEA/SAS services between London and Copenhagen on every night except Saturdays.

All of these services were Viscount-operated at the commencement of the schedules, but from the end of November 1961 the Argosies began to take over the flights. By May 1962 the only remaining Viscount all-cargo operations were those from London to Amsterdam and to Zurich, and the Manchester-Belfast service. Two Argosies were initially utilised on the scheduled services, with the third one being used for training flights and as a standby aircraft.

The summer 1963 timetable featured Argosy international services from London to Paris (Le Bourget), Milan (Linate), Copenhagen, and Frankfurt via Düsseldorf. They were also used on domestic flights from London to Manchester, Jersey and Guernsey. There was still a place in the cargo schedules for the Viscounts. They operated night services

The BEA Cargo sheds in the Central Area at Heathrow. In the foreground the North Office Block of Terminal 3 is under construction. (BEA photo-copyright British Airways, via Brian A.L. Jones)

from London to Brussels (in competition with SABENA Dakotas), to Zurich (alongside Swissair Convair 440s), and the six nights-weekly Manchester-Belfast route.

On 1 November 1964 a new Argosy service between London and Gothenburg was inaugurated. It initially operated three times each week, but in 1965 the frequency was increased to six times-weekly and the routeing was amended to London-Copenhagen-Gothenburg-London. During the financial year 1963/4 BEA's flown cargo tonnage increased by 19 per cent to 58,259 tons, but the airline never made a profit from the srs 102s, mainly because of the poor economics of operating a fleet of just three examples. Between March and July they were returned to the manufacturer in part exchange for a fleet of five upgraded srs 222s. These featured enlarged door openings to permit the carriage of the standard 108in wide pallets used on long-haul cargo jets. Their fuselages were 47 ft long and they could each carry up to 14 tons of freight. The contract for the srs 222s, signed on 21 September 1964, was worth £4 million.

Merchantman G-APEM being loaded at Nicosia. Trident 2E G-AVFL in the background. (BEA photo-copyright British Airways, via Anthony Kelly)

In the summer of 1965 the Argosy srs 222s were to be seen operating UK domestic cargo services in addition to their international duties. On every night except Sundays they operated London-Manchester and return, and on Tuesdays, Wednesdays and Fridays they flew evening schedules between London and Glasgow. The Channel Islands were served by afternoon round trips from London to Jersey on Tuesdays and Thursdays, and from London to Guernsey on Mondays and Fridays. The Manchester- Belfast route was still Viscount-operated, with a round trip on every night except Saturdays.

On 4 July 1965 Argosy srs 222 G-ASXL crashed into high ground at Costalba in Italy whilst inbound to Milan. Two crew members were injured, and the aircraft was declared a write-off. Its loss resulted in srs 101 G-APRM being leased back from Hawker Siddeley Aviation until replacement srs 222 G-ATTC joined BEA in November 1966.

More new Argosy routes were introduced during 1966. On 7 May a weekly London-Athens-Nicosia routeing commenced, and on 1 November Argosies replaced Viscounts on the weekly London-Vienna cargo run. On the same date a joint BEA/ Lufthansa schedule from Manchester to Düsseldorf and Frankfurt was introduced. BEA Argosies were used for some of these flights, with leased Douglas DC-4s operating the others. For the summer of 1967 the Argosies were operated on routes out of London to Amsterdam, Athens, Copenhagen, Frankfurt and Düsseldorf, Gothenburg, Milan, Athens and Nicosia, Paris, and Stockholm, and Vienna, but another example was to be lost before the year's end.

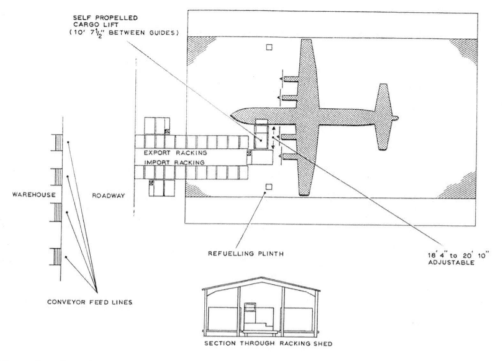

Illustrations from the BEA Merchantman ground operations manual. (via Author)

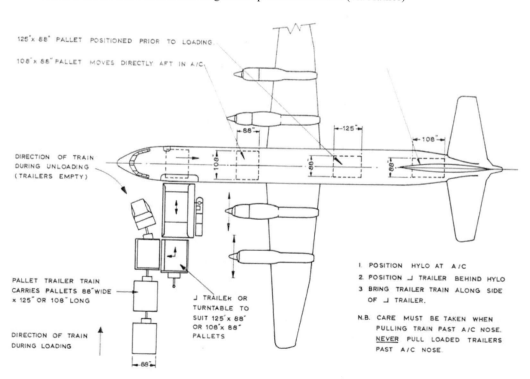

Merchantman G-APEO being loaded at night, with a BOAC Boeing 707 freighter in the background. (BEA photo-copyright British Airways, via Anthony Kelly)

On 4 December 1967 G-ASXP departed Stansted on a training sortie. Just after it left the ground, power was reduced to simulate a failure of the no.4 engine. The aircraft went out of control and crashed, probably as a result of the propeller going into fine pitch when the engine was throttled back. Among the three injured crew members was the co-pilot Ian Bashall, who had also been co-pilot on G-ASXL when it crashed near Milan in 1965. G-ASXP was also declared a write-off, but this time no replacement machine was ordered. A further Argosy came close to being destroyed on 17 February 1968, when G-ATTC suffered a failure of the reduction gear to its no.4 engine whilst *en route* from Milan to London. The propeller detached itself from the engine and caused severe damage to the no. 3 engine and the fuselage side. The aircraft made an emergency landing at Paris (Le Bourget), where further damage was sustained, but it was repaired and eventually returned to service.

On 1 April 1968 the Argosies entered service on the London-Belfast route, but they were to enjoy only two more years of service before retirement. During the financial year 1968/9 BEA handled some 132,000 tonnes of cargo, one-fifth of all the cargo flown within Europe.

Since 1966 BEA had been conducting trials with Vanguards in the all-cargo role, commencing with Saturday night newspaper charter flights between Manchester and Belfast that year. The type was used on twice-weekly London-Dublin freight flights from 1 October 1969, by which time the first of the Merchantman conversions was almost ready for its first flight. Five Vanguards had been earmarked for conversion to Merchantman configuration, with the first two conversions being carried out by Aviation Traders Engineering Ltd, and the remainder by BEA's own engineers using kits supplied

Merchantman G-APEG in its final BEA livery. (The A.J. Jackson Collection)

by Aviation Traders. The cost of each conversion was in the region of £128,000, and the most prominent feature was a large freight door, 139 in long by 81 in high, cut in the left side of the forward fuselage. The cabin windows were blanked out, the cabin floor beams and fuselage frames were strengthened, and the cabin floor was fitted with rollers for the easy movement of pallets. To aid night operations additional lighting was provided at the cargo door entrance. The main cabin was divided into eleven bays, each capable of accepting a 108 in by 88 in Hawker Siddeley Universal Cargo Pallet conforming to the International Air Transport Association (IATA) standard specification. To transport bulkier loads, three of these pallets in the overwing positions could be replaced by two 125 in by 88 in pallets. Under the cabin floor, the lower holds provided a usable volume of 621 cu ft forward and 572 cu ft aft. Each aircraft was provided with an external tail steady, to limit the aftward tilting of the fuselage to one degree during loading and unloading.

After allowing 1400 kg deadweight for the pallets and cargo nets a maximum freight capacity of 18,500 kg could be transported over the aircraft's optimum sector lengths of up to 800 statute miles. Such sectors included those from London to Amsterdam, Belfast, Brussels, Copenhagen, Dublin, Düsseldorf, Frankfurt, Glasgow, Gothenburg, Manchester, Paris, and Zurich, as well as Manchester-Frankfurt and Stockholm-Gothenburg. The first Aviation Traders conversion was G-APEM, which first flew in its new configuration on 10 October 1969. This was followed by G-APEO on 1 February 1970. BEA's first conversion was G-APEK, which entailed some 60,000 man-hours by the airline's engineering staff. Prior to the introduction of the Merchantman on scheduled services, BEA stripped Vanguard G-APEL of its seats and front airstairs and used it on some cargo services to Copenhagen, Milan and Paris with freight loaded into the main passenger cabin. Over a period of time most of the remaining passenger Vanguards also had their front airstairs removed to enable them to operate as makeshift freighters if the need arose.

A Merchantman being loaded at Genoa. (BEA photo-copyright British Airways, via Anthony Kelly)

Meanwhile the Argosies soldiered on for a while longer, being used to inaugurate London-Turin services on 1 November 1969 and to re-introduce London-Malta flights on the same date. By February 1970 the Merchantman fleet was entering service, and the final Argosy schedule was operated on 30 April 1970, from Jersey to London. Since 1965 the Argosy srs 222 fleet had flown a total of 51,415 hours in BEA service.

The first Merchantman commercial service took place on 7 February 1970 when G-APEM flew the London-Stuttgart-Vienna service, also inaugurating BEA cargo services to Stuttgart. This was followed by the first Merchantman services from London to Amsterdam on 9 March, and to Paris, Gothenburg and Stockholm during February/March 1970. Guernsey received Merchantman service from 5 April, and from 1 November the Manchester-Amsterdam route was served by the type.

On 9 December 1969 the new joint BOAC/BEA Cargo Centre at Heathrow, known as CargoCentre Europe, was handed over, and became officially operational on 10 January 1970. At the end of March 1970 the BEA Cargo Unit moved in. At each aircraft stand, fixed racking was provided, consisting of eleven export and eleven import pallet bays. Export pallets were transported from the warehouse to the stand prior to the aircraft's arrival, and import pallets were unloaded directly from the aircraft to the racking shed, prior to despatch to the warehouse. At the racking shed a special transporter was in use, and during loading and unloading the pallets were transferred between the aircraft and the transporter by a Houchin high lift platform.

For BEA's summer 1971 schedules eight Merchantman aircraft were in service, and their international routes included a Birmingham-Manchester-Paris (Orly) flight on Wednesdays, Fridays and Saturdays, a weekday Glasgow-Frankfurt schedule, services from Manchester to Amsterdam on Thursdays and Saturdays, and from Manchester to

Frankfurt five times each week. On the domestic front the type operated out of London to Belfast, Dublin, Glasgow, Manchester and the Channel Islands, but Viscounts still maintained the Manchester-Belfast services, which operated nightly except Saturdays.

During the early 1970s many BEA cargo services were operated in conjunction with other national carriers. Alitalia DC-9 freighters flew the joint Manchester-Birmingham-Milan services, SAS DC-9s operated the Manchester-Birmingham-Copenhagen route, and TAP used a Boeing 727 freighter between London and Lisbon. There was also a London-Manchester-Helsinki service, which was operated by Finnair, but utilised a piston-engined Douglas DC-6B of Kar-Air. BEA's own aircraft were used on the joint services from Manchester to Germany, and on the routes linking London with Gothenburg, Stockholm, Zurich, Nicosia and Brussels.

CHAPTER TWELVE

BEA Airtours

Almost from its formation, BEA had been selling blocks of seats on its services to holiday destinations to travel agents and tour operators, but on 1 April 1964 the airline launched its own tour operating subsidiary called Silver Wing Holidays. By 1966 the Silver Wing Holidays brochure was offering two-week package holidays to the Costa Brava for as little as £46.13.0, and two weeks in Morroco for just £84.12.0. By the end of the 1960s, however, BEA was losing a lot of traffic on the holiday routes to the many charter airlines, who could undercut its scheduled service seat rates. The Comet 4B fleet was about to be retired, and the opportunity was taken to use these aircraft to set up a BEA charter airline subsidiary. BEA Airtours was accordingly formed on 24 April 1969, with Captain W. Baillie (formerly head of flight operations at BEA) as its managing director. Peter McKeown was appointed flight manager, hangar space was aquired at Gatwick, and operations commenced from there on 6 March 1970.

The inaugural service was operated by Comet 4B G-ARJL from Gatwick to Palma, and by the end of the year BEA Airtours had purchased nine Comet 4Bs from BEA. In addition to those examples, G-APME was operated on lease from BEA until early 1972.

BEA Airtours began its first season of operations with 375 staff, of whom 111 were aircrew, and only twenty-eight were not either pilots, cabin crew or engineers. The Comets were fitted with 109 seats of the type used in BEA Super One-Elevens, and their cabin decor was designed by Charles Butler Associates. The carpet was royal blue, the bulkheads blue, and the curtains yellow. The seats were finished in blocks of colour; royal blue, orange and yellow. During the first summer season charters were operated out of Gatwick for tour companies such as Exchange Travel, Thomas Cook, Inghams, and the National Union of Students Travel Service, to Alicante, Gerona, Ibiza, Malaga, Nicosia, Palma, Pisa, Rimini, Tenerife, Trieste and Venice. The only non-Gatwick departures were a weekly series of charters from Birmingham to Palma, inaugurated by G-ARJN on 16 May 1970. More than 350,000 seats were sold on over 4300 round trips, and the airline announced that by the following summer it hoped to capture 20 per cent of the UK holiday charter market.

By the end of the summer 1970 season BEA Airtours was already looking round for larger aircraft to replace the Comets. In November 1970 it was announced that it would be aquiring a fleet of seven Boeing 707-123Bs from American Airlines for £10.4 million, but political pressure for the purchase of surplus BEA or BOAC aircraft instead led to the cancellation of the order. During the quiet winter months of 1970/1 the Comets were utilised extensively on BEA scheduled services, to cover for the late delivery of Trident 3Bs. From 13 to 18 November they also flew for the BEA subsidiary Northeast Airlines, operating scheduled services and inclusive-tour charters out of Newcastle while the

Comet 4B G-ARJL of BEA Airtours on take-off. (Kev Darling)

BEA Airtours Comet 4B G-APMC at Heathrow, possibly while on lease to BEA. (Kev Darling)

Northeast Tridents were being stripped of their former BKS Air Transport livery and repainted. During their first year of operation the BEA Airtours Comets had carried 650,000 passengers, and the airline had made a small profit of £154,140. BEA Airtours had meanwhile purchased a fleet of Boeing 707-436s from BOAC, and the first one was delivered in December 1971. By the summer of 1972 two examples were in use on holiday charters out of Gatwick, but all the Comet 4Bs were also still in service.

BEA Airtours Boeing 707-465 G-ARWD at Liverpool in May 1973. (Author)

BEA Airtours Comet 4B G-ARCP. (The A.J. Jackson Collection)

see your Travel Agent for

'All-in' holidays on the Continent

You have so little to bother about when you arrange a flying 'All-in' holiday. Your Travel Agent sees to everything : your air travel, all your hotel bookings and bills. But he not only saves you trouble, he saves you money — you couldn't book such a holiday for yourself, at such low cost! Don't think anything is skimped. It isn't. Most flights are by the famous VISCOUNT or the luxurious ELIZABETHAN. And don't think you are shepherded or dragooned. You're not. (Everything is arranged for you *individually*.) Yes, an 'All-in' holiday is an unforgettable experience.

flying **BEA** BRITISH EUROPEAN AIRWAYS

January 1954 advertisment for BEA 'All-inclusive' holidays. (via Author)

BEA Airtours Comet 4B G-APMD was sold to Dan-Air in 1972. (Kev Darling)

BEA Airtours Boeing 707-436 G-APFD. (Kev Darling)

BEA Airtours Boeing 707-436 G-APFH at Gatwick. In the background can be seen a TWA Boeing 707, BEA Airtours Comet 4B, two Dan-Air Comet 4s, and a Boeing 737. (Kev Darling)

Landing shot of a BEA Airtours Boeing 707-436. (Mick West)

During the winter of 1972/3 two more Boeing 707s were delivered, and BEA Airtours began to use them on transatlantic charters and on the airline's first round-the-world charter flight. The aircraft used for this was G-APFL, under the command of Captains Peter McKeown and Maurice Barnet. Two first officers were also carried, and the same crew stayed with the aircraft and its passengers throughout its global tour. Flight KT001 departed Gatwick on 26 January 1973 and routed via Teheran, Delhi, Colombo, Singapore, Bangkok, Hong Kong, Guam, Nandi, Auckland, Pago Pago, Honolulu, Mexico City and Bermuda before finally arriving back at Gatwick on schedule on 25 February. Additional flight crew joined the flight at Hong Kong to assist with the long trans-Pacific legs. Another three-week, round-the-world charter was also operated during that winter.

By the summer of 1973 seven Boeing 707s were in service, flying to Spain, Greece, Tunisia, Morroco and the Canary Islands from Gatwick, and operating fortnightly charters from Newcastle to Athens and Corfu. By then, the Comet fleet had been reduced to five aircraft. The final Comet 4B service was operated by G-ARJL, the aircraft that had flown BEA Airtours' inaugural service in March 1970. On 31 October 1973 this machine flew Paris (Le Bourget)-Gatwick on behalf of NUS Travel Service. In total, the Comets had carried around two million passengers for BEA Airtours. When BEA and BOAC were finally amalgamated in 1974, the charter arm was renamed British Airtours Ltd.

CHAPTER THIRTEEN

BEA's Structure

Upon its formation in 1946 BEA had an initial staff of 1641, 625 of whom had been transferred from BOAC. The airline was initially divided into two divisions:

The UK Division, based at Speke Airport, Liverpool, because this had been the base of the AAJC.
The Continental Division, based at Northolt.

In 1947 the UK Division was sub-divided into the English Division, still based at Liverpool, and the Scottish Airways Division, based at Renfrew Airport, Glasgow. From 1 January 1949 the English Division was renamed the British Division, the head office of the English Division at Liverpool was closed down, and its managers were relocated to Keyline House at Ruislip, where the activities of both Divisions were to be centralised. The maintenance base at Speke Airport was also closed, and the work transferred to Renfrew.

From May 1948 the UK independent airlines were allowed for the first time to operate scheduled services on domestic routes, under BEA Associate Agreements. These stipulated that the routes in question were not in competition with BEA, would not hamper the state airline's plans for expansion, and that the operating airline would maintain services for a minimum of two years. In reality, many of the routes granted were never flown.

During 1950 BEA ran a staff competition to find individual names for all the aircraft in its fleet (new names in the case of the Vikings, which were to be renamed). Twenty-three staff members submitted suggestions, and the winning names were announced in the September 1950 issue of *BEA Magazine*. All the aircraft were to be named after famous British men from history, or after Scottish clans, with different themes for each aircraft type. There was no outright winner. Instead, prizes were awarded to six staff members, who each won two free return tickets for either the first weekend Elizabethan service to Paris, or a Viscount proving flight during Easter 1951, or a Viking or Pionair service to Paris, Jersey, Scotland or Belfast.

In another BEA reorganisation, the British and Continental divisions were scrapped on 1 January 1951 and all the airline's activities were split between seven departments:

Commercial, Traffic, Flight Operations, Aircraft Movements and Schedules, Engineering, Finance and Property, and Administration. By 1951, BEA's staff had grown to around 7000.

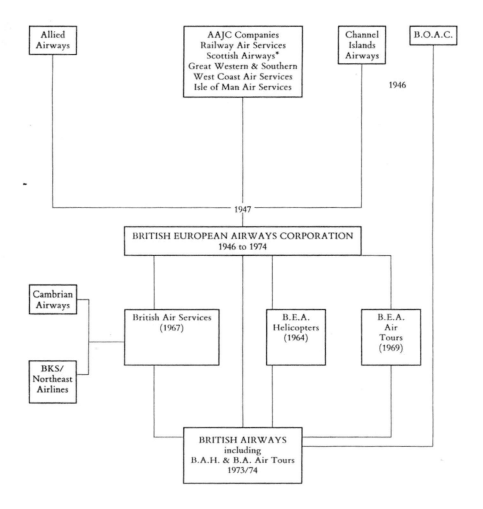

(*Scottish Airways includes Highland Airways and Western Isles Air Services)
Also included was the dormant North Eastern Airways

BEA's genealogical tree 1946-1974. (via Phil Lo Bao)

In 1953 the Conservative government of the day removed BEA's effective monopoly on domestic scheduled services. From then onwards, subject to licencing agreements, the independent airlines could operate domestic services free of the constraints of the BEA Associate Agreements, and by the summer of 1954 some twenty airlines were doing so.

On 1 April 1953 Tourist Class services were introduced on routes within Europe and from Europe to the Middle East. At first, however, BEA could not take full commercial advantage of this, as its Viscounts were not initially configured with Tourist Class seating.

In 1957 the image of the Union flag had to be temporarily removed from the covers of BEA timetables because 'there are places on our routes where it is slightly embarrassing', and it was replaced by the silhouette of an aircraft. BEA's staff in Greece and the Middle East had been warned by their head office that some potential passengers might be deterred from booking by the image of the national flag. Despite the redesign of the timetables, the Union flag image continued to adorn the tails of BEA aircraft.

The BEA Annual Report for 1959/60 showed that the airline employed 746 pilots, 119 radio operators and 584 cabin staff, along with aound 11,000 ground staff based at 82 stations throughout the world. In 1962, however, BEA finally dispensed with its remaining radio operators, who were all offered jobs elsewhere within the airline. Some were retrained as pilots, and others went to work in Traffic or Flight Operations. Yet another reorganisation in 1967 saw BEA being split into three divisions, Traffic and Sales, Operations, and Scottish. Each Division became a profit centre, and was supported in its role by centralised departments covering Finance, Personnel, Public Relations and Air Safety. In 1969 the German internal network also became a Division and profit centre. Under Chairman Henry Marking the profit centre concept was extended in April 1971 to cover the whole of the airline. Ten new Divisions were created:

BEA Mainline: responsible for all international services out of London, plus services from London to Belfast, Edinburgh and Glasgow.

Super One-Eleven: responsible for all international services out of Manchester, plus the German internal network, and also all domestic services out of Manchester with the exception of those to the Channel Islands.

Scottish Airways: responsible for all Scottish internal services, plus the routes from Aberdeen and Inverness to London, plus the Glasgow-Belfast route.

Channel Islands Airways: responsible for all Channel Islands services, plus all international and domestic services out of Birmingham, plus the operation of the single Viscount based in Gibraltar on lease to Gibair.

BEA Cargo

BEA Helicopters Ltd

British Air Services: responsible for the operations of subsidiaries Cambrian Airways and Northeast Airlines.

Travel Sales: responsible for BEA sales offices worldwide, plus inclusive-tour sales and BEA advertising.

BEA Airtours

Sovereign Group Hotels: responsible for all BEA's hotel interests worldwide, including minority interests in Excelsior Hotels at Manchester, Birmingham and Glasgow airports, the Phoenicia and Imperial hotels in Malta, and the Plaza Athenee, George V, and La Tremoile hotels in Paris.

Throughout its history, BEA took a financial interest in many overseas and UK regional airlines. In April 1946 an agreement was reached between the British and Irish governments, whereby all scheduled air services between the two countries would be operated by Aer Lingus. In return, BEA would take a 30 per cent shareholding in Aer Lingus, with BOAC holding 10 per cent and the Irish government the remaining 60 per cent. (BOAC's shareholding was later sold to BEA). Aer Lingus took over all UK-Ireland schedules services with effect from 1 July 1946. The Italian state airline Alitalia, which commenced operations on 7 May 1947, was originally founded in Italy on 16 September

1946, with BEA holding 40 per cent of the shares. On 21 March 1947 BEA also aquired a 15 per cent stake in the Greek airline TAE. By May 1947 the holding company BEA Associated Companies had interests that included a 41 per cent shareholding in Alitalia, a reduced 30 per cent share of Aer Lingus, a 44 per cent stake in Cyprus Airways, 51 per cent of Gibraltar Airways, 34 per cent of Malta Airways, and 15 per cent of TAE. This last shareholding was sold to Trans World Airlines of the USA during the financial year 1947/8.

On 5 October 1953 BEA took over the operation of the Gibraltar Airways service between Gibraltar and Tangier, using Dakota G-AGHP. This aircraft was replaced by a Viscount 701 from April 1959. A new agreement between BEA and Aer Lingus was signed on 1 September 1956, granting BEA traffic rights to Dublin from April 1957, in return for a reduction in BEA's shareholding in Aer Lingus to 10 per cent. BEA operations between London and Dublin commenced on 14 April 1957, and on the following day BEA Pionairs inaugurated Birmingham-Dublin services. BEA was to retain a diminishing financial interest in Aer Lingus until 1964, when the remaining 2.7 per cent shareholding was sold off.

On 7 February 1958 BEA aquired a one-third interest in the UK independent carrier Cambrian Airways. This led to the leasing to Cambrian of three BEA Pionairs, and their eventual sale to that airline in 1959. In 1964 BEA took a 30 per cent shareholding in another UK independent airline, BKS Air Transport. On 2 February 1967 British Air Services was set up as a holding company for Cambrian Airways and BKS. The whole of the share capital of both airlines was transferred to British Air Services, thus effectively making them subsidiaries of BEA and giving them access to financial support from the state airline. It also led to the upgrading of their fleets, with BEA Viscount 806s being transferred to both carriers.

By 1971 BEA still held a 23 per cent interest in Cyprus Airways, 49 per cent of Gibraltar Airways, and 34 per cent of Malta Airways.

CHAPTER FOURTEEN

BEA's Financial and Operating Performance

In its first financial year, up to March 1947, BEA employed 5731 people and made a loss of £2,157,937, about £30 for each passenger carried. However, the airline was expanding rapidly, and in July 1950 BEA earned more than £1 million in a single month for the first time in its history, the actual figure being £1,005,583. The 1951/2 Annual Report and Accounts revealed that for the first time more than one million passengers (1,135,579 to be precise) had been carried during a financial year. BEA's losses, however, had risen to £1,459,131. Much of this was attributed to an aircraft shortage during 1951, with its resultant loss of traffic and increased costs.

Despite the setbacks BEA continued to expand, and on 30 October 1952 it carried its five-millionth passenger. In August 1953 it carried a record 248,000 passengers in a single month, and on 31 March 1955 completed its first financial year of profitable operation. The operating profit was £552,314, and the nett profit £63,039. During the financial year 1955/6 an all-time record passenger load factor of 69.4 per cent was achieved. This was the first financial year in which more than two million passengers (2,224,747) were carried. A profit of £603,614 was recorded, with most of this due to the increased revenue generated by the Viscount fleet. In July 1956 BEA flew 100 million passenger-miles in a single month for the first time.

The Annual Report for 1959/60 showed it to be BEA's most successful financial year thus far, with a profit of £2,086,000 being recorded. On 25 June 1959 the airline carried its 20-millionth passenger. The fortieth anniversary of British scheduled international airline services was marked on 25 August 1959, and during the financial year BEA carried 3,289,606 passengers – 1,864,122 on international routes and 1,425,484 on domestic services.

On 27 September 1960 BEA transported its 25-millionth passenger, but the results for the financial year 1961/2 showed a loss of £1,488,065, BEA's first loss for seven years. This was attributed to several causes. Too many flights had been scheduled for the summer of 1961, and traffic had been lost to Air France's Caravelles on the London-Paris route and to the daily Pan-American Airways Boeing 707 services between London and Frankfurt. There were also the introductory costs of the Comet, Vanguard, Herald and Argosy fleets to be absorbed, which amounted to some £3 million.

During the year ending 30 June 1962, BEA's six busiest routes were: London-Glasgow (362,000 passengers), London-Paris (334,000), London-Belfast (267,000), London-Manchester (266,000), London-Jersey (210,000), and London-Edinburgh (201,000). All but one of these routes were UK internal services.

By the time of the publication of the 1969/70 Annual Report BEA's fortunes had been restored. During that financial year the airline had achieved ticket sales of £126 million, and made a profit of £6,532,000. This was its biggest profit to date, and nearly double that of the previous year. BEA was the world's seventh-largest airline, the other six all being based in the USA. In terms of passengers carried, it was the world's second largest international carrier.

During its last financial year, 1973/4, BEA carried 8.74 million passengers and produced its best ever financial result, a profit of £6,699,000. However this figure excluded the loss-making Scottish Airways Division and Channel Islands Division, which were by then part of the British Airways Regional Division.

CHAPTER FIFTEEN

BEA's Fleet Policy

BEA's original fleet plans envisaged the use of up to seventy Vikings on international routes, with internal services being maintained by a mixed fleet of Dakotas and Rapides. Future fleet procurement plans included seventy-five examples of the Vickers VC-2 (a thirty-two-seat, four-engined turboprop design that would evolve into the Viscount), and a number of Bristol 170s that would be operated in both passenger and freighter configurations. The Rapides were to be replaced by twenty-five Cunliffe Owen Concordias (a ten-seat, low-wing design with two piston engines). In the event, however, only two Concordias were to be built, and none were operated by BEA. The Viking order was reduced to forty aircraft, and the Airspeed Ambassador was ordered in preference to the Vickers VC-2.

On 31 March 1952 BEA's fleet comprised: forty-nine Vikings, six Elizabethans, thirty-eight Pionairs, eight Pionair-Leopards, two Dart-Dakotas, eighteen Rapides, one Bristol 170 and various small helicopters.

In 1956, with the Viscount in successful service, BEA Chairman Lord Douglas of Kirtleside stated publicly that the core of the fleet would continue to be British-built turboprops. Less than nine months later, however, he would have to concede that BEA would have to purchase jets in order to remain competitive. The September 1957 Three-Year Plan stated that the remaining Elizabethans were to be withdrawn during that year and replaced by Viscount 701s. The same type was to replace the remaining Pionairs by 1960, and the Viscount 701s were to be converted to sixty-eight-seaters, with built-in airstairs. Viscount 802s and 806s were to be purchased to take over from the srs 701s on front-line services, and Vickers Vanguards were to supplement the Viscounts on high-density routes. The DH 121 jet was to be the future flagship of the fleet, but until it was ready for service in 1963, a fleet of Comet 4Bs was to be delivered in 1959 as a stop-gap measure.

During the financial year 1966/7 the BEA fleet logged a total of 204,030 flying hours, a 10 per cent increase on the previous year. Some 7,323,970 passengers were carried, three million of them on domestic routes, and a 63 per cent load factor was achieved. The fleet recorded its highest annual aircraft utilisation figure to date, an average of 2144 hours per aircraft. By type, the highest utilisation was achieved by the Argosy fleet (2839 hours per aircraft), followed by the Vanguards (2420 hours), Comets (2295 hours), Viscounts (2147 hours) and Tridents (1903 hours).

On 27 January 1967 BEA ordered a fleet of BAC One-Eleven srs 500 jets. This brought the total of Weybridge-designed Vickers and BAC aircraft purchased by BEA to 161, comprising fifty-three Vikings, seventy Viscounts, twenty Vanguards and eighteen One-Elevens.

During 1970 the BEA subsidiary British Air Services researched the possibilities of opening up a network of UK commuter routes using small turboprop aircraft with good short-field performance. The Saunders ST27, de Havilland Canada Twin Otter and Short Skyliner were evaluated, and a route network based around four hubs was mapped out. The first hub was to be Cambridge, which was to be linked to Sheffield, Birmingham, London and Southampton. Birmingham was to have services to Southend, Heathrow, Southampton, Liverpool, Blackpool, Manchester, Newcastle, Leeds and Hull. From Bristol, routes would extend to Southampton, Bournemouth, Exeter, Plymouth, Cardiff, Swansea, Liverpool, Wolverhampton and the Surrey Docks in London. Finally, Sheffield would be linked to Newcastle, Tees-Side, Hull, the Surrey Docks, Birmingham, Wolverhampton, Bolton, Preston and Carlisle. Where airports did not already exist in places such as Preston and Bolton, purpose-built airstrips were to be constructed. Demonstration flights took place under the project name Interstol, and British Air Services even produced a projected timetable of services, but the economic climate was not ready for the launch of such an ambitious scheme and the plans were shelved.

In late 1973 BEA was hit by a fuel crisis brought about by the ongoing Arab-Israeli dispute. In retaliation for their support of Israel, the countries of the West had their supplies of Arab oil severely restricted, causing the price of fuel in some places to rise by almost 300 per cent. Before long there was not enough fuel available to meet all the demands, and the UK government ordered all the country's airlines to reduce their consumption by 40 per cent between 20 November and 31 December 1973. In order to comply, BEA had to cancel many flights, and re-route or combine many others. On domestic services, Tridents were replaced by the more fuel-economical Vanguards wherever possible. Fares were increased to cover rising fuel costs, and the charter subsidiary BEA Airtours levied a £3 fuel surcharge on each of its passengers. The situation soon became chaotic. Some BEA stations ran out of fuel completely, and BEA Operations Departments set up special units to monitor the availability of fuel supplies throughout the network and re-route flights via airports where fuel could be uplifted. By the beginning of 1974 the situation had eased somewhat, but fuel prices did not go down again, and neither did air fares.

At the end of March 1974 the BEA fleet was divided as follows:

Mainline Division – based at Heathrow with sixty-one Tridents and three Vanguards.
Super One-Eleven Division – based at Manchester with eighteen Super One-Elevens.
Channel Islands Division – based at Birmingham with twelve Viscount 802s and one One-Eleven srs 400.
Scottish Airways Division – based at Glasgow with seven Viscount 802s and two Short Skyliners.
Cargo Division – based at Heathrow with nine Merchantmen.

Of the subsidiary companies, British Air Services (Cambrian Airways and Northeast Airlines) had a fleet of nine One-Eleven srs 400s, fourteen Viscount 806s and four Trident 1Es. BEA Airtours had seven Gatwick-based Boeing 707-436s. BEA Helicopters operated a fleet of Sikorsky S-61Ns and smaller types from bases around the UK.

CHAPTER SIXTEEN

BEA Livery Changes

The original 1946 BEA livery was very simple. The aircraft were natural metal finish overall, with the airline name along the fuselage above the cabin windows. The BEA 'flying key' insignia was painted on the tail fins and below the cockpit windows.

In 1950 the colour scheme was modified to feature a white top to the fuselage and a red and white cheatline. The tail fin was now white, and bore the Union flag and the aircraft's registration letters. The nose was red, and the new BEA 'shield' insignia and the individual aircraft's name were carried beneath the cockpit windows.

A major livery change occurred in 1959. The white top to the fuselage was retained, but a black strip now ran the length of the fuselage at cabin window level and over the nose. Under the black strip the lower fuselage was initially still in natural metal finish, but was later painted light grey instead. The airline name disappeared from the fuselage, as did the 'shield' insignia and the aircraft's name. In their place was painted a small Union flag below the cockpit and BEA's new 'red square' logo (consisting of the letters 'BEA' in white on a red background) was transposed onto the front and rear ends of the black fuselage stripe. The logo also appeared in larger form on the white tail fin. The wing surfaces were painted red. The new 'Bealine' radio callsign for BEA flights was also introduced in 1959.

BEA's final aircraft livery was designed by Henrion Design Associates and was unveiled on 20 August 1968. The white fuselage top and light grey undersides were retained, but they were now separated by a peacock blue cheatline, with a stylised 'BEA' logo in new lettering in red on the top of the forward fuselage sides. The tail was also peacock blue, with a 'high-speed' half-Union Flag overlaid. The red wings were retained in an effort to keep costs down, but even so the cost of repainting the entire fleet was estimated at a minimum of £100,000. The first BEA fleet member to be seen in the new livery was actually a helicopter. Within days of the unveiling, Sikorsky S-61N G-AWFX was rolled out at Gatwick in the new colours after undergoing a major check there. The first fixed-wing aircraft to be repainted was Trident Two G-AVFI. To match the new aircraft livery, the cabin crews were issued with new uniforms designed by Hardy Amies. These featured a distinctive bright red topcoat for the stewardesses.

CHAPTER SEVENTEEN

Training BEA's Crews

BEA's crew training was initially carried out by BOAC, using Dakotas based at Aldermaston in Berkshire. On 1 May 1947 BOAC and BEA jointly formed Airways Training Ltd, again based at Aldermaston. However, this venture proved to be an economic disaster, losing £22,303 in its first year of operations, and it was closed down on 30 September 1948. BEA then established its own small training unit at Cranfield, comprising eight senior captains and four Avro 19 aircraft. The Avro 19s had originally been used for BEA scheduled services, but had proved unsuitable. Their narrow fuselages meant that the passenger seating had to be staggered, the mainspar passed through the passenger cabin (which was noisy and prone to vibration) and the toilet consisted of an Elsan chemical unit behind a curtain. In the training role, however, four examples continued to serve with BEA into the 1950s. BEA also acquired Avro Lancaster G-AJWM, which was used to train Lancastrian crews for Alitalia. Several Lancastrians were also purchased for the same purpose, but were passed on to Alitalia without being used by BEA. Cranfield was considered too remote from BEA's operating bases at Northolt and Glasgow, and the training base there was closed in October 1949. Crew training was then transferred to Northolt, where BEA's new Vikings were also available for training sorties. In later years, Blackbushe airport was also used for training, including Elizabethan circuit training.

Lancastrian G-AHCD was transferred to Alitalia in 1947. (The A.J. Jackson Collection)

Former Railway Air Services Avro 19 G-AHIC, used for crew training. (The A.J. Jackson Collection)

On 13th April 1951 BEA became the first British airline to place an order for flight simulators, ordering one for the Elizabethan fleet and one for the Viscounts. These relatively unsophisticated machines did not provide visual images, having their cockpit windows blanked out. They were initially based at Northolt, but in 1957 a new simulator building, housing one Elizabethan and two Viscount simulators, was opened at Heston. In November 1959 BEA's Comet 4B simulator entered service. This was the first BEA simulator to incorporate sound effects and movement in response to the flying controls, and was the first simulator to be approved for use before the real aircraft type entered service. BEA also used it to train Comet crews for Olympic Airways, and arranged training courses for many other airlines. During 1960 the training centre displayed at its entrance a board bearing the names of more than fifty airlines and other aircraft operators that had utilised BEA's training facilities. By 1961, simulators for the Viscount, Vanguard and Comet were in use, and one for the Trident was on order.

On 19 May 1961 HRH the Duke of Edinburgh opened the joint BEA/BOAC College of Air Training at Hamble. This had been set up to provide a source of new pilots to compensate for the diminishing supply of ex-service pilots previously available in large numbers to the state airlines. As a short-term measure, BEA sent an aircrew selection board to Canada and recruited thirty pilots from Trans-Canada Airlines and the Royal Canadian Air Force. The College operated a fleet of single-engined Chipmunks, and Beech Baron and Piper Apache twins. Its first graduates joined BEA in 1962 as second officers, then underwent type conversion training. During its first ten years, the College supplied 367 pilots to BEA and 252 to BOAC.

In 1962 BEA opened its new training centre at Heston. This comprised three main sections: classrooms and general training facilities; the simulator building; and Viking House, a residential hostel for the students. During that year around 200 to 300 students received training on any given day.

During the early 1960s, BEA found itself in need of a new base for type training on its various fleets, as Heathrow was too congested. Stansted was used for a while, but the unpredictable British weather restricted its use, so the airline looked around for an overseas training base where good flying weather was virtually guaranteed. Its first choice was Tripoli, but the high landing charges demanded by the airport authorities ruled it out, and Malta was selected instead. For the first time, BEA pilots were being trained overseas.

In April 1967 BEA Chairman Anthony Milward (a former Fleet Air Arm pilot) visited the College of Air Training, and piloted a Piper Cherokee on a twenty-minute sortie that included three landings. At that time, most cabin crew training was carried out at Heston, where a mock-up of a Trident passenger cabin was in use.

By 1970 the BEA Simulator Unit operated seven simulators, covering all the main types in service and the forthcoming Trident Three. This last one was a state of the art model, incorporating colour TV visual flight imagery. BEA was able to use it to train pilots for Category 3A all-weather automatic landings before the autoland system became operational on commercial services.

CHAPTER EIGHTEEN

BEA People

Many personalities (in the correct sense of the world) spent their entire careers with BEA and have many a tale to tell. Among these is Captain Noel Clark, who joined BEA from the RAF as a pilot in 1946 and did his Dakota training at Aldermaston. He was a first officer for about five years, and flew with many captains, some of whom had been inherited from companies such as Railway Air Services when BEA took over those

The entire crew of the first Royal flight by a BEA aircraft, to Malta in 1952. With Elizabethan G-AMAB outside the BEA engineering base at London Airport are (far left) Captain W. Baillie, then Captain Eric Poole. (via Mrs Angela Poole)

airlines. Among his Dakota schedules was a freighter service to Rome, which often returned to Northolt empty. It was thus diverted via other points on the way back if a load became available. On one occasion he brought back from Rome a coffin containing the body of a man who had died in Italy. *En route*, the flight was diverted to Montpelier to pick up a consignment of 3000 kg of live eels. During the flight to Northolt many of the eels escaped from their boxes and on arrival they were found wriggling all over the poor man's coffin. Not all of them made it to their final destination, as the radio officer took some home to his wife for his tea...

Later, after he had been promoted, Captain Clark was rostered to fly with HRH Prince Alexander of Yugoslavia, who was a BEA first officer at the time. They had operated an overnight freighter service from Rome to Athens, and were travelling to their hotel in the crew transport, when 'Alex' asked the driver to drop him off at the Royal Palace, as he wanted to stay the night with his 'Auntie Olga'. Captain Clark also transported many VIPs on Dakota passenger services, including Chancellor Willy Brandt of West Germany, and the famous conductor Sir Thomas Beecham.

Two BEA Stewardesses of the mid-1960s (on the left Nancy Elliott, nee Coulthwaite) pose with a cauldron made of Swiss chocolate at Zurich Airport, possibly on the occasion of the inaugural Trident service to Zurich. (via Michael Elliott)

BEA staff at Stornoway, as seen in local BEA newpaper advertisment of the 1960s. From left to right; Sandy Murray (Senior Traffic Officer), Second Officer Bob Hayward, Alex J Macrae (Traffic Assistant), Captain George Ebner and Robin Mackenzie (Station Superintendent). (via Robin Mackenzie)

From Dakotas he went on to fly Viscounts for five years, and then Vanguards. Among the visitors to his Vanguard cockpits were the Rolling Stones, and, later, HRH the Prince of Wales, who asked to sit on the flight deck for the landing of his flight from Glasgow to Heathrow. The approach to runway 10L took them over Windsor Castle, and HRH the Prince of Wales remarked that his mother often complained about aircraft noise.

Captain Clark's final type was the Trident, which he remembers as a wonderful aircraft to fly, and very fast. On many occasions they took off from Heathrow for Rome after the competing Pan American Boeing 707 flight, and landed there before it. He was 82 at the time of writing, and had been retired for twenty-eight years, having spent thirty years working for BEA and later British Airways.

BEA's first radio officer to attain a captaincy was Dennis Brewer. Having joined BEA from the armed forces in June 1947, he gained his Commercial Pilots' Licence and Instrument Rating on his own initiative in 1953. In June 1954 he joined BEA's pilot conversion programme, and was appointed a second officer in October 1954. Promotions to first officer and senior first officer came in 1956 and 1960 respectively, and he became a captain on 17 May 1965. During his career he flew on Pionairs, Elizabethans, Viscount 800s, Comet 4Bs and Tridents.

Robin Mackenzie was station superintendent at Stornoway in the 1960s, being at that time the youngest such officer on the Highlands and Islands network. He recalls many amusing moments, including the day when the stewardess came off the inbound Viscount to tell him she had a problem with an inebriated passenger who she could not waken. Between the two of them they managed to get him to wake up, only to be told, 'I am not getting off this aircraft until it lands at Stornoway'. They persuaded him to leave the Viscount and enter the terminal building, where the sight of his waiting wife sobered him up very quickly indeed!

During the 1950s the Heron flights were operated by pilots who were local legends, such as Captain Paddy Calderwood, Captain Eric Starling, and Captain David Barclay. Robin recalls that Captain Barclay used to enlist the help of his co-pilot to pick the mushrooms that grew in profusion on Stornoway aerodrome in those days, and also insisted that he joined him on a swim from the beautiful beach at the end of the runway. Part of the station superintendent's duties was to 'meet and greet' visiting VIPs. These included many government ministers, including one who, on arriving at Stornoway, remarked that it was nice to be on Skye!

Graham Stephenson joined BEA in September 1958 as a general apprentice (Course 2). He worked at Heathrow, Dorland Hall, the West London Air Terminal, and Glasgow (Renfrew) Airport, before also being posted to Stornoway. In 1963 he became one of the very first BEA aircraft despatchers. At that time the team, which was set up and trained by John Buckel, comprised about twenty staff, and was the first in any UK airline. He left BEA in 1966 to join BOAC.

Les Young commenced his employment with BEA in 1957 as a flight clerk on Pionair aircraft. He then transferred to the Traffic Department around 1960, remaining there for twenty years. On being transferred from Renfrew Airport to the St Enoch Square town terminal he met Andrena Marshall, a telephone operator at the reservations office at 40 Buchanan Street, Glasgow, and they subsequently married. Mr Young's father, Thomas, also worked for BEA, as an electrician at Renfrew Airport.

Eric A. Thomas joined BEA as a reservations clerk at Dorland Hall in 1949, and the same year undertook his first ever flight, a familiarisation flight to Paris in a Vickers Viking. During his time at Dorland Hall he noticed an oil painting of a BEA Viking hanging on the wall of the boardroom. The reservations department later moved to Wigmore Street, and it was there that he saw the painting again, this time in a dustbin, along with other victims of a general 'clear-out' of unwanted items during the move. He rescued it and took it to his office. Some years later he had it properly cleaned and restored, and it was rehung in his study at home. Mr Thomas went on to become BEA sales promotion manager.

Captain Eric Poole, a former Battle of Britain pilot, left the RAF and joined the Associated Airways Joint Committee (soon to become BEA) as a pilot in 1945. He was based at Liverpool (Speke), and initially flew Rapides on the Scottish routes. He then progressed onto the Croydon-Liverpool-Belfast route, flying Ju 52/3Ms for a short while before converting onto Vickers Vikings. In 1952 Captain Poole joined the Elizabethan fleet, and on promotion in 1957 he became BEA's youngest flight manager. After conversion to Viscount and then Comet aircraft, he transferred to the Trident fleet during 1961, being appointed flight development manager. In collaboration with Smiths Industries, Hawker Siddeley and his BEA colleagues, Captain Poole was responsible for the development and introduction into service of the Autoland system on BEA aircraft. In this role he commanded the world's first automatic landing on a scheduled passenger

Leslie Jones in BEA uniform in September 1948, in front of the original terminal building and No. 1 hangar at Manchester. (Leslie Jones)

service, on 10 June 1965. In 1976 he was awarded the Queen's Commendation for Valuable Service in the Air. He ended his flying career with BEA and British Airways with an Autoland landing at Heathrow, retiring as British Airways' chief technical services pilot, one of the world's foremost experts on civil all-weather operations, and the most senior pilot in all the British Airways Divisions. Captain Poole died in 2002 at the age of 85.

Captain Eric L R Poole in 1970. (via Mrs Angela Poole)

Leslie Jones entered the airline industry as an Air Traffic Clerk with the Associated Airways Committee at Liverpool Airport in 1944. His duties included passenger check-in and boarding, ticketing, the preparation of aircraft trim-sheets, recording aircraft movements, and assisting with the loading and unloading of baggage, cargo and mail. He was transferred to BEA in 1947 when the airline took over the AAJC services. During 1947 he applied for a relief posting to the civil Berlin Airlift, which was being managed by BEA. Whilst waiting, he was asked to go to BEA at Manchester (Ringway) Airport to help out for three weeks, and ended up staying for 18 years! When he first arrived at Ringway the BEA presence in the terminal building consisted of one check-in desk and two receptionists. During 1949 he was asked by the Airport Director at Ringway to provide a running commentary on the aircraft movements for the visitors to the airport's spectators enclosure. He was instrumental in the formation on 30 June 1953 of the Ringway Aero Club, set up to provide low-cost flying training for BEA personnel at Manchester. Leslie Jones retired from BEA in 1965 as Station Cashier at Manchester.

CHAPTER NINETEEN

The British Airways Amalgamation

A merger of the two state airline corporations BOAC and BEA was the subject of discussions and rumours from 1959 onwards, but successive BEA (and BOAC) chairmen always declared themselves opposed to the idea. In the 'Chairman's Page' of the December 1962 edition of *BEA Magazine*, Lord Douglas of Kirtleside wrote:

> Much has been made during the past fourteen years of the possible economies which might accrue from combining certain functions of the two Corporations. When one comes to work out actual figures, there are in fact few savings to be made, and they would certainly not add up to the amounts which have been mentioned. The suggestion that two million pounds a year might be saved is absurd. Against any possible savings in expenditure must be set, among other things, the large amounts of money which BEA earns abroad through our interline connections. We are currently earning about fifteen million pounds a year overseas, including more than seven million dollars a year in the United States and Canada. This important contribution to the United Kingdom's dollar earnings, which comes largely from our interline agreements with the major American carriers, would be placed in jeopardy if BEA and BOAC were merged. BEA gets this business because we are the only major European airline not in competition with the American long-haul carriers. The US airlines would obviously not put such business in the way of a direct competitor, which is what a merged Corporation would become.

He went on to say:-

> BEA has had stability for fourteen years – hence its success. This desire to dig up the plant of British air transport and examine its roots, which has been going on continuously since air transport first started, must be resisted. It can only lead to frustration and confusion and in the end can do nothing but harm to the British airline industry.

On 5 May 1969 the Report of the Committee of Enquiry into Civil Air Transport (the so-called 'Edwards Report') recommended the setting up of a National Air Holdings Board to supervise the activities of BEA, BOAC and British Air Services. Two months after becoming BEA chairman on 1 January 1971 Sir Henry Marking said, whilst speaking of proposals to merge BEA and BOAC: 'There will always be misguided people in the world who, from time to time, try to raise this old thing. It comes up every so many years, but one has learned to discount it.' On 5 August 1971, however, such a board was established, and named the British Airways Board. It immediately set about the task of trying to co-ordinate the activities of the two airlines to avoid waste and duplication. Whilst doing so, it was encouraged by the government of the day to consider the best way in which a merger might be achieved.

In 1972 the British Airways Board proposed the setting up of seven operating divisions under its overall management. These divisions comprised:

BEA Division (subdivided into Mainline, Super One-Eleven, Cargo, and Airtours divisions)

BOAC Division

British Air Services Division (including Cambrian Airways, Northeast Airlines, Scottish Airways Division, and Channel Island Airways Division)

British Airways Helicopters

British Airways Engineering

British Airways Associate Companies (to include all BEA and BOAC associate companies)

International Aeradio

These Divisions became functional on 1 September 1972.

In November 1972 the single trading name of British Airways was proposed. This was adopted from 1 September 1973, with BEA then becoming the British European Airways Division of British Airways. A target date of 1 April 1974 was set for the full implementation of the amalgamation, and a new colour scheme for the merged airline was devised. BEA aircraft were to wear British Airways titling above the cheatline on the forward portion of the fuselage, but the BEA tail logo was retained for the time being. The first BEA aircraft to carry the revised markings was Trident Three G-AWZC, in December 1973.

At midnight on 31 March 1974 BEA and BOAC formally ceased to exist, under the terms of the Air Corporations (Dissolution) Order 1973. No official record exists of the last-ever BEA service, but it is believed to have been the Trident-operated flight BE943 from Dublin to Heathrow, which landed at 2330 hrs on 31 March 1974.

CHAPTER TWENTY

BEA's UK Bases

Cranfield

Early in 1948 the BEA Gust Research Unit was established at Cranfield airfield, in collaboration with the Meteorological Office and other government departments. Two RAF de Havilland Mosquito PR34A aircraft were civilian-registered as G-AJZE and G-AJZF and allocated to the Unit. Specially fitted with weather radar and three accelerometers each, they flew all over Europe at altitudes in excess of 20,000 ft, investigating Clear Air Turbulence in preparation for the introduction of the Vickers Viscount turboprop fleet. The first such sortie was a flight from Cranfield to Lisbon on 22 April 1948, and over the next eighteen months or so a total of seventy-seven flights were

Mosquito PR34A G-AJZE of the BEA Gust Research Unit. (The A.J. Jackson Collection)

made and 247 flying hours accumulated. The last flight took place in November 1949, after which the government halted funding. The Unit was closed in January 1950 and, after overhaul by Marshalls of Cambridge, the Mosquitoes were returned to the RAF.

Gatwick

At the beginning of 1949 the Ministry of Civil Aviation was preparing to de-requisition Gatwick Airport. On 18 March BEA wrote to the Controller of Ground Services at the Ministry, requesting that Gatwick be designated as its primary diversion airport for London, instead of Stansted. BEA was also concerned that the planned transfer of all its services from Northolt to London Airport in the mid-1950s would cause congestion there. The airline was interested in using Gatwick for some of its scheduled routes that flew southwards from London. The airport's rail link with central London was also considered an advantage, but in the event Gatwick was mainly only used on a sustained basis by BEA for services to the Channel Islands.

Liverpool

In February 1947 BEA took over the Associated Airways Joint Committee engineering base at Speke Airport, Liverpool. This then became the main base of BEA's English Division, responsible for maintenance of the Rapide, Avro 19 and Dakota fleets. Services at that time included a Croydon-Liverpool-Belfast route using Junkers Ju 52/3Ms, and other services to the Isle of Man and Belfast. By the end of 1947 the Avro 19s and the Ju 52/3Ms had been withdrawn, and the Rapide fleet reduced in order to standardise on Dakota operations wherever possible. During the winter of 1947/8 a once-daily Liverpool-Manchester-Northolt service was operated by Dakotas, but this was withdrawn

Dakota G-AGJZ, seen from the spectators terrace at Liverpool. (Air-Britain)

Ju 52/3M G-AHOF was used for Croydon–Liverpool–Belfast services. (The A.J. Jackson Collection)

with the introduction of the summer 1948 schedules. These included five daily Dakotas round trips to the Isle of Man, and two weekday services to Belfast (reducing to one round trip on Saturdays and Sundays).

The 1948 review of BEA operations resulted in the amalgamation of the English and Scottish Divisions to form the British Division, based at Glasgow, and the closure of the Liverpool engineering base from January 1949. On 11 April 1949 a weekday service between Liverpool and Cardiff with optional stops at Hawarden (near Chester) and Valley in Anglesey was inaugurated with Rapide aircraft, the service being suspended for the winter months. From 1 June 1950 the route to Cardiff became a helicopter service with Sikorsky S-51 equipment. An optional call at Wrexham was included, but ceased in 1951 when Cambrian Airways took over the Liverpool-Cardiff route under a BEA Associate Agreement and reverted to Rapide fixed-wing aircraft. During the summer of 1951 BEA operated a Sunday service to Jersey with 'Pionair' class Dakotas.

The summer of 1953 saw BEA operating three daily round trips to the Isle of Man with Pionairs, with Belfast being served by four services each weekday and one round trip on Saturdays and Sundays. Some of the Belfast services also called at the Isle of Man *en route*. To operate these services, BEA had two Pionairs stationed at Liverpool and maintained at the Airwork engineering base there. Vickers Vikings also appeared on a few Isle of Man-Liverpool-Isle of Man flights, utilising the stopover time of the aircraft used for direct London-Isle of Man services.

On 26 May 1953 BEA's Dart-Dakota G-AMDB became the first turboprop aircraft to visit Liverpool, and on 25 March 1955 the first Viscount landed there, namely BEA's srs 701 G-AMOC. This was probably a weather diversion. Scheduled turboprop services

Speke airport is the aerial crossroads to the Isle of Man, Northern Ireland, Scotland and Eire. Here, you see a group of pilots and flying officers, some of the men who maintain the network of flying schedules now covering the British Isles, photographed as they met at the airport yesterday. They are left to right): Captain D. S. Yapp, Radio Officer G. T. Ross, Captain G. T. Greenhalgh, Senior Traffic Officer W. T. Ainscough, Captain E. Poole, and Mr. H. P. Snelling, Traffic Superintendent. Inset is Captain J. P. Higgins, the veteran pilot and pioneer of the Isle of Man Airways.

Newspaper cutting from 1945/6, showing a group of pilots at Speke Airport, Liverpool. (via Mrs Angela Poole)

Rapide G-AGUG and a Ju 52/3m at Liverpool in January 1947. (via Mrs Angela Poole)

commenced on 1 April 1960, when Viscounts replaced Pionairs on the routes from Liverpool to the Isle of Man and Belfast, and Viscount 800s passed through on a Birmingham-Liverpool-Belfast day return service.

On 1 April 1963 Cambrian Airways took over the BEA Irish Sea routes out of Liverpool, using former BEA Viscount 701s. BEA aircraft continued to appear at Liverpool on an irregular basis, however, as the airport was the airline's designated weather diversion for Manchester flights.

Blackbushe

As well as being used in the 1950s for crew training, Blackbushe Airport was also the venue for demonstrations of the FIDO fog dispersal system, using BEA and BOAC aircraft. During November and early December 1952, fog at London's airports wreaked havoc with the BEA schedules. A total of 2029 flights were cancelled, and countless others were diverted to Birmingham, Manchester and Bournemouth. BEA had long been campaigning for the introduction at London Airport of the FIDO system, which had been pioneered during World War Two. This system used perforated pipes, laid alongside the runway edges. Petrol was pumped into the pipes and ignited, and the resultant heat caused the fog to lift temporarily. On 11 November 1952 demonstration flights were laid on at Blackbushe, using BEA Elizabethan G-ALZY and Viking G-AHPM, as well as BOAC Avro York G-AGJC. Members of the press were carried on these demonstrations, the first time that the public had been allowed on board during FIDO landings.

Manchester

Writing in the May 1967 edition of *BEA Magazine*, Stanley Thirlwall recalled that in May 1947 the BEA base at Ringway Airport, Manchester, handled ten services each day, four to Belfast, four to the Isle of Man and two to Croydon. These were mostly operated by Rapide aircraft. Passenger handling was carried out in the pre-war building, which contained BEA and KLM check-in desks, a restaurant, the control tower and administration offices. The cargo section was housed in a wooden hut nearby. By late 1947 Avro 19s and Ju 52/3Ms were also to be seen operating BEA services.

During 1948 BEA flew 22,346 passengers and 710 tons of freight out of Manchester. On 19 August 1949 Dakota G-AHCY (under the command of Captain Frank Pinketon) departed Nutts Corner airport in Belfast on the 1150 hrs scheduled passenger service to Manchester. The visibility at Ringway was good at the time, but there was cloud over the hills on the approach. The Dakota collided with Wimberry Rocks at Dovestones near Oldham at a height of aproximately 1700 ft. Out of the twenty-nine passengers and three crew members aboard there were twenty-four fatalities, and the remaining eight occupants were all injured.

In February 1952 the BEA Manchester town terminal was located at Airways Terminal, in St Peter's Square. For the summer 1953 timetable BEA Pionairs flew direct from Manchester to Paris (Le Bourget) on Tuesdays, Thursdays and Saturdays. On the other four days the service was operated via Birmingham. 'Admiral' class Vikings flew the Manchester-Amsterdam-Düsseldorf service on three days of the week, and also operated Manchester-Zurich services. On the domestic scene, Pionairs were responsible for twice-daily Manchester-Belfast services, supplemented by additional Viking flights over the same route in the mornings and evenings.

BEA engineers installing a new engine on Dakota G-AGZB in hangar 6 at Manchester on 10 August 1951. (Leslie Jones)

By 1955 BEA's town terminal had relocated to the Air Terminus at Royal Exchange in Manchester. Viscount turboprops were in widespread service by the commencement of the summer 1956 schedules, and operated to Amsterdam on three days each week in the peak season. They also maintained weekday Glasgow-Manchester-Paris services, and operated on the Manchester-Birmingham-Düsseldorf route twice-weekly, with an additional direct Manchester-Düsseldorf flight on Saturdays. They were also utilised on twice-weekly Night Tourist services to Zurich and Milan during the peak season. In May 1957, twice-weekly Viscount flights to Palma were operated, and the type was also to be seen on Manchester-Dublin services on Tuesdays, Wednesdays and Thursdays. In 1962 new terminal facilities were opened at Manchester Airport. The first BEA passenger to check in was Mr John Davies, on a flight to Glasgow. To mark the occasion he was presented with a free ticket for his next trip to Glasgow by BEA Station Manager Gerry Payne.

Until 1 November 1966, Viscount Check 1s were carried out by the BEA engineering staff at Manchester, but from that date they commenced the same checks on Trident aircraft instead.

Birmingham

In 1952 BEA's Birmingham town terminal was situated at New Street Station, but by the summer of 1953 it had moved to the Air Terminal at the Civic Centre, off Broad Street. The airline's Pionairs operated a daily round trip to Belfast, reducing to weekdays only from 1 September. On four days of each week the same type flew the Birmingham-Paris service, and on Fridays, Saturdays and Sundays they operated services to Guernsey and Jersey. There was also a weekday Pionair service to Northolt, departing in the morning and returning in the evening. From April 1954 the service to London was operated on a daily basis (operated by Viscount turboprops to the new London Airport) and supplemented on weekdays by an afternoon Pionair round trip to Northolt.

For the summer of 1956, weekday Viscount services operated Glasgow-Birmingham-Paris (Le Bourget) and return. On Mondays and Wednesdays the same type flew Manchester-Birmingham-Düsseldorf and back.

In May 1957 the Pionairs were still operating to Belfast, twice each weekday and once on Saturdays and Sundays. They also flew to Dublin on three days each week. Viscounts operated the daily round trip to London Airport.

In 1966 BEA's staff at Birmingham totalled 116, compared with just nine in 1949. During the summer of 1966 120 services, to ten destinations, were scheduled at Birmingham Airport each week.

BEA Sales and Reservations Offices

Throughout its history, BEA maintained a network of town terminals and sales offices thoughout the UK and overseas. In 1950 it had a New York sales office, manned by just two staff. Clive Adams was the BEA Representative, North America, and he was assisted by June Scheller, his secretary. She had previously been based at Keyline House, Ruislip, and Airways Terminal, Victoria, London, during the early days of BEA. As well as taking reservations from US travel agents, the sales office in New York also handled interline bookings from other airlines. During June 1950, 2500 passengers were booked onwards from London to continental Europe by transatlantic carriers such as Trans World Airlines, Pan American Airways, Trans-Canada Airlines and of course BOAC.

In September 1954 the list of BEA UK town offices included:

4 Donegall Square East, Belfast
133 George Street, Edinburgh
122 Vincent Street, Glasgow
The Railway Station, Inverness
The Joint Station, Aberdeen
3 Bold Street, Liverpool
Whitchurch Airport, Bristol
20 Castle Arcade, Cardiff

By the financial year 1971/2, BEA's Travel Sales Division had twenty-two UK sales offices open to the public, plus sales offices in most of the airline's European destination cities. A 24-hour telephone reservations service was also in operation.

BEA in London

BEA's first head office was set up in Bourne Junior School, on the eastern side of Northolt Airport, under the approach to runway 26. The school had opened in September 1939, but with the onset of hostilities its location near the approaches to the airfield was judged to be too dangerous and its pupils were evacuated. BEA moved in during 1946 and soon renamed it Keyline House, after the airline's 'flying key' logo. It was further renamed Bealine House in 1959, and remained as BEA's administrative headquarters until the amalgamation into British Airways. In its early days BEA also maintained a supplies depot at White Waltham in Berkshire, which was later transferred to Wembley.

The first BEA booking office in central London was a collection of six rooms within BOAC's Berkeley Square premises. BOAC also allowed BEA to use its Victoria Air Terminal for check-in and coach transport to Northolt. The use of these facilities continued until 1948, when BEA's own premises became ready. In May 1948 the BEA reservations department moved to Dorland Hall in Lower Regent Street, and on the 31st of that month the airline opened its first London town terminal, the Kensington Air Station. Eric Thomas (who eventually retired as Sales Promotions Officer at the West London Air Terminal) was a booking clerk at Dorland Hall in 1950, and recalls the times when he was the sole clerk on duty on the overnight shift. The rats from the restaurant kitchen next door would come in and scour the wastepaper baskets for the remains of sandwiches and other edibles.

On 3 March 1953 BEA installed a mechanical reservations system called 'Flightmaster', which was capable of displaying seat availability on 32,000 flights at a time. On 19 May the Kensington Air Station was replaced by the Waterloo Air Station at 18 York Road, London SE1. This could handle 2000 passengers and twenty coach departures each hour, and came into regular service on 21 May. When it opened the coach journey time to London Airport was reduced by fifteen minutes. The building itself had

Map showing the location of BEA's new Waterloo Air Terminal, July 1953. (via Author)

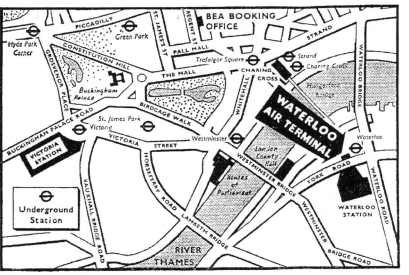

WATERLOO AIR TERMINAL
LONDON

B.E.A.'s new London terminal is situated at 18, York Road, S.E.I. (facing Waterloo railway station)   Telephone :- WATerloo 8030.

Buses 46 and 76 pass the door. Escalators direct to terminal from Waterloo Underground Station.

A BEA Bedford VAL coach, used in 1970 for transferring diverted passengers and for transporting aircrew to their overnight hotels. (David Bowler)

originally been erected for the Festival of Britain celebrations and was regarded as only a temporary location, as the land on which it stood was earmarked for the eventual National Theatre. During 1953 BEA obtained a plot of land on Cromwell Road in Kensington as the site for its future new London town terminal once the Waterloo premises had to be vacated.

Construction work on the new terminal in Cromwell Road commenced in 1956, and on 6 October 1957 the Waterloo Air Station was closed and replaced by the West London Air Terminal, as the new premises were named. The initial structure was a temporary one, for check-in and airport coach services only, and it was superseded by the first phase of the permanent buildings in July 1960. The new air terminal was well placed for public transport links, being close to Gloucester Road underground station. For the time being, the reservations department remained at Dorland Hall until the new computerised reservations system, ordered in 1961 and called Beacon (short for BEA Computer Network), became operational at the West London Air Terminal. In the interim BEA introduced its 'Sell and Report' booking system. This dispensed with the need (except in the peak season) for travel travel agents to telephone BEA for every individual booking. Instead, they could report seat sales in batches at specified intervals.

On 6 November 1963 HRH the Duke of Edinburgh officially opened the permanent West London Air Terminal buildings. The £5 million multi-storey complex was constructed over the London Transport Underground rail junction at Gloucester Road. On

Terminal One – standing for Number One service

The brand new Terminal 1 at London Airport is the centre of BEA's Inter-Britain network and from early summer it will also be used for our International flights. Here you can change planes for destinations all over the country, quickly and conveniently in complete comfort. With everything necessary for a smooth transit laid on under one roof. Terminal One is the most modern, most advanced passenger terminal in Europe. It's symbolic of the Number One service that's standard with BEA, Europe's Number One airline.

BEA

No.1 in Europe

1969 Advertisment for the new Terminal One at Heathrow. (via Author)

the ground floor were check-in desks and lounge facilities for BEA and the twenty-four other airlines it represented. The administration offices were on the second floor, and on floors three to eight were offices for almost 2000 staff who were relocated from Dorland Hall and Terminal House in Victoria. The third floor was also earmarked for the two Univac computers for the Beacon reservations system. The new terminal boasted a 17,000 sq ft main passenger concourse, with shops, a bookstall and a creche. The coach stands were served from sixteen numbered departure gates. On the mezzanine floor were the advance reservations unit, bank, left luggage office, bar, buffet, restaurant and late check-in facilities. The terminal was served by its own telephone exchange, capable of handling 10,000 calls each day. A major setback occurred during the night of 6/7 December 1963, when a serious fire at the complex caused extensive damage to the upper floors. By the evening of 9 December, however, some facilities for passengers had been restored in the arrivals hall and the baggage areas.

At 1500 hrs on 17 April 1965, the Beacon computerised reservations system became operational. The reservations staff at Dorland Hall were then transferred to the West London Air Terminal, occupying 216 telephone sales positions there. Beacon was only the fourth system of its kind in the world, the other three being located in the USA. It processed all BEA's flight reservations with the exception of those for the German internal services and some UK domestic flights. It could also be used for room reservations at BEA associated hotels throughout the world. By 1971 it was linked to 350 desks in the central booking hall at the West London Air Terminal and to 250 other BEA locations.

On 1 August 1965 BEA introduced its new Executive Express coach service. This operated directly from West London Air Terminal to the boarding steps of BEA aircraft on peak hour services from Heathrow to Aberdeen, Belfast, Edinburgh and Glasgow, and vice versa. It was restricted to passengers with hand-baggage only, and the bypassing of the airport lounges and baggage areas resulted in significant end-to-end time savings. This was at a price, as the Executive Express fare of ten shillings was double that of BEA's ordinary airport coach service. The service was eventually discontinued on 31 March 1973.

During 1967 Timesaver Tickets were introduced for BEA's credit account business customers. These tickets, which could only be used for UK domestic routes, were issued in books to the clients, who made a telephone booking with a BEA reservations agent and obtained a booking reference number before writing out their own ticket.

On 7 May 1969 Terminal One at London (Heathrow) Airport was opened for the exclusive use of BEA. The first inbound service was a flight from Palma, which arrived at 0635 hrs. The new terminal was initially used by BEA international flights only, but by the end of 1969 it was also handling domestic services and the flights of BKS Air Transport, Cambrian Airways, Aer Lingus and Cyprus Airways, all of whom used BEA as their handling agent. The building was fitted with gate piers with extending gateways, but for technical reasons these could not be used by Viscount aircraft. Britain's first Power Operated Gangway had in fact been introduced on an experimental basis by BEA at Heathrow as far back as November 1965, being used on Trident services to Paris.

On 1 April 1973 BEA ceased providing specific airport coach services for each flight, and instead operated coaches between Heathrow and central London at ten-minute intervals between 0620 hrs and 2200 hrs each day. Check-in facilities at the West London Air Terminal were withdrawn on 1 January 1974, after a steady decline in their use over the years.

BEA Coaches

BEA relied on BOAC to provide transport for its passengers between central London and Northolt until 16 July 1947, when it assumed control of its own coach services. Rather than take on the responsibility of operating its own coaches the airline awarded a contract to the London Passenger Transport Board, with the contract passing to the London Transport Executive from 1 January 1948. The initial equipment was a fleet of Commer Commando coaches acquired from BOAC. These seated eighteen passengers, with the rear portion of the seating being raised above a large luggage compartment.

In 1951 BEA ordered forty (later increased to sixty-five) AEC Regal IV chassis coaches, with special bodies designed to meet the airline's requirements. These were also one-and-a-half deckers, carrying thirty-seven passengers. The front portion of the body contained seating on two decks and the seats in the rear half were again raised above an enlarged baggage hold. The coaches were finished in blue-grey and dove-grey livery, with a cream-coloured band in between. The BEA shield logo was painted on each side of the coaches and also embossed above the radiator filter. Destination blinds at the front of the

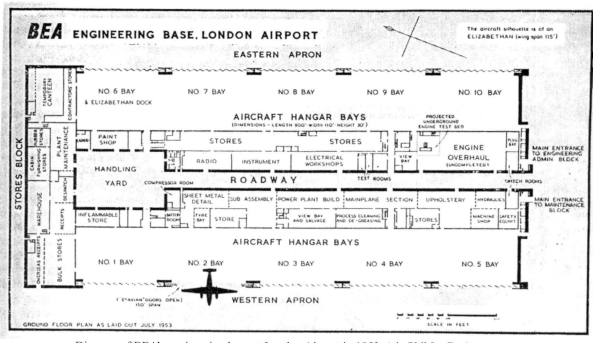

Diagram of BEA's engineering base at London Airport in 1953. (via Phil Lo Bao)

1969 view of Terminal 1 at Heathrow, also showing part of the roof terraces on the Queens Building. BEA Tridents, Vanguards and Viscounts and a Comet 4B are among the parked aircraft. (via Mrs Angela Poole)

coach displayed the flight destination and the airline operator concerned. The first few examples were delivered during the summer of 1952.

Although BEA ceased flight operations from Northolt in 1954, the airline's motor transport section remained based there for a further two years or so before relocating to London Airport. BEA adopted a new 'red-square' livery in 1959, and the coach fleet was gradually repainted in the revised colour scheme.

During 1963 an order was placed for a fleet of fifty-seven-seater Routemaster double-decker buses, although it was to be the latter half of 1966 before the first examples were delivered. The Routemasters did not have built-in luggage holds. Instead, they towed baggage trailers, which could be taken out onto the tarmac at Heathrow for their contents to be loaded directly onto the waiting aircraft. A supply of spare trailers was stationed at both Heathrow and the West London Air Terminal to speed turnrounds. From 1969 onwards, the Routemasters and the single-decker Executive Express coaches were repainted in the final BEA livery.

The Heathrow Engineering Base

In July 1950 work started on the initial phase of a £2 million pre-stressed concrete engineering complex for BEA. It was to consist of five bays, was to be 1000 ft long when completed, and was to be the home of the future Elizabethan and Viscount fleets. The first two bays were scheduled for completion in August 1951, but it was quickly decided that an additional five bays were going to be needed. As a temporary measure, aluminium hangars were erected in preparation for the arrival of the Elizabethans. On 17 March 1952 BEA's first Elizabethan was moved into the first completed bay, named the Elizabethan Dock, and this signalled the start of the transfer of all BEA's facilities from Northolt. The move was officially completed by 17 April 1952, although some electrical and instrument workshops remained at Northolt for the time being. Five bays were in use by the end of 1952, and the remaining five became operational during 1953. The total floor area of the new base was 458,405 sq ft. It was used for Viscount and Elizabethan maintenance only, with major work on the Pionair and Viking fleets being carried out at Glasgow. The lack of canteen facilities and the poor public transport links initially caused staff discontent at the new engineering complex.

In late 1956 BEA announced plans for a new extension to the base that would almost double the total floor area to 958,000 sq ft. At that time the engineering complex was operating to full capacity, as Pionair maintenance work had been transferred from Glasgow during July and August 1956. Also, major overhauls were being conducted on all the current BEA aircraft types, apart from the Rapides and Herons. Construction work on the extension began in October 1956, with completion scheduled for 1960, in time to accommodate the forthcoming Vanguard fleet.

In 1958 the base featured unique permanent maintenance docks, each consisting of a series of platforms and decks providing easy access to all parts of the airframe. Each dock was self-contained, with its own electrical supply, compressed air and lubrication points. The engineering base was a popular venue for guided visits from schools and groups of aviation enthusiasts, with 5250 people being shown around during the financial year 1958/9.

By the mid-1960s the complex comprised two large maintenance buildings containing twenty hangar bays, the largest of which measured 180 ft by 110 ft. There were two engine testbeds, and the engineering staff numbered over 4000. The base was to continue to expand and develop until its amalgamation into British Airways in the 1970s.

APPENDICES

Appendix 1: BEA Chairmen

1 August 1946 to 1947 Sir Harold Hartley
1947 to February 1949 Gerard d'Erlanger
March 1949 to 31 March 1964 Lord Douglas of Kirtleside
1 April 1964 to 31 December 1970 Anthony Milward
1 January 1971 to September 1972 Henry Marking
September 1972 to November 1972 Ken Wilkinson
November 1972 to January 1974 P.C.F. Lawton
January 1974 to 31 March 1974 Roy Watts

Appendix 2: Selection of BEA Scheduled Services in 1952

Selection of BEA scheduled services for period February/March 1952, taken from *Bradshaws International Air Guide*

Northolt–Glasgow (Renfrew). Four Pionair round trips each weekday.

Northolt–Edinburgh. Daily Pionair round trip.

Northolt–Belfast. Three daily Viking round trips.

Northolt–Isle of Man-Belfast. Daily Dakota round trip.

Northolt–Paris (Le Bourget). Eight daily Viking round trips.

London Airport–Paris (Le Bourget). Two daily Viking round trips.

Northolt–Brussels. Three daily Viking round trips.

Northolt–Amsterdam. Two daily Viking round trips.

Northolt–Istanbul. Viking service BE760 departed at 0944 hrs on Tuesdays, Thursdays, Saturdays and Sundays. Flew via Nice, Rome (nightstop) and Athens. Arrived at 1605 hrs on following day.

Northolt–Oslo. Dakota service BE530 departed at 0924 hrs on Tuesdays, Thursdays, Fridays and Sundays, arriving at 1515 hrs.

Northolt–Copenhagen–Stockholm. Viking service BE550 departed at 1036 hrs daily, except Wednesday and Sunday, arriving at 1810 hrs.

Northolt–Düsseldorf–Berlin. Daily Dakota round trip BE842/3.

Northolt–Nice–Rome–Athens. Weekday Viking service BE740. Departed at 1032 hrs, arriving at 1150 hrs on following day after nightstop in Rome.

Manchester–Birmingham–Paris (Le Bourget). Pionair round trip service BE303/4 on Mondays, Wednesdays and Fridays.

Glasgow–Aberdeen–Orkney–Shetland. Weekday Dakota round trip service S204/S205.

Aberdeen–Wick. Weekday round trip by 'Islander' class Rapide.

Inverness–Wick–Orkney. Two round trips each weekday by 'Islander' class Rapide.

Appendix 3: Route Maps illustrating the Development of the Network

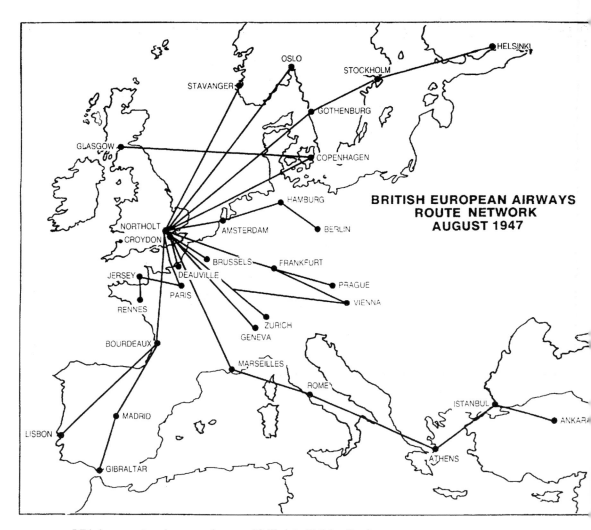

BEA International routes August 1947. (via Phil Lo Bao)

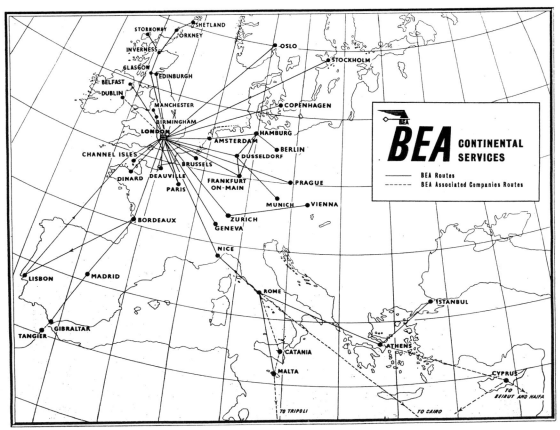

BEA route network August 1949. (via Helaine Michaels)

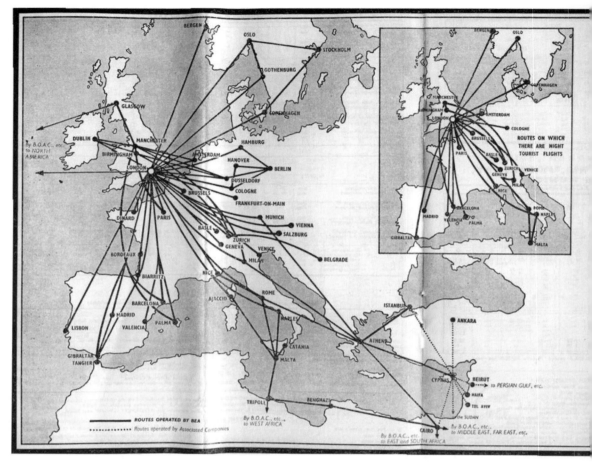

BEA International routes 1957. (via author)

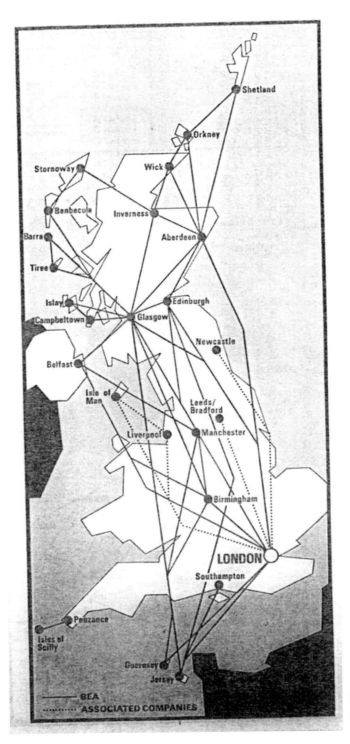

BEA Domestic route
network 1969. (via author)

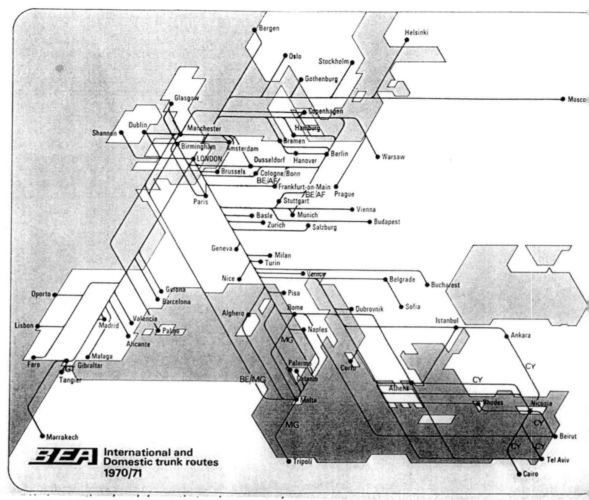

BEA International and domestic trunk routes 1970/1. (via author)

Appendix 4: Technical Details of Major Aircraft Types

Brief technical and operational details of major aircraft types operated by BEA

De Havilland DH 89A Dragon Rapide
Wingspan 48 ft   Length 34 ft 6 in   Height 10 ft 3 in
Cruising speed 132 mph   Range 578 miles

Powered by two DH Gipsy Six (also known as Gipsy Queen) in-line piston engines.

A biplane capable of carrying up to eight passengers, the Dragon Rapide (usually shortened to Rapide) was a development of the DH84 Dragon, but incorporating the experience gained in designing the larger, four-engined DH86 Express to meet the requirements of Australian operators. It first flew on 17 April 1934, and was supplied pre-war to the state airlines of Turkey, Persia and Romania. With the outbreak of World War Two, many Rapides were impressed into the RAF, and 523 examples of a military version known as the Dominie were built for use as radio trainers and communications aircraft. Production ended in 1946, after a total of 728 machines had been completed. Post-war, many Dominies were converted for civil use as light airliners and for air taxi operations. In these roles they served in countries throughout the world. BEA used a large number as the 'Islander' class on routes within Scotland and on Channel Islands and Scilly Isles services. Some are still flying today in the UK.

Douglas Dakota
Wingspan 95 ft   Length 64 ft 5 in   Height 16 ft 11 in
Cruising speed 207 mph   Range 2125 miles

Powered by two Pratt & Whitney Twin Wasp radial piston engines.

One of the most important transport aircraft ever built, the Dakota began life as the Douglas Sleeper Transport, a development of the Douglas DC-2, and built to meet American Airlines requirement, for an aircraft with sleeper berths that could fly New York–Chicago non-stop. The Douglas Sleeper Transport made its first flight on 17 December 1935, and a total of forty were built. The aircraft was noteworthy for its time as it was a low-wing monoplane with a retractable main undercarriage. More commercially successful was the DC-3 day version of the design, capable of accommodating twenty-one seated passengers, and it was in this layout that the type entered service with American Airlines on 25 June 1936. Before the attack on Pearl Harbor, Douglas built nearly 400 DC-3s, powered by either Wright Cyclone or Pratt & Whitney Twin Wasp engines.

With the USA's entry into World War Two, large scale production of the type for the US military began. The type was used for every type of transport duty, serving with the USAAF as the C-47 Skytrain and the US Navy as the R4D. It was also supplied to the RAF, where it was known as the Dakota. A total of 10,655 were built in the USA, plus a further 2500 or so in the Soviet Union and Japan.

After the war, thousands of military machines were declared surplus and sold to almost every airline in the world, including BOAC, from whom BEA acquired its first examples. After long service in both passenger and cargo roles, the BEA Dakota fleet was disposed of. Many examples stayed in the UK to serve with independent airlines such as Derby Aviation and East Anglian Flying Services. Many other Dakotas, acquired from other sources, served with the profusion of British charter operators of the 1960s. Today, the type is still to be seen at UK airshows, operated by the Air Atlantique Historic Flight and the Battle of Britain Memorial Flight.

Vickers Viking

Wingspan 89 ft 3 in   Length 65 ft 2 in   Height 19 ft 6 in
Cruising speed 210 mph   Range 1700 miles
Powered by two Bristol Hercules 634 radial piston engines
(All data refers to srs 1B)

The Vickers VC1 (later named the Viking) was designed in response to Specification 17/44, issued by the Ministries of Supply and Aircraft Production in 1944 for a civil conversion of the Wellington bomber. The aircraft utilised Wellington wings and the tail surfaces of the Vickers Warwick Mk V. The prototype made its maiden flight on 22 June 1945, becoming the first post-war airliner design to fly in Britain. On 5 April 1946 the Ministry of Aircraft Production placed an order for fifty examples, to be operated by BEA. The type was also ordered by Central African Airways, South African Airways, British West Indian Airways and Iraqi Airways. Military variants were also built for the RAF as the Valetta transport and the tricycle-undercarriage Varsity navigation trainer. Including these variants, production totalled 167 machines. On 6 April 1948 a Viking converted to a test bed for Rolls-Royce Nene turbojet engines became the world's first jet-powered transport aircraft.

After retirement, the BEA Viking fleet became the backbone of the early UK charter airlines such as Eagle Aviation and BKS Air Transport. Examples acquired from other sources also served in large numbers with other independent airlines, including Autair, Hunting-Clan Air Transport and Airwork. Former BEA Viking srs 1A G-AGRU passed through a number of owners and was at one time in use as a cafe at Soesterberg in Holland, before being rescued for preservation in the UK. It is now on show in its original BEA livery at Brooklands.

Airspeed AS 57 Ambassador

Wingspan 115 ft   Length 82 ft   Height 18 ft 3 in
Cruising speed 272 mph   Range 1550 miles
Powered by two Bristol Centaurus 661 radial piston engines

The AS 57 was one product of the Brabazon IIA specification of 1943, and the design was eventually defined as a large medium-haul airliner with twice the payload of a DC-3. It was a high-wing monoplane of all-metal stressed-skin construction, with very clean lines, a fully pressurised cabin and a tricycle undercarriage. Two prototypes were ordered by the Ministry of Aircraft Production in September 1945, and the type was given the name Ambassador. It made its first flight on 10 July 1947. In September 1948 BEA placed an order for twenty examples of the developed Ambassador 2; this was to be the sole order for the Ambassador. In BEA service the type was known as the 'Elizabethan' class. After premature retirement from BEA, owing to the overwhelming success and popularity of the turboprop Viscount, the Ambassador fleet went on to give sterling service with UK independent airlines BKS Air Transport, Autair and Dan-Air, and served as an executive and VIP transport with Shell and the Royal Jordanian Air Force. Examples of the type were also converted to serve as test beds for the Bristol Proteus, Rolls-Royce Tyne, and Napier Eland turboprop engines. The sole surviving example of the Ambassador, G-ALZO, is under restoration at Duxford in its Dan-Air livery.

Vickers Viscount

Wingspan 93 ft 8 in   Length 81 ft 2 in   Height 26 ft 9 in
Cruising speed 316 mph   Range 1690 miles
Powered by four Rolls-Royce Dart 505 turboprops
(All data refers to srs 701)

The Vickers Type 609 was designed to meet the 1944 Brabazon IIB requirement for a turboprop transport for European operations. Out of three competing concepts presented, in April 1945 the Ministry of Aircraft Production selected the Vickers design for a pressurised aircraft capable of carrying twenty-four passengers over 1040 miles at an altitude of 20,000 ft, powered by four Rolls-Royce Dart engines. Two prototypes were ordered under specification C.8/46, but with their range and speed reduced to 700 miles and 276 mph respectively. The type was originally to have been called Viceroy, but after the partition of India in 1947 it was renamed the Viscount.

The prototype first flew on 16 July 1948, but at first attracted little interest from BEA, the airline preferring the Airspeed Ambassador. However, the appearance of the Rolls-Royce RDa3 engine with 40 per cent more power led to the design of the fifty-three-seat Viscount srs 700, the prototype of which made its first flight on 28 August 1950. An order from BEA for the developed Viscount srs 701 was followed by further orders for the larger and more powerful srs 802 and srs 806 versions. The later srs 810 variant was not ordered by BEA, but was purchased by Lufthansa, South African Airways, Pakistan International Airways, and Continental Airlines in the USA. The final Viscount version was the srs 843, built for CAAC of China. Total Viscount production was 444. New examples of the various models were delivered to airlines worldwide, including Air France, KLM, and Aer Lingus. There were also breakthrough sales in North America to Trans-Canada Airlines and Capital Airlines. There was also a jet-powered Viscount, converted to two Rolls-Royce Tay engines in 1950 and used for research into electrically signalled flight control systems. After retirement, several of BEA's Viscounts were passed on to BEA subsidiaries BKS Air Transport and Cambrian Airways. Preserved examples of former BEA Viscount srs 701s can be seen in their original liveries at Duxford and Cosford.

de Havilland DH 106 Comet 4B

Wingspan 107 ft 10 in   Length 118 ft   Height 29 ft 5 in
Cruising speed 535 mph   Range 2600 miles
Powered by four Roll-Royce Avon 525 turbojets

The Comet 4B was a short-haul version of the Comet 4, which had itself emerged as a redesign of the original world-beating Comet 1, grounded after a series of catastrophic crashes in 1954. In fact, the Comet 4B was virtually identical to the Comet 4A, a model ordered for short-haul services within the USA by Capital Airlines, but not proceeded with due to financial problems at Capital. Compared with the Comet 4, the 4B model featured a considerably stretched fuselage, but had shorter wings, with the pinion fuel tanks deleted. Only eighteen Comet 4Bs were built, the model also serving with Olympic Airways. The final development of the Comet was the 4C model. This mated the longer fuselage of the srs 4B with the larger wing and greater fuel capacity of the Comet 4. Twenty-eight examples were built, the customers including Sudan Airways and Kuwait Airways. Two airframes remained unsold; these were greatly modified during construction to emerge as prototypes of the Hawker Siddeley HS801 maritime reconaissance aircraft, later to be named Nimrod. After retirement, former BEA Comet 4Bs were used on inclusive-tour charter flights by BEA subsidiary BEA Airtours and by Channel Airways. They were also used for this purpose by Dan-Air. In 1966 Dan-Air purchased two Comet 4s from BOAC. The airline went on to acquire almost all the surviving Comet 4s, 4Bs and 4Cs.

Vickers Vanguard
Wingspan 118 ft 7 in   Length 122 ft 10 in   Height 34 ft 11 in
Cruising speed 425 mph   Range 1830 miles
Powered by four Rolls-Royce Tyne 512 turboprops

The Vanguard was designed to meet BEA's requirement for a larger successor to the Viscount, with superior economics and performance. In July 1956 BEA ordered twenty examples of the initial V951 model. This was followed in January 1957 by an order from Trans-Canada Airlines for twenty examples, designated V952s. The airline later ordered three more. No further orders followed, as at that period all the major airlines wanted jets; propeller-powered aircraft were seen as unattractive to passengers. Including the prototype, Vanguard production totalled just forty-four machines. BEA later amended its order to include all but the first six examples as the V953 variant, with an increased payload where maximum range was not required. The Vanguard's capacious 'double-bubble' fuselage made it ideal for freight carrying, and by 1967 Air Canada (as Trans-Canada Airlines had been renamed) had converted the first of several of its Vanguards to freighter configuration. BEA was to follow suit, with the 'Merchantman' cargo conversion. After withdrawal from service by Air Canada and British Airways, Vanguards were used in both passenger and cargo roles by Europe Aero Service, Air Bridge Carriers (later Hunting Cargo), Invicta International and Merpati Nusantara. A former BEA V953 Vanguard, G-APEP, is preserved at Brooklands in Hunting Cargo livery.

de Havilland DH 121 Trident
Wingspan 98 ft   Length 131 ft 2 in   Height 28 ft 3 in
Cruising speed 550 mph   Range 1094 miles
Powered by three Rolls-Royce Spey 512 turbojet engines plus RB162 booster engine
(All data refers to Trident 3B)

In 1957 BEA issued a specification for a short-haul jet. Three main contenders emerged, all advanced designs, and BEA selected the DH 121. In its original form it was to have been powered by three Rolls-Royce RB140 bypass engines and to carry up to 111 passengers on stage lengths of 260–865 miles. At that time both Boeing and Douglas in the USA were pre-occupied with their long-haul 707 and DC-8 jets, and Lockheed had selected the turboprop Electra as its next project. The opportunity therefore existed for Britain to capture the bulk of the world market with a short-haul jet. De Havilland's own market research estimated possible worldwide sales of up to 550 aircraft by 1965. However, BEA insisted on a scaled-down design, tailored too closely to its own requirements, and the resulting Trident was too small to compete with the Boeing 727 that emerged as its main competitor for worldwide sales. Further versions of the Trident for BEA were the srs 2E and the considerably more capable srs 3B, and BEA's operations with the type were noteworthy for the pioneering of the Autoland system for all-weather services. Other Trident sales included srs 1Es to Kuwait Airways, Pakistan International Airways, Air Ceylon, Iraqi Airways, and Channel Airways. Cyprus Airways purchased two srs 2Es, and CAAC of China bought thirty-three Trident 2Es and two srs 3Bs. Trident 2E G-AVFB is preserved in the BEA 'red square' colour scheme at Duxford.

BAC Super One-Eleven

Wingspan 93 ft 6 in   Length 107 ft   Height 24 ft 6 in
Cruising speed 541 mph   Range 1705 miles
Powered by two Rolls-Royce Spey 512 turbojets

The origins of the BAC One-Eleven lie in the thirty-two-seat Hunting H107 of 1956. This was to have been powered by two Bristol Orpheus 12B engines. Hunting was absorbed into the British Aircraft Corporation in 1960. The project was reworked, firstly as the BAC 107 and then as the definitive BAC One-Eleven, powered by Rolls-Royce Spey engines and seating up to sixty-nine passengers. The first order came from British United Airways, for ten srs 100s with options on a further five. The aircraft then broke into the American market, with an order from Braniff International for six examples. The prototype of the srs 200 made its first flight on 20 August 1963, but was lost in October of that year, a victim of the deep-stall phenomenon. Srs 200s were ordered by Aer Lingus and Mohawk Airlines of the USA. This model was followed by the more powerful srs 300 and srs 400, the latter being tailored to meet US requirements. American Airlines ordered a fleet of srs 400s and operated them on US internal routes as '400 Astrojets'.

The 'stretched' srs 500 incorporated a lengthened fuselage, increased wing area, and uprated Spey engines. The first production example of the srs 510ED for BEA was ARB certificated in 1968, and the fleet entered BEA service as the Super One-Eleven. Srs 500 production was later transferred to ROMBAC in Romania. The later One-Eleven srs 475 combined the standard fuselage of the srs 300/400 with the increased wingspan of the srs 500. All of BEA's Super One-Elevens were transferred to British Airways. After eventual retirement by British Airways, many examples were acquired by European Air Charter. Other UK airlines to use One-Elevens of various marks included Court Line Aviation, Laker Airways, Dan-Air and British Caledonian.

Appendix 5: BEA Fleet List

Compiled from fleet list kindly supplied by Derek A. King, and from other sources.

Author's note: I do not profess to be an expert on individual aircraft histories, and apologise in advance for any omissions.

Abbreviations
AAJC = Associated Airways Joint Committee
A/L = Airlines
A/S = Air Services
A/T = Air Transport
A/W = Airways
BA = British Airways
Convtd = Converted
c/n = constructors number
D/D = Delivery date
LAC = Lancashire Aircraft Corporation
Lsd = leased
MCA = Ministry of Civil Aviation
MoS = Ministry of Supply
MTCA = Ministry of Transport and Civil Aviation
RAS = Railway Air Services
Regn = Aircraft registration letters
W/O = Written off in accident

Airspeed AS 57 Ambassador ('Elizabethan' Class)

Regn	c/n	D/D	Aircraft name	Disposal
G-ALFR	5210	24.5.51	Golden Hind	On loan from manufacturer until 7.51
G-ALZN	5212	22.8.51	Elizabethan	Sold to Overseas Aviation 10.3.61
G-ALZO	5226	25.11.52	Christopher Marlowe	Sold to Jordanian Air Force 5.59
G-ALZP	5318	28.2.52	Sir Richard Grenville	Sold to Jordanian Air Force 14.9.60
G-ALZR	5214	13.2.52	Sir Walter Raleigh	Sold to Rolls-Royce 2.59
G-ALZS	5215	25.1.52	William Shakespeare	Sold in Norway 1.6.60
G-ALZT	5216	27.1.52	Sir John Hawkins	Sold to BKS A/T 5.5.58
G-ALZU	5217	5.3.52	Lord Burghley	W/O Munich Airport 6.2.58
G-ALZV	5218	12.4.52	Earl of Leicester	Sold to Overseas Aviation 10.3.61
G-ALZW	5219	28.4.52	Sir Francis Walsingham	Sold to BKS A/T 5.58
G-ALZX	5220	29.5.52	Sir John Norris	Sold to Butler A/T 6.6.57
G-ALZY	5221	10.7.52	Sir Philip Sydney	Sold to Jordanian Air Force 26.12.59
G-ALZZ	5222	9.8.52	Edmund Spencer	Sold in Norway 1.6.60
G-AMAA	5223	5.9.52	Sir Francis Knollys	Sold to Shell Aviation 1.60
G-AMAB	5224	4.10.52	Sir Francis Bacon	W/O near Düsseldorf 8.4.55
G-AMAC	5225	1.11.52	Sir Robert Cecil	Sold to BKS A/T 17.6.60

Regn	c/n	D/D	Aircraft name	Disposal
G-AMAD	5211	20.3.52	Sir Francis Drake	(previously loaned for route proving 10.5.51-14.5.51) Sold to BKS A/T 23.7.57
G-AMAE	5227	18.12.52	Earl of Essex	Sold to Butler A/T 6.57
G-AMAF	5228	17.1.53	Lord Howard of Effingham	Sold to Overseas Aviation 10.3.61
G-AMAG	5229	4.2.53	Sir Thomas of Gresham	Sold to Shell Aviation Division 8.2.59
G-AMAH	5230	6.3.53	Sir Christopher Hatton	Sold to Butler A/T 6.6.57

Armstrong Whitworth AW 650 Argosy (No Class Name)

Regn	c/n	D/D	Type	Disposal
G-AOZZ	6651	19.12.61	srs 101	Leased from manufacturer. Returned 1.10.68
G-APRM	6653	23.11.61	srs 101	Leased from manufacturer. Returned 11.66
G-APRN	6654	6.11.61	srs 101	Leased from manufacturer. Returned 3.5.65
G-ASXL	6800	28.1.65	srs 222	W/O near Milan 4.7.65
G-ASXM	6801	2.3.65	srs 222	Sold to Transair 6.70
G-ASXN	6802	26.3.65	srs 222	Sold to Transair 7.70
G-ASXO	6803	28.4.65	srs 222	Sold to Transair 4.70
G-ASXP	6804	16.6.65	srs 222	W/O Stansted Airport 15.12.67
G-ATTC	6805	21.11.66	srs 222	Sold to Transair 29.4.70

Avro XIX srs 1 (No Class Name)

Regn	c/n	D/D	Disposal
G-AGUD*	1275	—	Transferred to MCA 27.5.47
G-AGUX*	1277	—	Transferred to MCA 6.10.47
G-AGVA*	1278	—	Transferred to MCA 6.10.47
G-AHIB*	1317	—	Transferred to MCA 30.4.47
G-AHIC*	1318	—	Transferred to MCA 28.5.47
G-AHID*	1319	—	Transferred to MCA 11.6.47
G-AHIE*	1320	—	Transferred to MCA 30.4.47
G-AHIF*	1321	—	Transferred to MCA 11.6.46
G-AHIG*	1322	—	Regd to BEA Flying Club 21.8.47–21.12.47, then to BEA. Transferred to MCA 14.5.48
G-AHIH*	1323	—	Transferred to MCA 11.6.47
G-AHII*	1324	—	Sold to Airways Training 26.8.47
G-AHIJ*	1325	—	Regd to BEA Flying Club 5.7.47. Transferred to MCA 11.11.47
G-AHIK*	1326	—	Sold to Airways Training 26.8.47
G-AHXL*	1352	10.48	Ex-Airways Training. Sold in Sweden 25.7.50
G-AHXM*	1353	10.48	Ex-Airways Training. Sold to Sperry Gyroscope 14.9.50

*Inherited from RAS 1.2.47

Avro 683 Lancaster

Regn	c/n	Disposal
G-AJWM	ex-RAF PP741	Regd to BEA 4.6.47. Used for training Alitalia crews. Transferred to Alitalia 11.48

Avro 691 Lancastrian III

Regn	c/n	D/D	Disposal
G-AHBX	1292/Set 75	2.47	Transferred to Alitalia 2.48
G-AHBY	1293/Set 76	2.47	Transferred to Alitalia 11.47
G-AHCB	1296/Set 79	1.47	Transferred to Alitalia 7.47
G-AHCD	1298/Set 81	5.47	Transferred to Alitalia 12.47
G-AHCE	1299/Set 82	2.47	Transferred to Alitalia 8.47

Boeing 707-436

Used by BEA Airtours only. All ex-BOAC. All transferred to British Airtours 1.4.74

Regn	c/n	D/D
G-APFB	17703	27.03.74
G-APFD	17705	16.02.73
G-APFG	17708	31.03.73
G-APFH	17709	15.1.72
G-APFK	17712	30.12.71
G-APFL	17713	1.12.72
G-APFO	17716	15.11.72

Boeing 707-465

Used by BEA Airtours only. Ex-BOAC.

Regn	c/n	D/D	Disposal
G-ARWD	18372	15.1.73	Transferred to British Airtours 1.4.74

Bristol 170 Mk 21

Regn	c/n	D/D	Aircraft name	Disposal
G-AICS	12762	16.8.50	Yeoman/Sir George White	Leased to Silver City A/W from 6.52 and sold to them 30.4.57

British Aircraft Corporation BAC One-Eleven srs 510ED. (No Class Name)

(All examples transferred to British Airways on merger 1.4.74)

Regn	c/n	D/D
G-AVMH	136	12.6.69
G-AVMI	137	2.4.69
G-AVMJ	138	29.8.68
G-AVMK	139	16.9.68
G-AVML	140	4.10.68
G-AVMM	141	25.10.68
G-AVMN	142	20.11.68
G-AVMO	143	27.11.68
G-AVMP	144	11.12.68

Regn	c/n	D/D
G-AVMR	145	5.5.70 (Used for Autoland trials prior to delivery).
G-AVMS	146	13.1.69
G-AVMT	147	28.3.69
G-AVMU	148	19.3.69
G-AVMV	149	21.4.69
G-AVMW	150	2.5.69
G-AVMX	151	20.6.69
G-AVMY	152	21.7.69
G-AVMZ	153	15.8.69

Also loaned to BEA as required were Cambrian Airways srs 400s G-AVGP, G-AVOE, G-AVOF, G-AWBL and G-BBMG.

De Havilland DH 89 and D H 89A Rapide ('Islander' class)

Regn	c/n	D/D	Aircraft name	Disposal
G-ACPP (DH 89)	6254	1.2.47		Inherited from Great Western and Southern A/L. Sold to Aircraft and Engineering Services 4.48
G-ADAJ (DH 89)	6276	1.2.47		Inherited from Scottish A/W. Sold in France 4.48
G-AERN	6345	1.2.47		Inherited from West Coast Air Services. To Gibraltar A/W 11.47
G-AEWL	6367	1.2.47		Inherited from Scottish A/W. Sold to C. Allen 14.5.48
G-AFEZ	6408	1.2.47	Lord Shaftesbury	Inherited from Isle of Man A/S. Sold to Airviews 5.6.56
G-AFOI	6450	1.2.47		Inherited from Scottish A/W. To Gibraltar A/W 7.6.48
G-AFRK	6441	1.2.47	Rudyard Kipling	Inherited from Scottish A/W. Sold to Airviews 16.5.56
G-AGDG	6547	1.2.47		Inherited from Scottish A/W. Sold in France 21.11.47
G-AGDM	6584	12.4.47		Inherited from Allied A/W. Sold to C. Allen 5.48
G-AGEE	6622	1.2.47		Inherited from Great Western and Southern A/L. To Gibraltar A/W 11.47
G-AGHI	6455	12.4.47		Inherited from Allied A/W. Sold to C. Allen 1.7.48
G-AGIC	6522	1.2.47		Inherited from Scottish A/W. Sold in France 20.11.47
G-AGIF	6509	1.2.47		Inherited from Scottish A/W. Sold to Ulster Aviation 4.48
G-AGJF	6499	1.2.47		Inherited from Scottish A/W. W/O at Barra 6.8.47

Regn	c/n	D/D	Aircraft name	Disposal
G-AGJG	6517	1.2.47		Inherited from Scottish A/W. Sold to Adie Aviation 10.48
G-AGLE	6784	1.2.47		Inherited from RAS. Sold to C. Allen 8.6.48
G-AGLP	6780	1.2.47		Inherited from RAS. Sold to C. Allen 8.6.48
G-AGLR	6781	1.2.47		Inherited from RAS. Sold to Lees Hill Aviation 21.6.48
G-AGOJ	6850	1.2.47		Inherited from Scottish A/W. Sold to LAC 18.6.48
G-AGPH	6889	1.4.47	Sir Henry Havelock	Inherited from Channel Islands A/W. Damaged beyond repair, Barra, 6.12.51
G-AGPI	6885	1.4.47		Inherited from Channel Islands A/W. Sold to Lees Hill. Aviation 5.48
G-AGSH	6884	1.4.47	James Keir Hardy	Inherited from Channel Islands A/W. Sold to Airviews 4.5.56, but re-purchased 12.1.62 and given new name 'Lord Baden Powell'. Sold to British Westpoint A/L 2.5.64
G-AGSJ	6888	1.2.47		Inherited from Isle of Man A/S. Sold to Island A/S 25.5.48
G-AGSK	6887	1.4.47	Lord Kitchener	Inherited from Channel Islands A/W. To Gibraltar A/W 15.12.52
G-AGUF	6855	1.4.47		Inherited from Channel Islands A/W. Sold to Island A/S 18.6.48
G-AGUG	6859	1.4.47		Inherited from Channel Islands A/W. Sold to LAC 18.6.48
G-AGUP	6911	1.2.47	Sir Robert Keel	Inherited from Isle of Man A/S. Sold to Jersey A/L 18.8.51
G-AGUR	6910	1.2.47	Lord Roberts	Inherited from Scottish A/W. Sold to C.E. Harper Aviation 10.11.53
G-AGUU	6908	1.2.47	Sir Colin Campbell	Inherited from Great Western and Southern A/L. Sold to Malayan A/W 8.52.
G-AGUV	6912	1.2.47	General Gordon	Inherited from Great Western and Southern A/L. To Gibraltar A/W 6.1.53
G-AHGF	6903	1.2.47		Inherited from RAS. Sold to Lees Hill Aviation 21.6.48
G-AHGH	6934	1.2.47		Inherited from RAS. Sold to Patrick Duval Aviation 21.6.48
G-AHGI	6935	1.2.47		Inherited from RAS. Sold to Patrick Duval Aviation 21.6.48
G-AHKR	6824	1.2.47		Inherited from Isle of Man A/S. W/O Isle of Man 15.4.47
G-AHKS	6812	1.2.47	Robert Louis Stephenson	Inherited from AAJC. Sold to Eagle Aviation. 25.4.55

Regn	c/n	D/D	Aircraft name	Disposal
G-AHKT	6811	1.2.47	Lord Tennyson.	Inherited from Isle of Man A/S. Sold to A. J. Whittemore Aviation 4.53
G-AHKU	6810	1.2.47	Cecil John Rhodes	Inherited from Isle of Man A/S. Sold to British Westpoint A/L 2.5.64
G-AHKV	6792	1.2.47	Sir James Outram	Inherited from Isle of Man A/S. Sold to A.J. Whittemore Aviation 4.53
G-AHLL	6576	1.2.47	Sir Henry Lawrence	Inherited from Scottish A/W. Damaged beyond repair St. Just, Lands End, 21.5.59
G-AHLM	6708	1.2.47		Inherited from Scottish A/W. Sold to Marshalls of Cambridge. 3.48
G-AHLN	6754	1.2.47		Inherited from Scottish A/W. Sold to Ulster Aviation 4.48
G-AHXV	6747	1.2.47		Inherited from AAJC. W/O North Ronaldsay 15.1.49
G-AHXW	6782	1.2.47	John Nicholson	Inherited from AAJC. Sold to A.J. Whittemore Aviation 13.3.53
G-AHXX	6800	1.2.47		Islander Inherited from AAJC. Sold to Malayan A/W 9.52
G-AHXY	6808	1.2.47		Inherited from AAJC. W/O Renfrew 27.12.48
G-AHXZ	6825	1.2.47	Charles Dickens	Inherited from AAJC. W/O Renfrew 28.8.51
G-AIHN	6498	1.2.47		Inherited from RAS. To Gibraltar A/W 11.47
G-AJCL	6722	12.6.59	Sir Henry Lawrence	Ex-Butlins Ltd. Sold to British Westpoint A/L 2.5.64
G-AJSK	6500	1.5.49	Lord Lister	Ex-Fields Aviation. To Gibraltar A/W 30.12.52
G-AJXB	6530	17.12.48	William Gilbert Grace	Ex-Fields Aviation. Sold to Eagle Aviation 25.4.55
G-AKDX	6898	25.8.47		Ex YI-ABE Sold to Adie Aviation 7.49
G-AKZB	6790	8.2.49	Lord Baden Powell	W/O St Just, Lands End 12.12.61

de Havilland DH 106 Comet 4B (No Class Name)

Regn	c/n	D/D	Aircraft name	Disposal
G-APMA	6421	20.12.59	Sir Edmund Halley	Stored at Cambridge 31.3.69 but returned to service. Stored again at Cambridge 4.71. Sold to R.J. Coley for scrap 8.7.72
G-APMB	6422	9.11.59	Walter Gale	Stored at Cambridge 5.10.69. Sold to Channel A/W 15.6.70
G-APMC	6423	16.11.59	Andrew Crommelin	Leased to Olympic A/W 19.5.60 – 1.9.69. To BEA Airtours 12.3.70. To Dan-Air 5.11.73
G-APMD	6435	29.3.60	William Denning	To BEA Airtours 31.3.70. To Dan-Air 9.9.72

Regn	c/n	D/D	Aircraft name	Disposal
G-APME	6436	10.5.60	John Tebbutt	To BEA Airtours 7.8.70. To Dan-Air 24.2.72
G-APMF	6426	27.1.60	William Finlay	To BEA Airtours 1.4.70. To Dan-Air 30.1.73
G-APMG	6442	31.7.60	John Grigg	To BEA Airtours 16.3.70. To Dan-Air 19.1.73
G-APYC	6437	20.8.69		ex-SX-DAK of Olympic A/W. To Channel A/W 26.1.70
G-APYD	6438	1.9.69		ex-SX-DAL of Olympic A/W. To Channel A/W 26.1.70
G-APZM	6440	9.10.69		ex-SX-DAN of Olympic A/W. Stored at Cambridge 27.10.69. To Channel A/W 14.5.70
G-ARCO	6449	13.4.61	John Hind	Destroyed by bomb in flight 12.10.67
G-ARCP	6451	19.4.61	William Brooks	To BEA Airtours 22.5.70. To Dan-Air 22.10.73
G-ARDI	6447	5.11.69		ex-SX-DAO of Olympic A/W. Stored at Cambridge, then to Channel A/W 25.4.70
G-ARGM	6453	6.5.61		To BEA Airtours 5.3.70. To Dan-Air 1.11.73
G-ARJK	6452	15.5.61		To BEA Airtours 5.3.70. To Dan-Air 5.10.73
G-ARJL	6455	31.5.61		Leased to Olympic A/W 2.64-2.70. To BEA Airtours 1.3.70. To Dan-Air 9.11.73
G-ARJM	6456	26.6.61		W/O Ankara 21.12.61
G-ARJN	6459	5.8.61		To BEA Airtours 25.3.70. To Dan-Air 15.2.73

de Havilland DH 114 Heron 1B

Regn	c/n	D/D	Aircraft name	Disposal
G-ANXA	14044	23.2.55	John Hunter Renamed Sister Jean Kennedy.	Leased to Sierra Leone A/W 26.9.73. To Peters Aviation 9.4.74
G-ANXB	14048	12.2.55	Sir James Young Simpson	Withdrawn from use 3.4.73 To Peters Aviation 24.10.73
G-AOFY	14099	13.4.56	Sir Charles Bell	W/O Port Ellen, Islay 28.9.57

Douglas C47 Dakota ('Pionair' and 'Pionair-Leopard' Classes)

Regn	c/n	D/D	Aircraft name	Disposal
G-AGHH	9187	24.1.49		Leased from BOAC until 10.2.49
G-AGHJ	9413	1.8.46	Albert Ball	To Jersey A/L 28.3.61
G-AGHL	9407	1.8.46	Lanoe Hawker	To Field Aircraft Services 23.3.60
G-AGHM	9623	21.12.51	Edward Maitland	Leased to Cambrian A/W 16.4.61. Sold to Cambrian A/W

Regn	c/n	D/D	Aircraft name	Disposal
G-AGHP	9408	17.12.48	Bert Hinkler	Convtd to Pionair-Leopard. W/O near Chatenoy, France 16.5.58
G-AGHS	10099	17.12.48	Horace Short	Leased to Cambrian A/W 2.3.61. Sold to Cambrian A/W
G-AGHU	9863	17.8.46		Leased from BOAC until 9.7.47
G-AGIO	11907	1.8.46		Leased from BOAC until 28.7.47
G-AGIP	11903	1.8.46	Horatio Philipps	Leased to Cambrian A/W 31.1.60. Sold to Cambrian A/W
G-AGIS	12017	1.8.46	Ross Smith	Sold to Aero Services London Ltd. 8.9.53
G-AGIT	11921	1.8.46		Leased from BOAC until 30.7.47
G-AGIU	12096	20.9.46	Edward Busk	Sold to Ministry of Aviation (for Air Mali) 21.3.61
G-AGIW	12186	1.8.46		W/O Mill Hill, Middlesex 17.10.50
G-AGIX	12053	1.8.46		W/O near Sywell, Northants 31.7.48
G-AGIZ	12075	22.6.49	Oliver Swann	Convtd to Pionair-Leopard. Sold to Field Aircraft Services 1.2.54
G-AGJV	12195	1.8.46	John Porte	Sold to Derby Airways 2.12.60
G-AGJW	12199	1.8.46	Wilfred Parke	Sold to BOAC Associated Companies 5.11.58
G-AGJZ	12014	1.8.46	John Stringfellow	Sold to Field Aviation Services 22.3.60
G-AGNF	15534/ 26997	1.8.46		Sold to Field Aviation Services 14.10.49
G-AGNG	15552	1.8.46		Leased from BOAC until 20.5.48
G-AGNK	15540/ 26895	28.9.51	Edward Mannock	Sold to East Anglian Flying Services 26.5.61
G-AGYX	12472	1.8.46	George Holt Thomas	Sold to Autair 21.4.61
G-AGYZ	12278	1.2.47	Charles Kingsford Smith	Convtd to Pionair-Leopard. Sold to Eagle Aviation 29.3.54
G-AGZB	12180	1.2.47	Robert Smith-Barry	Sold to East Anglian Flying Services 8.12.60
G-AGZC	12222	19.8.46	Samuel Cody	Sold to Ministry of Aviation (for Air Mali) 26.2.61
G-AGZD	12450	1.8.46	Percy Pilcher	Sold to East Anglian Flying Services 26.7.60
G-AGZE	12416	19.8.46		Leased from BOAC until 16.9.47
G-AHCS	12348	1.8.46		W/O Oslo 7.8.46
G-AHCT	12308	1.8.46	Hiram Maxim	Sold to Eagle Aviation 29.3.54
G-AHCU	13381	1.8.46	Charles Ulm	Convtd to Pionair-Leopard. Sold to East Anglian Flying Services 18.5.62
G-AHCV	12443	1.8.46	George Cayley	Sold to East Anglian Flying Services 8.6.61
G-AHCW	13308	1.8.46.		W/O near Coventry 19.2.49
G-AHCX	13335	1.8.46	Spencer Gray	Convtd to Pionair-Leopard. Sold to Yemen Airlines 27.6.62
G-AHCY	12355	1.8.46		W/O near Oldham, Lancs 19.8.49
G-AHCZ	11924	1.8.46	Charles Sampson	Leased to Cambrian A/W 2.3.59. Sold to Cambrian A/W

Regn	c/n	D/D	Aircraft name	Disposal
G-AHDA	12177			Purchased for spares only 9.46
G-AHDB	12077			Purchased for spares only 9.46
G-AHDC	13481			Purchased for spares only 9.46
G-AIWD	13475	26.2.51	John Dunne	Sold to BKS A/T 17.5.60
G-AJDE	13182	1.1.51	David Henderson	Sold to Martins Air Charter 6.2.61
G-AJHY	13388	23.8.47	William Henson	Sold to Westpoint Aviation 20.6.61
G-AJHZ	12421	10.7.47	Bentfield Hucks	Sold to Jersey A/L 28.3.61
G-AJIA	12208	24.6.47	John Alcock	Sold to Ministry of Aviation (for Air Mali) 22.3.61
G-AJIB	9624	30.7.47	Griffith Brewer	Sold to East Anglian Flying Services 26.2.60
G-AJIC	9487	22.5.47	Roy Chadwick	Sold to Autair 29.3.61
G-AKJH	13164	29.11.50	Edward Hillman	Sold to Derby A/W 17.4.61
G-AKNB	9043	13.11.50	Sefton Brancker	Sold to Silver City A/W 11.12.59
G-ALCB	9878			Purchased for spares only 9.46
G-ALCC	10106	12.4.49	Harry Hawker	Leased to Cambrian A/W 2.4.61 Sold to Cambrian A/W
G-ALLI	19351	17.5.49	Samuel Instone	Sold to Travelair 4.3.60
G-ALPN	12158	17.11.50	Godfrey Paine	Sold to Silver City A/W 18.11.59
G-ALTT	12000	5.7.49	Charles Grey	Convtd to Pionair-Leopard. Sold to Autair 13.11.62
G-ALXK	16080/ 32828	2.6.50	Rex Pierson	Sold to North South A/L 8.7.61
G-ALXL	16487/ 33235	19.5.50	Charles Rolls	Leased to Cambrian A/W 3.5.60 Sold to Cambrian A/W
G-ALXM	16465/ 33213	26.4.50	William Rhodes-Moorhouse	Sold to Martins Air Charter 1.7.60
G-ALXN	14661	22.9.50	Henry Royce	Convtd to Pionair-Leopard. Convtd to Dart-Dakota 51. Reverted to piston engines 11.53 Sold to East Anglian Flying Services 25.5.62
G-ALYF	19350	9.12.50	Pionair	Sold to Westpoint Aviation 22.3.61
G-AMDB	14987/ 26432	10.10.50	Claude Johnson	Convtd to Pionair-Leopard. Convtd to Dart-Dakota 51. Reverted to piston engines 11.53. Sold to Westpoint Aviation 16.3.62
G-AMDZ	12911	21.1.51	Frank Barnwell	Sold to East Anglian Flying Services 4.4.60
G-AMFV	10105	11.12.50	Richard Howard-Flanders	Leased to Cambrian A/W
		16.3.59		Sold to Cambtrian A/W
G-AMGD	9628	3.11.50	George Brackley	Sold to Autair 8.4.60
G-AMJX	15635/ 27080	11.5.51	Reginald Mitchell	Leased to Cambrian A/W 20.3.59. Sold to Cambrian A/W

Regn	c/n	D/D	Aircraft name	Disposal
G-AMJY	16808/ 33556	11.5.51	James McCudden	Sold to Air Ceylon 11.11.59
G-AMKE	14483/ 25928	11.6.51	Frederick Lanchester	Sold to Air Links 4.7.61
G-AMNV	16833/ 33581	14.1.52	Eric Geddes	Sold to Tyne Tees Air Charter 21.6.62
G-AMNW	14177/ 25622	14.1.52	Frank Searle	Sold to East Anglian Flying Services 29.5.62
G-AMYB	16598/ 33346	4.56	Lord Hood	Leased from Eagle Aviation until 11.56

Handley Page HPR7 Herald

Regn	c/n	D/D	Disposal
G-APWA	149	20.1.62	Loaned from manufacturer until 4.62 for use on HRH Prince Philip's South American Tour
G-APWB	150	10.3.62	Leased from MoS. Sold to Autair International 28.11.66
G-APWC	151	9.1.62	Leased from MoS. Sold to Autair International 28.11.66
G-APWD	152	30.4.62	Leased from MoS. Sold to Autair International 28.11.66

Hawker Siddeley Trident 1C (No Class Name)

Regn	c/n	D/D	Disposal
G-ARPA	2101	18.8.65	Transferred to BA 1.4.74
G-ARPB	2102	30.6.64	Used by HSA for autoland trials. Transferred to BA 1.4.74
G-ARPC	2103	9.9.64	Transferred to BA 1.4.74
G-ARPD	2104	8.1.65	Transferred to BA 1.4.74
G-ARPE	2105	10.7.64	Transferred to BA 1.4.74
G-ARPF	2106	19.12.63	Transferred to BA 1.4.74
G-ARPG	2107	19.2.64	Transferred to BA 1.4.74
G-ARPH	2108	25.3.64	Transferred to BA 1.4.74
G-ARPI	2109	2.5.64	W/O Staines 18.6.72
G-ARPJ	2110	26.5.64	Transferred to BA 1.4.74
G-ARPK	2111	26.6.64	Transferred to BA 1.4.74
G-ARPL	2112	6.8.64	Transferred to BA 1.4.74
G-ARPM	2113	9.10.64	Transferred to BA 1.4.74
G-ARPN	2115	4.12.64	Transferred to BA 1.4.74
G-ARPO	2116	31.1.65	Transferred to BA 1.4.74
G-ARPP	2117	25.5.65	Transferred to BA 1.4.74
G-ARPR	2119	12.4.65	Transferred to BA 1.4.74
G-ARPS	2120	1.6.65	W/O in cabin fire, Heathrow 29.7.69
G-ARPT	2121	9.7.65	W/O on ground, Heathrow 3.7.68
G-ARPU	2122	25.8.65	Transferred to BA 1.4.74
G-ARPW	2123	15.10.65	Transferred to BA 1.4.74
G-ARPX	2124	25.5.66	Transferred to BA 1.4.74
G-ARPZ	2128	1.7.66	Transferred to BA 1.4.74

Hawker Siddeley HS 121 Trident 1E

Regn	c/n	D/D	Disposal
G-ASWU	2114	4.1.72	Ex 9K-ACF Kuwait A/W. To Cyprus A/W as 5B-DAD 15.3.73
G-AVYE	2139	20.1.72	Leased from BKS A/T until 14.2.72

Hawker Siddeley Trident 2E
(All transferred to BA 1.4.74 unless otherwise stated)

Regn	c/n	D/D	Disposal
G-AVFA	2140	23.12.69	
G-AVFB	2141	6.6.68	To Cyprus A/W as 5B-DAC 20.6.72
G-AVFC	2142	6.8.68	
G-AVFD	2143	16.4.68	
G-AVFE	2144	8.5.68	
G-AVFF	2145	30.5.68	
G-AVFG	2146	4.7.68	
G-AVFH	2147	1.8.68	
G-AVFI	2148	27.11.68	
G-AVFJ	2149	21.12.68	
G-AVFK	2150	17.1.69	
G-AVFL	2151	18.2.69	
G-AVFM	2152	25.4.69	
G-AVFN	2153	23.5.69	
G-AVFO	2156	23.6.70	
G-AZXM	2154	18.10.72	

Hawker Siddeley HS 121 Trident 3B
(All transferred to BA 1.4.74)

Regn	c/n	D/D
G-AWYZ	2301	23.3.72
G-AWZA	2302	11.5.71
G-AWZB	2303	24.2.71
G-AWZC	2304	18.2.71
G-AWZD	2305	26.3.71
G-AWZE	2306	8.4.71
G-AWZF	2307	11.5.71
G-AWZG	2308	12.6.71
G-AWZH	2309	15.7.71
G-AWZI	2310	9.8.71
G-AWZJ	2311	16.9.71
G-AWZK	2312	16.10.71
G-AWZL	2313	25.11.71
G-AWZM	2314	16.12.71
G-AWZN	2315	20.1.72

Regn	c/n	D/D
G-AWZO	2316	16.2.72
G-AWZP	2317	21.3.72
G-AWZR	2318	13.4.72
G-AWZS	2319	5.5.72
G-AWZT	2320	6.6.72
G-AWZU	2321	10.7.72
G-AWZV	2322	9.8.72
G-AWZW	2323	29.11.72
G-AWZX	2324	29.1.73
G-AWZZ	2326	19.4.73
G-AYVF	2325	14.3.73

Junkers Ju 52/3m (Jupiter Class) (No individual names)

All converted by Shorts at Belfast (conversion numbers in brackets)
All broken up 2.48 unless otherwise stated.

Regn	c/n	D/D	Disposal
G-AHBP	6750 (SH7C)	1.2.47	Inherited from RAS
G-AHOC	501441 (SH16C)	1.2.47	Inherited from RAS
G-AHOD	131150 (SH10C)	1.2.47	Inherited from Scottish A/W. Spares use only
G-AHOE	(SH8C)	1.2.47	Inherited from RAS
G-AHOF	8685 (SH9C)	1.2.47	Inherited from RAS
G-AHOG	3317 (SH17C)	1.2.47	Inherited from RAS
G-AHOH	641364 (SH14C)	1.2.47	
G-AHOI	641227 (SH13C)	1.2.47	
G-AHOJ	500138 (SH15C)	1.2.47	
G-AHOK	2998 (SH12C) W/O Renfrew	26.1.47	whilst still in service with Scottish A/W
G-AHOL	641213 (SH11C)	1.2.47	

Short SC7 Skyliner

Regn	c/n	D/D	Disposal
G-ASZJ	SH1831	9.71	Loaned from manufacturer for trials
G-AZYW	SH1903	8.3.73	Transferred to BA 1.4.74
G-BAIT	SH1908	20.4.73	Transferred to BA 1.4.74

Vickers V498 Viking Mk 1A

Regn	c/n	D/D	Aircraft name	Disposal
G-AGON*	4/104	2.5.47		Used for training only. To MoS 19.8.47
G-AGRM*	5/105	16.6.47		Used for training only. To MoS 15.8.47
G-AGRN*	6/106	17.6.47		Used for training only. To MoS 22.8.47
G-AGRO*	7/107	11.6.47		To MTCA 2.2.48
G-AGRP*	8/108	18.6.47		To MTCA 2.2.48
G-AGRS*	110	14.8.46		To MTCA 18.12.47

Regn	c/n	D/D	Aircraft name	Disposal
G-AGRU	112	9.8.46	Vagrant	To British West Indian Airways 2.2.48
G-AGRV	114	11.8.46	Value	To MTCA 2.2.48
G-AGRW	115	8.8.46	Vagabond	To MTCA 2.2.48
G-AHON	116	15.8.46	Valentine	Sold to Trans World Air Charter 10.1.48
G-AHOP	117	19.8.46	Valerie	To MTCA 2.2.48
G-AHOR	118	29.8.46	Valet	To MTCA 2.2.48
G-AHOS	119	7.9.46	Valiant	To MTCA 2.2.48
G-AHOT	121	12.9.46	Valkyrie	Sold to Trans World Air Charter 10.1.48
G-AHOU	122	27.9.46	Valley	To British South American Airways 2.2.48
G-AHOV	123	1.10.46	Valour	To MoS/MCA 2.2.48
G-AHOW	124	11.10.46	Vanessa	To MoS/MCA 2.2.48

* All above were registered to BOAC (BEA Division) and operated on lease from MOS/MTCA/

Vickers V614 Viking Mk 1

Regn	c/n	D/D	Aircraft name	Disposal
G-AHOX	125	21.10.46	Vanguard	To MoS/MCA 10.9.47
G-AHOY	128	7.11.46	Vanity	To MoS/MCA 2.2.48
G-AHOZ	129	12.11.46	Vantage	To MoS/MCA 2.2.48
G-AHPA	130	23.11.46	Varlet	To MoS 15.8.47
G-AHPB	132	20.11.46	Variety	To MCA 2.2.48
G-AHPC	133	21.11.46	Vassal	To MCA 2.2.48
G-AHPD	134	3.12.46	Vampire	To MCA 2.2.48
G-AHPE	137	6.12.46	Vandal	To MCA 2.2.48
G-AHPF	138	7.12.46	Vedette	To MCA 2.2.48

Vickers V621 Viking Mk 1A

Regn	c/n	D/D	Disposal
G-AIJE	127	10.3.48	Loaned by MoS until 23.9.48 and from 12.48 until 18.2.51

Vickers V610 Viking Mk 1B and V629 Viking Mk 1B ('Admiral' Class)

Regn	c/n	D/D	Aircraft name	Disposal
G-AHPK	148	15.4.47	Veracity	W/O Ruislip 6.1.48
G-AHPL	149	16.4.47	Verdant	Convtd to 'Admiral' class 51 as 'Lord Anson' To Central African Airways 10.4.53
G-AHPM	152	26.4.47	Verderer	Convtd to 'Admiral' class 51 as 'Lord Rodney' To Eagle Aviation 15.7.53
G-AHPN	155	24.3.47	Ventnor	W/O Heathrow 31.10.50
G-AHPO	157	12.3.47	Venturer	Convtd to 'Admiral' class 51 as 'Sir Edward Howard'. Renamed 'Lord Dundonald'. Used by Eagle Aviation from 21.4.53. Damaged at Nuremberg 20.12.53. To Eagle Aviation for spares 24.12.53

Regn	c/n	D/D	Aircraft name	Disposal
G-AHPP	160	15.4.47	Venus	Convtd to 'Admiral' class 51 as 'Sir Peter Parker'. Renamed 'Sir Charles Saunders'. Sold in Germany 25.2.56
G-AHPR	164	28.4.47	Verily	Convtd to 'Admiral' class 51 as 'Prince Rupert'. Sold to Field Aircraft Services 16.11.55
G-AHPS	167	14.5.47	Verity	Convtd to 'Admiral' class 51 as 'Sir Doveton Sturdee'. Sold in Germany 26.10.55
G-AIVB	215	16.5.47	Vernal	Convtd to 'Admiral' class 51 as 'Robert Blake'. Sold to First Air Trading 2.12.55
G-AIVC	216	16.5.47	Vernon	Convtd to 'Admiral' class 51 as 'Lord Collingwood'. Sold to Eagle Aircraft Services 3.6.54
G-AIVD	217	16.5.47	Veteran	Convtd to 'Admiral class' 51 as 'Lord Duncan'. Sold in Germany 3.56
G-AIVE	218	31.5.47	Vestal	W/O near Largs, Scotland 21.4.48
G-AIVF	219	30.5.47	Vibrant	Convtd to 'Admiral class' 51 as 'Sir James Somerville'. Sold in Germany 28.3.56
G-AIVG	220	30.5.47	Viceroy	Convtd to 'Admiral class' 51 as 'Sir George Rooke'. W/O Le Bourget, Paris 12.8.53
G-AIVH	221	30.5.47	Vicinity	Convtd to 'Admiral' class 51 as 'Lord Howe'. Sold to Eagle Aviation 1.9.54
G-AIVI	222	4.6.47	Victor	Convtd to 'Admiral' class 51 as 'Viking'. Sold to First Air Trading 9.5.55
G-AIVJ	223	18.7.47	Victoria	Convtd to 'Admiral' class 51 as 'Lord Jellicoe'. Sold in Germany 23.1.56
G-AIVK	224	23.6.47	Victory	Convtd to 'Admiral' class 51 as 'Lord Keyes'. Sold to British International Airlines 14.4.55
G-AIVL	225	25.6.47	Vigilant	Convtd to 'Admiral' class 51 as 'Lord Hawke'. Sold to Eagle Aviation 25.4.55
G-AIVM	226	8.7.47	Vigorous	Convtd to 'Admiral' class 51 as 'George Monck'. Sold in Germany 24.11.55
G-AIVN	227	27.7.47	Violet	Convtd to 'Admiral' class 51 as 'Sir William Penn'. Renamed 'Edward Boscawen'. Sold to Central African Airways 10.9.54
G-AIVO	228	18.8.47	Villain	Convtd to 'Admiral' class 51 as 'Edward Vernon'. Sold to Eagle Aircraft Services 7.2.55
G-AIVP	229	9.8.47	Vimy	W/O near Berlin 5.4.48
G-AJBM	239	9.8.47	Vincent	Convtd to 'Admiral' class 51 as ' Sir Charles Knowles'. Renamed 'Charles Watson'. Sold to Argentine Air Force 26.1.56

Regn	c/n	D/D	Aircraft name	Disposal
G-AJBN	240	11.9.47	Vindictive	Convtd to 'Admiral' class 51 as 'Lord Nelson'. Sold to First Air Trading 5.11.55
G-AJBO	241	11.9.47	Vintage	Convtd to 'Admiral' class 51 as 'John Benbow'. Sold to Eagle Aviation 1.9.54
G-AJBP	242	16.9.47	Vintner	Convtd to 'Admiral' class 51 as 'Sir Hyde Parker'. Renamed 'Sir Edward Spragge'. Sold to First Air Trading 1.12.55
G-AJBR	243	24.9.47	Virginia	Convtd to 'Admiral' class 51 as 'Sir Bertram Ramsay'. Sold to BKS A/T 27.1.55
G-AJBS	244	25.9.47	Virgo	Convtd to 'Admiral' class 51 as 'Sir Cloudesley Shovell'. Sold to Argentine Air Force 26.1.56
G-AJBT	245	19.9.47	Viper	Convtd to 'Admiral' class 51 as 'Sir Thomas Troubridge'. To Central African Airways 22.4.55
G-AJBU	246	16.1.48	Virtue	Convtd to 'Admiral' class 51 as 'Lord Bridport'. Sold to Field Aircraft Services 16.11.55
G-AJBV	247	23.1.48	Viscount	Convtd to 'Admiral' class 51 as 'Sir Henry Morgan'. Sold to Iraqi A/W 22.5.53
G-AJBW	248	21.1.48	Vista	Convtd to 'Admiral' class 51 as 'Sir William Cornwallis'. Sold to Eagle Aviation 17.5.55
G-AJBX	249	27.1.48	Vital	Convtd to 'Admiral' class 51 as 'Sir Edward Hughes'. Sold to Eagle Aircraft Services 1.6.54
G-AJBY	250	10.1.48	Vitality	Convtd to 'Admiral' class 51 as 'Sir Richard Strachan'. Renamed 'Lord Torrington'. Sold in Germany 26.1.56
G-AJCA	252	7.2.49	Vixen	Convtd to 'Admiral' class 51 as' Sir Thomas Allin'. Renamed 'Sir John Leake'. Sold to Misrair 10.6.54
G-AJCD	255	17.2.49	Vizor	Convtd to 'Admiral' class 51 as 'Sir Charles Douglas'. Renamed 'Lord Barham'. To Eagle Aviation 31.8.54
G-AJCE	256	24.3.48	Vivacious	Convtd to 'Admiral' class 51 as'Lord Exmouth'. Sold to Eagle Aircraft Services 26.1.55
G-AJDI	258	25.4.49	Volatile	Convtd to 'Admiral' class 51 as 'Sir Christopher Cradock'. Renamed 'Lord Keith'. Sold to Argentine Air Force 26.1.56
G-AJDJ	259	1.3.49	Volley	Convtd to 'Admiral' class 51 as 'Lord Beatty'. Sold to Misrair 9.6.54

Regn	c/n	D/D	Aircraft name	Disposal
G-AJDK	260	22.3.49	Volunteer	Convtd to 'Admiral' class 51 as 'Richard Kempenfelt. Sold to Eagle Aircraft Services 23.10.53
G-AJDL	262	30.3.49	Vortex	Convtd to 'Admiral' class 51 as 'Lord St Vincent'. W/O Nutts Corner, Belfast 5.1.53
G-AJJN	289	13.12.49	Vulcan	Convtd to 'Admiral' class 51 as 'Sir Charles Napier'. Sold to BKS A/T 13.12.54
G-AKBG	263	25.4.49	Votary	Convtd to 'Admiral' class 51 as 'Sir Richard Bickerton'. Renamed 'Sir Thomas Hardy'. Sold to Hunting-Clan A/T 21.4.55
G-AKBH	264	25.4.49	Voyager	Convtd to 'Admiral' class 51 as 'Lord Hood'. Sold to Eagle Aircraft Services 7.2.55

Vickers V635 Viking Mk 1B ('Admiral' Class)

NB Dates shown are dates of registration, not delivery. All were purchased from South African Airways (SAA).

Regn	c/n	D/D	Aircraft name	Disposal
G-AMGG	290	19.12.50	Sir Robert Calder	Ex-ZS-BNE of SAA. Sold to Eagle Aviation 1.7.55
G-AMGH	293	19.12.50	Sir John Duckworth	Ex-ZS-BNH of SAA. Sold in Germany 1.10.55
G-AMGI	297	19.12.50	Sir Henry Harwood	Ex-ZS-BNL of SAA. Sold to Eagle Aviation 29.6.55
G-AMGJ	295	19.12.50	Sir John Warren	Ex-ZS-BNJ of SAA. Sold to First Air Trading 2.12.55
G-AMNJ	296	27.11.51	Lord Fisher	Ex-ZS-BNK of SAA. Sold in Germany 13.9.55
G-AMNR	291	4.1.52	Lord Charles Beresford	Ex-ZS-BNF of SAA. Sold to Eagle Aviation 25.4.55
G-AMNS	294	4.1.52	Sir Dudley Pound	Ex-ZS-BNI of SAA. Sold to Argentine Air Force 26.1.56
G-AMNX	292	15.1.52	Sir Phillip Broke	EX-ZS-BNG of SAA. Sold to Eagle Aviation 16.5.55

Vickers V630 Viscount

Regn	c/n	D/D	Disposal
G-AHRF	1	29.7.50	On loan from manufacturer for route proving until 23.8.50

Vickers V700 Viscount

Regn	c/n	D/D	Disposal
G-AMAV	3	8.52	On loan from manufacturer until 2.53 for route proving, and from 10.53 to 11.53 for London–New Zealand Air Race

Vickers V701 Viscount ('Discovery' Class)

Regn	c/n	D/D	Aircraft name	Disposal
G-ALWE	4	3.1.53	Discovery	W/O Wythenshawe, Manchester 14.3.57
G-ALWF	5	13.2.53	Sir John Franklin	Sold to Channel A/W 6.12.63
G-AMNY	6	20.2.53	Sir Ernest Shackleton	W/O Luqa, Malta 5.1.60
G-AMNZ	20	3.10.53	James Cook	Sold to Cambrian A/W 26.6.63
G-AMOA	9	17.4.53	Sir George Vancouver	Sold to Cambrian A/W 23.12.63
G-AMOB	11	24.4.53	William Baffin	Sold to VASP 30.8.62
G-AMOC	13	4.6.53	Richard Chancellor	Sold to Channel A/W 6.12.63
G-AMOD	15	26.6.53	John Davis	Sold to VASP 30.8.62
G-AMOE	17	13.7.53	Sir Edward Parry	Leased to Channel A/W 13.3.64-12.64. Sold to Channel A/W 20.1.65
G-AMOF	19	8.8.53	Sir Martin Frobisher	Sold to VASP 30.8.62
G-AMOG	7	27.3.53	Robert Falcon Scott	Sold to Cambrian A/W 28.1.63
G-AMOH	21	14.10.53	Henry Hudson	Sold to Channel A/W 6.12.63
G-AMOI	22	5.11.53	Sir Hugh Willoughby	Sold to VASP 30.8.62
G-AMOJ	23	30.11.53	Sir James Ross	Sold to Channel A/W 14.2.64
G-AMOK	24	22.12.53	Sir Humphrey Gilbert	Sold to LAV 19.2.63
G-AMOL	25	1.1.54	David Livingstone	Sold to Cambrian A/W 1.4.63
G-AMOM	26	27.1.54	James Bruce	W/O Blackbushe 20.1.56
G-AMON	27	11.3.54	Thomas Cavendish	Sold to Cambrian A/W 28.12.62
G-AMOO	28	19.12.53	John Oxenham	Leased to Channel A/W 4.64-11.66 Sold to Cambrian A/W 11.66
G-AMOP	29	16.2.54	Mungo Park	Sold to Cambrian A/W 28.12.62

Vickers V701C Viscount ('Discovery' Class)

Regn	c/n	D/D	Aircraft name	Disposal
G-ANHA	61	19.10.54	Anthony Jenkinson	Sold to VASP 30.8.62
G-ANHB	62	21.11.54	Sir Henry Stanley	Sold to VASP 30.8.62
G-ANHC	63	19.12.54	Sir Leo McLintock	W/O near Anzio, Italy 22.10.58
G-ANHD	64	4.5.55	Sir William Dampier	Sold to VASP 30.8.62
G-ANHE	65	29.6.55	Gino Watkins	Sold to VASP 30.8.62
G-ANHF	66	11.7.55	Matthew Flinders	Sold to VASP 30.8.62
G-AOFX	182	27.7.56	Sir Joseph Banks	Sold to VASP 30.8.62

Vickers V732 Viscount ('Discovery' Class)

Regn	c/n	D/D	Aircraft name	Disposal
G-ANRS	78	19.11.55	George Bass	Leased from BOAC Associated Companies until 31.3.56

Vickers V736 Viscount ('Discovery' Class)

Regn	c/n	D/D	Aircraft name	Disposal
G-AODG	77	15.12.55	Fridtjof Nansen	Leased from Fred Olsen until 25.3.57
G-AODH	78	15.12.55	Roald Amundsen	Leased from Fred Olsen until 22.4.57

Vickers V745D Viscount

Regn	c/n	D/D	Aircraft name	Disposal
G-APNF	225	18.6.58	Philipp Carteret	Leased from Vickers until 16.8.58
G-APNG	228	26.6.58	James Lancaster	Leased from Vickers until 6.8.58

Vickers V779D Viscount

Regn	c/n	D/D	Disposal
G-APZP	250	26.3.60	Leased from Fred Olsen until 28.2.61
G-ARBW	247	19.6.60	Leased from Fred Olsen until 28.2.61

Vickers V802 Viscount ('Discovery' Class)

Regn	c/n	D/D	Aircraft name	Disposal
G-AOHG	156	20.2.57	Richard Hakluyt	Transferred to BA 1.4.74
G-AOHH	157	5.3.57	Sir Robert McClure	Transferred to BA 1.4.74
G-AOHI	158	11.3.57	Sir Charles Montagu Doughty	W/O Ben More, Scotland 19.1.73
G-AOHJ	159	27.3.57	Sir John Mandeville	Transferred to BA 1.4.74
G-AOHK	160	2.4.57	John Hanning Speke	Transferred to BA 1.4.74
G-AOHL	161	17.4.57	Charles Sturt	Transferred to BA 1.4.74
G-AOHM	162	27.6.57	Robert Machin	Transferred to BA 1.4.74
G-AOHN	163	1.5.57	Alexander Gordon Laing	Transferred to BA 1.4.74
G-AOHO	164	4.5.57	Samuel Wallis	Transferred to BA 1.4.74
G-AOHP	165	17.5.57	James Weddel	W/O near Copenhagen 17.11.57

Regn	c/n	D/D	Aircraft name	Disposal
G-AOHR	166	4.6.57	Sir Richard Burton	Transferred to BA 1.4.74
G-AOHS	167	22.6.57	Robert Thorne	Transferred to BA 1.4.74
G-AOHT	168	3.7.57	Ralph Fitch	Transferred to BA 1.4.74
G-AOHU	169	11.7.57	Sir George Strong-Nares	W/O Heathrow 7.1.60
G-AOHV	170	25.7.57	Sir John Barrow	Transferred to BA 1.4.74
G-AOHW	253	1.8.57	Sir Francis Younghusband	Transferred to BA 1.4.74
G-AOJA	150	14.2.57	Sir Samuel White Baker	W/O Nutts Corner, Belfast 23.10.57
G-AOJB	151	6.2.57	Stephen Borough	Transferred to BA 1.4.74
G-AOJC	152	19.1.57	Robert O'Hara Burke	Transferred to BA 1.4.74
G-AOJD	153	11.1.57	Sebastian Cabot	Transferred to BA 1.4.74
G-AOJE	154	26.1.57	Sir Alexander Mackenzie	Transferred to BA 1.4.74
G-AOJF	155	8.2.57	Sir George Somers	Transferred to BA 1.4.74
G-AORC	254	17.8.57	Richard Lauder	W/O Craigie, Scotland 28.4.58
G-AORD	171	7.9.57	Arthur Philipp	Transferred to BA 1.4.74

Vickers V806 Viscount ('Discovery' Class)

Regn	c/n	D/D	Aircraft name	Disposal
G-AOYG	256	29.3.58	Charles Darwin	Sold to Cambrian A/W 8.9.70
G-AOYH	311	23.12.57	William Harvey	Sold to BKS A/T 31.7.68
G-AOYI	257	1.1.58	Sir Humphrey Davy	Sold to Cambrian A/W 31.7.68
G-AOYJ	259	8.1.58	Edward Jenner	Leased to Cyprus A/W 28.10.65–16.11.69. Sold to Mandala A/W 5.70
G-AOYK	260	12.2.58	Edmund Cartwright	Leased to Cyprus A/W 20.1.65–16.11.69. Sold to Mandala A/W 5.70
G-AOYL	261	15.2.58	Lord Joseph Lister	Sold to BKS A/T 5.68
G-AOYM	262	19.3.58	John Loudon McAdam	Sold to Cambrian A/W 8.11.71
G-AOYN	263	26.3.58	Sir Isaac Newton	Sold to Cambrian A/W 30.12.71
G-AOYO	264	3.4.58	Adam Smith	Sold to BKS A/T 29.5.68
G-AOYP	265	16.5.58	John Napier	Sold to Cambrian A/W 20.1.71
G-AOYR	266	11.4.58	Sir Richard Arkwright	Sold to BKS A/T 29.12.69
G-AOYS	267	13.6.58	George Stephenson	Sold to Cambrian A/W 22.10.71
G-AOYT	268	2.5.58	James Watt	Sold to Winner A/W 5.69
G-APEX	381	24.6.58	John Harrison	Sold to BKS A/T 29.12.69
G-APEY	382	18.7.58	William Murdoch	Sold to BKS A/T 4.68
G-APIM	412	23.6.58	Robert Boyle	Sold to Cambrian A/W 11.71
G-APJU	413	2.8.58	Sir Gilbert Blane	Sold to Mandala A/L 8.8.70
G-APKF	396	12.7.58	Michael Faraday	Sold to Lao A/L 9.69
G-APOX	418	11.4.59	Isambard Brunel	Sold to Mandala A/L 6.70

Vickers V951 Vanguard ('Vanguard' Class) (Names not carried)

Regn	c/n	D/D	Aircraft name	Disposal
G-APEA	704	27.3.61	Vanguard	Broken up Heathrow 1.73
G-APEB	705	17.3.61	Bellerophon	Broken up Heathrow 6.73
G-APEC	706	13.1.61	Sirius	W/O near Ghent 2.10.71
G-APED	707	30.1.61	Defiance	Loaned to BEA for proving flights 3.60–14.10.60 prior to delivery. Broken up Heathrow 1.73
G-APEE	708	2.12.60	Euryalus	W/O Heathrow 27.10.65
G-APEF	709	13.12.60	Victory	Sold to Templewood Aviation 17.4.72

Vickers V953 Vanguard ('Vanguard' Class) (Names not carried)

Regn	c/n	D/D	Aircraft name	Disposal
G-APEG	710	19.5.61	Arethusa	Convtd to Merchantman 7.71. Transferred to BA 1.4.74
G-APEH	711	21.6.61	Audacious	Sold to Merpati Nusantara A/L 31.3.74
G-APEI	712	20.7.61	Indefatigable	Transferred to BA 1.4.74
G-APEJ	713	15.8.61	Ajax	Convtd to Merchantman 6.71. Transferred to BA 1.4.74
G-APEK	714	16.9.61	Dreadnought	Convtd to Merchantman 2.70. Transferred to BA 1.4.74
G-APEL	715	7.10.61	Leander	Convtd to Merchantman 10.70. Transferred to BA 1.4.74
G-APEM	716	3.11.61	Agamemnon	Convtd to Merchantman 10.69. Transferred to BA 1.4.74
G-APEN	717	14.11.61	Valiant	Sold to Templewood Aviation 18.12.73
G-APEO	718	27.11.61	Orion	Convtd to Merchantman 2.70. Transferred to BA 1.4.74
G-APEP	719	13.12.61	Superb	Convtd to Merchantman 3.71. Transferred to BA 1.4.74
G-APER	720	16.1.62	Amethyst	Transferred to BA 1.4.74
G-APES	721	24.1.62	Swiftsure	Convtd to Merchantman 4.70. Transferred to BA 1.4.74
G-APET	722	21.2.62	Temeraire	Convtd to Merchantman 10.72. Transferred to BA 1.4.74
G-APEU	723	30.3.62	Dauntless	Transferred to BA 1.4.74

Helicopters operated by BEA Helicopter Experimental Unit and BEA Helicopters.

Augusta Bell 47J ('King Arthur' Class)

Regn	c/n	D/D	Aircraft name	Disposal
G-APTH	1058	2.4.59	Sir Lucan	Sold to R.A. Wade 2.4.65

Augusta Bell 206A Jet Ranger

Regn	c/n	D/D	Disposal
G-AWGU	8044	27.4.68	Transferred to BA Helicopters

Bell 47B-3 ('King Arthur' Class)

Regn	c/n	D/D	Aircraft name	Disposal
G-AKFA	69	24.7.47	Sir Balin	W/O Gatwick 4.1.55
G-AKFB		24.7.47	Sir Balin	Sold to Antair Helicopters

Bell 212

Regn	c/n	D/D	Disposal
G-BAFN	30550	1.11.72	Transferred to BA Helicopters.

Bristol 171 Sycamore Mk 3A ('King Arthur' Class)

Regn	c/n	D/D	Aircraft name	Disposal
G-ALSR	12886	9.11.51	Sir Gareth	On loan from MoS until 15.10.54
G-AMWG	13068	26.5.53	Sir Gawain	Sold to Ansett ANA 12.7.56
G-AMWH	13069	30.6.53	Sir Geraint	Sold 4.8.64

Sikorsky S-51 ('King Arthur' Class)

Regn	c/n	D/D	Aircraft name	Disposal
G-AJHW	5117	8.8.49	Sir Baudwin	Sold to Autair Helicopters 12.7.53
G-AJOR	5132	26.8.47	Sir Owen	Sold to Autair Helicopters 16.7.53
G-AJOV	5135	13.10.47	Sir Lamorel	Sold to Autair Helicopters 9.6.54
G-AKCU	5128	9.10.47		W/O Croesor Dam, North Wales 24.5.49

Sikorsky S-61N

Regn	c/n	D/D	Disposal
G-ASNL	61220	28.1.64	Transferred to BA Helicopters
G-ASNM	61221	5.2.64	W/O North Sea 15.11.70
G-ATBJ	61269	8.4.65	Transferred to BA Helicopters
G-ATFM	61270	8.10.65	Transferred to BA Helicopters
G-AWFX	61216	5.9.68	Transferred to BA Helicopters
G-AYOM	61143	7.1.71	Transferred to BA Helicopters
G-AYOY	61476	22.2.71	Transferred to BA Helicopters
G-AZCF	61488	22.8.71	Transferred to BA Helicopters

Westland-Sikorsky WS-55 ('King Arthur' Class)

Regn	c/n	D/D	Aircraft name	Disposal
G-ANFH	WA-15	2.11.54	Sir Ector	Sold to Bristow Helicopters 13.8.65
G-ANUK	WA-39	10.2.54	Sir Kay	Sold to Christian Salvesen Ltd 14.5.57
G-AOCF	WA-56	29.8.55	Sir Lionel	Sold in Libya 24.10.66

Aircraft Used by BEA Gust Research Unit

de Havilland DH 98 Mosquito PR34A

Regn	c/n	D/D	Disposal
G-AJZE	ex RG231 (RAF)	1.3.48	Returned to RAF 19.10.50
G-AJZF	ex RG238 (RAF)	9.6.48	Returned to RAF 19.10.50

Aircraft Used by BEA Communications Flight 1946–49

Avro 652A Anson 1

Regn	c/n	D/D	Disposal
G-AHBN	ex NK270 (RAF)	1.8.46	To Alitalia 7.48

de Havilland DH 60G Moth

Regn	c/n	D/D	Disposal
G-AAWO	235	1.2.47	Inherited from Scottish A/W. Presented to Capt. Ted Fresson on his leaving BEA in 9.48

De Havilland DH 84 Dragon 1

Regn	c/n	D/D	Disposal
G-ACIT	6039	1.2.47	Inherited from Scottish A/W. To Speedbird Flying Club 1.49

Miles M28 Mercury 6

Regn	c/n	D/D	Disposal
G-AHAA	6268	1.8.46	Sold to K.E. Millard & Co. 3.48

Auster J/1 Autocrat

Regn	c/n	Disposal
G-AGVM	1872	To BEA Aero Club
G-AGYO	2006	To Speedbird Flying Club
G-AHCN	1980	To BEA Aero Club
G-AIBR	2151	–

Bibliography

In the preparation of this work I made use of the following sources of reference, many of which are, alas, out of print, but are recommended to anyone wishing to find out more about aspects of BEA.

Books

Annals of British and Commonwealth Air Transport. John Stroud. Putnams. 1962
BAC One-Eleven. Malcolm L. Hill. The Crowood Press. 1999
The Viking, Valetta and Varsity. Compiled by Bernard Martin. Air-Britain (Historians) Ltd. 1975
British Airways – Its History, Aircraft and Liveries. Keith Gaskell, Airlife. 1999
The Story of Aberdeen Airport 1934–1984. James D. Ferguson. Scottish Airports. 1984
The Vickers Viscount 700. Kenneth Munson. Profile Publications Ltd. 1966
London's Airports. Maurice Allward. Ian Allan Ltd.
London Airports. Maurice Allward and Roy McLeavy. Ian Allan Ltd. 1958
Golden Age – Commercial Aviation in Britain 1945–1965. Charles Woodley. Airlife. 1992
Golden Gatwick – 50 Years of Aviation. John King and Geoff Tait. Rae Gatwick Branch and BAA. 1980
Vickers Viscount 700. P. St. John Turner. Airline Publications and Sales. 1973
Channel Silver Wings. Ian Scott-Hill and George Behrend. Jersey Artists Ltd. 1972
British Independent Airlines Since 1946. (1st Edition). A.C. Merton-Jones. LAAS International/M.A.S. 1976
An Illustrated History of Liverpool Airport. P. H. Butler. MAS. 1983
Croydon to Concorde. Capt. R.E. Gillman. John Murray (Publishers) Ltd. 1980
Classic Civil Aircraft 5 – Hawker Siddeley Trident. Max Kingsley-Jones. Ian Allan Ltd. 1993
An Illustrated History of British European Airways. Phil Lo Bao. Browcom Group plc. 1989
The Challenge of BEA. Garry May. Wolfe Publishing Ltd. 1971
Railway Air Services. John Stroud. Ian Allan Ltd. 1987

Magazine Articles

There's Something About St. Mary's. Mike J. Ingham. Aircraft Illustrated. Feb 2000
The New Renaissance. Derek James. Aeroplane Monthly. Apr 2003
Northolt – The Civil Years. Geoffrey Negus. Air-Britain Digest. Spring 1966
The Day Veracity Died. David Kennedy. Propliner. Spring 1993
Lost Opportunity. Richard Payne. Air-Britain Digest. Autumn 2001
A Turning Point In History. Guy Warner. Air-Britain Digest. Summer 2002

Plus: various editions of BEA Magazine. Bradshaws International Air Guide Feb 15th–Mar 14th 1952 and the websites of Air-Britain, Museum of Flight – East Fortune, Argosy Air, David Young's Comet Website, Trident Preservation Society, Aviation Safety Network.

Index

Ambassador, Airspeed (also 'Elizabethan' class) 7, 32, 33, 34, 35, 36, 37, 38, 39, 42, 44, 45, 46, 72, 77, 86, 100, 117, 137, 143, 146, 147, 151, 152, 161, 169, 178, 179

Argosy, Armstrong Whitworth 8, 122, 123, 124, 125, 127, 129, 141, 143

Associated Airways Joint Committee 11, 13, 15, 89, 99, 152, 154, 158

Autoland System 7, 70, 71, 73, 75, 77, 80, 148, 152, 153

Avro XIX 10, 15, 146, 158, 161

BAC Two-Eleven 74, 83
BAC Three-Eleven 83, 84
BEA Airtours 8, 56, 59, 131, 132, 136, 139, 144
BEA Associate Agreements 137, 138, 159
BEA Cargo Unit/Division 129, 139, 144
BEA Gust Research Unit 157, 158
BEA Helicopter Experimental Unit 8, 108, 109, 110, 111, 112, 113
BEA Helicopters Ltd 8, 103, 113, 115, 139, 144
Bealine House 164
Bell 47B3 108, 110, 114
BKS Air Transport (also Northeast Airlines) 39, 49, 72, 77, 131, 132, 140, 144, 156, 167
BOAC 7, 8, 10, 12, 13, 14, 15, 16, 47, 50, 62, 84, 129, 131, 132, 136, 137, 139, 146, 147, 152, 155, 156, 161, 164, 167
Boeing 707 8, 131, 132, 136, 141, 144, 151
Bristol Britannia 60, 62
Bristol 171, 110, 111,
Bristol 173, 112
British Air Services 139, 140, 144, 155, 156
British Airways (1935 version) 10
British Airways (1972 version) 8, 49, 66, 83, 84, 115, 151, 153, 156, 164, 169

Cambrian Airways 49, 88, 101, 140, 144, 156, 159, 161, 167
Channel Islands Airways Unit/Division 77, 100, 103, 139, 142, 144, 156
Comet 4B, de Havilland 7, 8, 21, 46, 49, 50, 51, 52, 53, 54, 55, 56, 59, 62, 63, 65, 67, 69, 72, 73, 87, 88, 131, 132, 136, 141, 143, 147, 151, 152, 179, 180
Croydon Airport 7, 9, 10, 13, 14, 16, 99, 152, 158, 161
Cyprus Airways 44, 46, 48, 49, 50, 52, 55, 140, 167

Dakota, Douglas (also Dart-Dakota, 'Pionair' class, and 'Pionair-Leopard' class) 7, 8, 11, 13, 14, 15, 16, 17, 18, 20, 21, 22, 25, 27, 29, 30, 32, 44, 47, 60, 69, 85, 86, 89, 90, 91, 92, 99, 100, 101, 102, 116, 117, 119, 121, 122, 124, 140, 143, 146, 149, 150, 151, 152, 158, 159, 161, 163, 169, 177, 178
Dorland Hall 152, 164, 165, 166

Gatwick Airport 10, 100, 101, 102, 110, 112, 113, 114, 115, 131, 132, 136, 145, 158

Heathrow Engineering Base 169
Herald, Handley Page 92, 98, 141
Heron, de Havilland 8, 91, 92, 94, 96, 97, 98, 100, 101, 105, 152, 169

Internal German Services 8, 80, 81, 85, 86, 87, 139

Ju52/3m, Junkers 10, 14, 90, 99, 152, 158, 161

Kensington Air Station 35, 164
Keyline House 137, 163, 164

Liverpool Airport Base 14, 109, 137, 152, 154, 158, 159
London-Christchurch (NZ) Air Race 7, 42
London-Paris Air Race 7, 51

Mainline Division 82, 139, 144
Malta Airlines 36, 37, 49, 63, 66, 140
Merchantman conversion 8, 66, 127, 128, 129, 144

Northolt Airport 7, 8, 13, 14, 15, 16, 17, 18, 19, 20, 21, 22, 25, 26, 27, 29, 30, 33, 39, 89, 90, 99, 100, 110, 111, 116, 117, 119, 137, 146, 147, 150, 158, 163, 164, 167, 169

Olympic Airways 48, 50, 52, 63, 147

Railway Air Services 10, 11, 14, 15, 149
Rapide, de Havilland (also 'Islander' class) 8, 10, 15, 89, 90, 91, 96, 99, 100, 104, 105, 106, 143, 152, 158, 159, 161, 169, 177
Rotodyne, Fairey 112, 113

Scottish Air Ambulance services 8, 96, 97, 98
Scottish Airways Division 93, 137, 139, 142, 144, 156
Sikorsky S-51 108, 109, 110, 111, 159
Sikorsky S-61N 8, 103, 106, 107, 113, 114, 115, 144, 145
Silver Wing Service 7, 10, 34, 35, 36, 46, 52

Skyliner, Short 94, 95, 144
South Bank Heliport 110, 112
Super One-Eleven, BAC 8, 56, 78, 79, 80, 81, 82, 83, 87, 88, 94, 95, 131, 143, 144, 181
Super One-Eleven Division 82, 139, 144

Terminal 1 Heathrow 167
Trident, de Havilland 7, 21, 49, 54, 65, 66, 67, 68, 69, 70, 71, 72, 73, 74, 75, 76, 77, 78, 79, 82, 83, 94, 131, 132, 143, 144, 145, 147, 148, 151, 152, 156, 162, 167, 180, 181
Vanguard, Vickers 7, 48, 55, 60, 61, 62, 63, 64, 65, 66, 75, 83, 92, 103, 127, 128, 141, 143, 144, 147, 151, 169, 180
Viking, Vickers (also 'Admiral' class) 7, 11, 15, 17, 18, 19, 20, 21, 25, 26, 27, 29, 32, 33, 34, 86, 90, 100, 137, 143, 146, 152, 159, 161, 169, 178
Viscount, Vickers 7, 8, 21, 32, 36, 37, 39, 40, 41, 32, 43, 44, 45, 46, 47, 48, 49, 50, 55, 60, 62, 68, 70, 78, 79, 83, 86, 87, 88, 92, 93, 94, 101, 102, 103, 117, 119, 120, 121, 123, 125, 130, 137, 138, 140, 141, 143, 144, 147, 151, 152, 157, 159, 161, 162, 163, 167, 169, 179

Waterloo Air Station/Terminal 164, 165
Westland-Sikorsky WS-55 106, 111, 112, 114
West London Air Terminal 152, 164, 165, 166, 167, 169